D0175544

MORE PRAISE FOR BEYOND
MEGACHURCH MYTHS

"One of the major transformations in American Christianity is the emergence of hundreds of megachurches in the latter part of the twentieth century. This is the first book to be published that is based on close empirical research and yet is written in a manner that is easily understood by individuals attempting to assess this trend."
—Donald E. Miller, professor of religion; executive director, Center for Religion and Civic Culture, University of Southern California

"No one who is serious about being informed on the American church scene will be able to ignore this book. It is an incredibly comprehensive description and analysis of an ongoing important spiritual and sociological phenomenon. Doctrinal orthodoxy, organizational behavior, leadership development, small group programming, worship style, communications—you name it—this book cross-references it with the megachurch to help us understand this important spiritual and sociological movement."
—Reggie McNeal, author, *The Present Future* and *Practicing Greatness*

"If the word 'megachurch' sounds frightening, impersonal, compromising, or worse, then this book may be for you. Scott Thumma and Dave Travis project a factual inside view and do a great job of demystifying the large church movement in North America."
—Greg Surratt, pastor, Seacoast Church

"Everyone has questions about megachurches such as 'Why is their number growing? How long will they last? What happens after the current pastor's tenure?' and many more. Scott Thumma and Dave Travis will be your Lewis and Clark as you explore all things megachurch in Beyond Megachurch Myths.*"*
—Dr. Samuel R. Chand, president, SRC Ministries

"This is the best available overview of the megachurch phenomenon. Thumma and Travis use several types of evidence to assess the conventional wisdom about megachurches, qualifying that wisdom when appropriate and challenging it when necessary. In the end, megachurches emerge as more diverse than many assume them to be. Anyone who wants to understand the nature of that diversity should read this book."
—Mark Chaves, professor, Department of Sociology, University of Arizona

"Packed with myth-defying information from two longtime observers of megachurches, this book offers an important assessment for anyone who is curious or concerned."
—Nancy T. Ammerman, Boston University

"Finally a data-based and fact-based look at the megachurch phenomena! These guys and their research get it. They go far beyond the standard anecdotal assumptions and superficial analysis to show us what's actually happening in each of the widely divergent streams of this thing called 'megachurch.'"
—Larry Osborne, pastor, North Coast Church; president, North Coast Training Network, Vista, California

JB JOSSEY-BASS

BEYOND
MEGACHURCH MYTHS

*What We Can Learn from
America's Largest Churches*

Scott Thumma

Dave Travis

Foreword by

Rick Warren

A LEADERSHIP ❖ NETWORK PUBLICATION

BICENTENNIAL
1807
⟨W⟩WILEY
2007
BICENTENNIAL

John Wiley & Sons, Inc.

Published by Jossey-Bass
A Wiley Imprint
989 Market Street, San Francisco, CA 94103-1741   www.josseybass.com

Wiley Bicentennial logo: Richard J. Pacifico

Jossey-Bass books and products are available through most bookstores. To contact Jossey-Bass directly call our Customer Care Department within the U.S. at 800-956-7739, outside the U.S. at 317-572-3986, or fax 317-572-4002.

Jossey-Bass also publishes its books in a variety of electronic formats. Some content that appears in print may not be available in electronic books.

Excerpt from Spinelli, Tony, and Brophy, Andrew. "Growing Protest over Church's Relocation," *Connecticut Post*, Copyright © (2006) by the Connecticut Post. Reprinted with permission.

Excerpt from Sheler, Jeff. "Interview: Alan Wolfe." *Religion & Ethics Newsweekly*, April 30, 2004. Reprinted with permission.

Excerpt from Brown, Patricia Lee. "Megachurch as Mini-Towns." *The New York Times*, Copyright © (2002) by the New York Times Co. Reprinted with permission.

Library of Congress Cataloging-in-Publication Data

Thumma, Scott, date.
 Beyond megachurch myths : what we can learn from American's largest churches / Scott Thumma, Dave Travis ; forword by Rick Warren. — 1st ed.
   p. cm.
 Includes bibliographical references and index.
 ISBN 978-0-7879-9467-9 (cloth)
 1.   Bign churches. I. Travis, Dave, date. II. Title.
 BV637.9.T48 2007
 250.973—dc22

                                                   2007019069

Printed in the United States of America
FIRST EDITION
HB Printing   10 9 8 7 6 5 4 3 2 1

LEADERSHIP NETWORK TITLES

The Blogging Church: Sharing the Story of Your Church Through Blogs, by Brian Bailey and Terry Storch

Leading from the Second Chair: Serving Your Church, Fulfilling Your Role, and Realizing Your Dreams, by Mike Bonem and Roger Patterson

The Way of Jesus: A Journey of Freedom for Pilgrims and Wanderers, by Jonathan S. Campbell, with Jennifer Campbell

Leading the Team-Based Church: How Pastors and Church Staffs Can Grow Together into a Powerful Fellowship of Leaders, by George Cladis

Organic Church: Growing Faith Where Life Happens, by Neil Cole

Off-Road Disciplines: Spiritual Adventures of Missional Leaders, by Earl Creps

Leading Congregational Change Workbook, by James H. Furr, Mike Bonem, and Jim Herrington

Leading Congregational Change: A Practical Guide for the Transformational Journey, by Jim Herrington, Mike Bonem, and James H. Furr

The Leader's Journey: Accepting the Call to Personal and Congregational Transformation, by Jim Herrington, Robert Creech, and Trisha Taylor

Culture Shift: Transforming Your Church from the Inside Out, by Robert Lewis and Wayne Cordeiro, with Warren Bird

A New Kind of Christian: A Tale of Two Friends on a Spiritual Journey, by Brian D. McLaren

The Story We Find Ourselves In: Further Adventures of a New Kind of Christian, by Brian D. McLaren

Practicing Greatness: 7 Disciplines of Extraordinary Spiritual Leaders, by Reggie McNeal

The Present Future: Six Tough Questions for the Church, by Reggie McNeal

A Work of Heart: Understanding How God Shapes Spiritual Leaders, by Reggie McNeal

The Millennium Matrix: Reclaiming the Past, Reframing the Future of the Church, by M. Rex Miller

Shaped by God's Heart: The Passion and Practices of Missional Churches, by Milfred Minatrea

The Missional Leader: Equipping Your Church to Reach a Changing World, by Alan J. Roxburgh and Fred Romanuk

The Ascent of a Leader: How Ordinary Relationships Develop Extraordinary Character and Influence, by Bill Thrall, Bruce McNicol, and Ken McElrath

Beyond Megachurch Myths: What We Can Learn from America's Largest Churches, by Scott Thumma and Dave Travis

The Elephant in the Boardroom: Speaking the Unspoken About Pastoral Transitions, by Carolyn Weese and J. Russell Crabtree.

CONTENTS

ABOUT LEADERSHIP NETWORK

SINCE 1984, LEADERSHIP NETWORK has fostered church innovation and growth by diligently pursuing its far-reaching mission statement: to identify, connect, and help high-capacity Christian leaders multiply their impact.

Although Leadership Network's techniques adapt and change as the church faces new opportunities and challenges, the organization's work follows a consistent and proven pattern: Leadership Network brings together entrepreneurial leaders who are focused on similar ministry initiatives. The ensuing collaboration—often across denominational lines—creates a strong base from which individual leaders can better analyze and refine their own strategies. Peer-to-peer interaction, dialogue, and sharing inevitably accelerate participants' innovation and ideas. Leadership Network further enhances this process through developing and distributing highly targeted ministry tools and resources, including audio and video programs, special reports, e-publications, and online downloads.

With Leadership Network's assistance, today's Christian leaders are energized, equipped, inspired, and better able to multiply their own dynamic Kingdom-building initiatives.

Launched in 1996 in conjunction with Jossey-Bass (a Wiley imprint), Leadership Network Publications present thoroughly researched and innovative concepts from leading thinkers, practitioners, and pioneering churches. The series collectively draws from a range of disciplines, with individual titles offering perspective on one or more of five primary areas:

1. Enabling effective leadership
2. Encouraging life-changing service
3. Building authentic community
4. Creating Kingdom-centered impact
5. Engaging cultural and demographic realities

For additional information on the mission or activities of Leadership Network, please contact:

Leadership Network
www.leadnet.org
(800) 765-5323
client.care@leadnet.org

FOREWORD BY RICK WARREN

Finally! I've waited for this book for a long time.

When Kay and I started Saddleback Church in 1980, we didn't plan on pastoring a megachurch. Our vision was to pastor a church that reached our community in Orange County. It sounds simple now, but we really just wanted to bring people into the membership, build them up to maturity, train them for their ministry, and send them out to fulfill their mission in the world. We were amazed at how quickly our church grew . . . and grew . . . and grew.

Along the way, I met other pastors of large churches and compared stories. These conversations—along with some convictions I had—helped form the Purpose Driven paradigm we teach at our conferences. As I talked to these pastors, it became clear that as our churches grew, so did the chorus of our detractors and critics. Now, I don't mind honest criticism. I think it helps take off our rough edges. But what drove all of us pastors crazy was that the critics had no real knowledge of the megachurches they were criticizing!

In *Beyond Megachurch Myths*, Scott Thumma and Dave Travis finally blow away the myths about megachurches and present facts based on real data and research. This book helps answer some of the most common misconceptions about megachurches. The underlying research confirms what I have been saying about the overlooked strengths of megachurches and what they can teach churches of all sizes.

I have a heart for pastors and a passion for growing healthy churches, big and small. There is no correlation between the size and health of a congregation. God's desire to use us is never limited by attendance. Every church, no matter the size, has a role to play in the work of God's kingdom, and I encourage you to read this book. We can learn a lot from each other.

May 2007   Rick Warren
Lake Forest, California   Pastor, Saddleback Church

ACKNOWLEDGMENTS

TWO VERY DIFFERENT PEOPLE wrote this book. So at times you may hear two distinctive voices in the text, one more an academic researcher and the other more a leadership consultant.

Scott Thumma is a professor at the respected Hartford Seminary in Hartford, Connecticut, and a researcher at the seminary's Hartford Institute for Religion Research. He spends his time teaching and researching current trends in American religious life. He regularly travels around the world to teach about megachurches.

Dave Travis is the executive vice president for church innovations at Leadership Network, a Dallas, Texas–based nonprofit organization. Dave's role is to lead the organization in identifying, connecting, and helping high-capacity Christian leaders such as pastors of megachurches. His work is based on his leadership of a team and his personal connection to pastors. He travels around the country visiting churches and consulting with pastors.

We are also alike in many ways. We both love "outsider art" and the Atlanta Braves. More important, both of us are enormously interested and invested in understanding the megachurch phenomenon. We both care passionately about churches and hope our work adds to their vitality and effectiveness. As such, we hope our commonalities give this book the unity of a single voice.

We are blessed to be supported in our research and writing by our respective organizations and great colleagues. We also have the heritage and legacy of Christian parents and siblings to thank for our grounding in the faith. We have supportive spouses and wonderful children to whom we are ever grateful for their love, encouragement, and understanding that it takes time to research and write. Scott's wife, Jennifer, and his children, Katy, Ben, and Maddie, provide this support abundantly. And Lynne, Stephanie, and Claire are supportive of all Dave does. We are truly blessed to have such wonderful families.

We have also greatly benefited from the work of other scholars and friends who have assisted us in the study of megachurches. While we have drawn from our own studies and observations for most of this work, we want to acknowledge a few other scholars and observers who have contributed to our insights.

Dave has spent considerable time with Lyle Schaller over the years, and Lyle's many books have shaped both of our thoughts. His book *The Very Large Church: New Rules for Leaders*, while known in the church world, is underappreciated outside of it. Lyle has thoughtfully observed and written about many of these churches over a forty-year period and has shared many insights with Dave.

Elmer Towns, cofounder of Liberty University, was for many years America's leading researcher of large churches. In 1969, his listing of America's ten largest churches in *Christian Life* magazine hit the evangelical world "like a bombshell," according to the magazine's editor Robert Walker. That same year, a related book, *The Ten Largest Sunday Schools*, became a bestseller. He wrote many other books related to large churches, including *Ten of Today's Innovative Churches*.

John Vaughan, who holds the distinction of having the first book with the word *megachurches* in the title, has continually encouraged us and the world to focus on megachurches as a distinct phenomenon. His book of a decade ago, *Megachurches and America's Cities*, gave early insights into this movement.

Warren Bird, research director at Leadership Network and our coauthor of the 2005 megachurch study, has provided inspiration, critiques, and unbounded energy to keep us on task. Other scholars who have shaped our thinking in their writings and in conversations include Nancy Ammerman, Carl Dudley, Nancy Eiesland, Nancy Martin, Donald Miller, David Roozen (and the entire Faith Communities Today group for their support of our megachurch research), Cynthia Woolever (and the sharing of the U.S. Congregational Life study data), and Ben Watts. At the end of this book, we provide a list of resources written by these scholars and others by which readers may broaden their picture of the megachurch movement.

We want to thank Sheryl Fullerton, Sandy Siegle, and the entire team at Jossey-Bass, as well as Greg Ligon, Mark Sweeney, and Stephanie Plage at Leadership Network for their great work on this project.

Finally, we want to thank all of the megachurch pastors, staff, and members who have patiently helped us understand their churches and the distinctiveness of these very large congregations, and we kindly request that in the future they all fill out our survey questionnaires.

INTRODUCTION

DRIVING NORTH ON MELROSE in Vista, California, a wide, multilane road lined with businesses in a mixed residential-commercial area, you don't see anything that looks like what we usually think of as a megachurch. As you approach the church's stated address, you pass a number of mobile home parks, single-story apartment buildings, and small houses. Climbing the hill toward the church, the scenery changes to a series of low-slung, prefab warehouse buildings occupied by auto services such as muffler and sound shops.

You see a small sign, "North Coast Church," and your eye travels to the same lettering and logo on the side of one of the buildings. You notice a stream of cars heading into an area just in front of one of the warehouses. While some cars are jockeying for space at this entrance, another sign points you and most of the other cars down the block to the next intersection toward parking. As you turn right on this side street and then right again into a large, newly paved parking lot, a smiling parking lot attendant in an orange vests greets you as he directs you to a parking spot.

You exit from your car and head back toward the warehouse you passed earlier. You enter a wide promenade, which looks much like an empty parking lot separating several of the warehouses. This driveway/parking lot is transformed during church hours from nondescript, storefront–strip mall parking into a mall promenade complete with informational booths and friendly faces. To your left, a large warehouse door is labeled "The Edge." Coming through the door is the sound of deep bass music. To the right, another warehouse shell is decorated with a painting of a lifeguard stand and is labeled "Tower 6." Further down the promenade is a door to the warehouse with a small, white wood frame symbol over it that reads "Traditions." Even further along are signs directing you to a "Children's Area," "Video Café," and "North Coast Live."

North Coast Church is a thirty-year-old congregation serving North San Diego County, California. As one of the megachurch pioneers of multivenue ministry, its weekend worship services serve over six thousand people. In addition to their multiple venues at the warehouse/strip-mall

Melrose campus, the church operates three other campuses in area schools both to handle the growing number of attendees and to reach into new communities.

Even more impressive, North Coast claims that over 80 percent of adult attendees participate in small groups that meet together for Scripture study, prayer, and sharing throughout the week. At least half of these small groups support, sponsor, or participate in ministry initiatives focused on serving the community outside the church. These initiatives include serving in schools and shelters, reaching out to military families, and tutoring. Additionally, the church sponsors an extensive recovery ministry, as well as a military spouse support ministry; bereavement and grief support ministries; seminary and college-level classes; programs for children, youth, and several age groups of single adults; "Life After Fifty" groups; and myriad other ministries.

North Coast's founding pastor of twenty-plus years is Larry Osborne: quiet, soft-spoken, bearded, and California born and bred. Although Larry has earned a doctorate from a respected seminary, his sandals and silk print shirt are his natural weekend attire in this beach community. He is a warmhearted leader who is often found between services out in the makeshift plaza greeting people with bear hugs and laughter.

Like most megachurch leadership teams in our experience, Larry and his staff have given considerable thought to most aspects of the church's life, but they also spontaneously experiment with new ideas. They reflect deeply on theological traditions, but they are also innovative pioneers at finding ways to adapt their church to its changing ministry context. Although Larry has written several books and speaks frequently at pastors' conferences, he is not a TV or radio preacher. He is loyal to his Evangelical Free tradition and helps the denomination's district and national office several times each year. However, the denominational label is not a part of the church's name. Many of the pastoral staff and other leaders come from different religious traditions. All prospective new members are plainly told of the connections and commitments to the denomination in the membership class, but this relationship is not easily discerned from the church's Web site.

We offer this brief story to give you a taste of what is to come throughout this book. In many ways, North Coast is typical of megachurches in the United States. However, we also offer it as a warning: there is no "typical" megachurch model. Rather, this book will focus on the diversity of churches within this phenomenon and dispel many of the mistaken assumptions about them. While we find several dominant "streams" or types of megachurches that fit our definition, we feel it is important for the reader both to have some sense of what makes these megachurches similar to each other and also where the distinctive differences lie. This is a hard task to adequately accomplish within one book. Our encouragement, therefore, is for you to go to the Web site at www.megachurchmyths.com and link to the entire list of U.S. megachurches. Go and visit several of them (either physically or virtually on their Web sites) and get a taste of this exciting development within American religion. Throughout this book, we will tell stories of various churches that we have visited along the way in order to give texture to our ideas. However, there is no substitute for visiting these churches in person as a way to create your own informed opinions about them, rather than relying on the often mistaken stereotypes of the megachurch.

Megachurches Matter

The purpose of this book is to explore why megachurches matter. These large churches are changing the landscape of American religion. Megachurches not only receive the attention of their leaders and attendees, but also of the leaders and membership in smaller churches, denominational officials, church consultants, and seminary faculties. Increasingly, they are the topic of conversation by municipal leaders, media reporters, political parties, and scholars. Yet they are some of the most misunderstood organizations in the country.

Much of the popular reporting and widespread public beliefs about these organizations is wrong. These false impressions are echoed, seconded, and passed on in other reports and works to the point that these mistaken ideas have become the common knowledge perspective on the subject. This book challenges many of these long-held assumptions by drawing both on our years of experience with megachurches and on several large academic studies of many of these churches.

We hope this book will help religious leaders not only to understand megachurches better but also to learn from them, even if they have no desire to become a megachurch. We also think there are significant lessons for leaders in business, government, education, and other nonprofit organizations that can be gleaned from the study of these churches. Above all, however, these groups must have a clear and accurate picture of the megachurch phenomenon.

While this work focuses on megachurches, we do not intend to suggest that the very large church model is the only viable one in modern America. Our work in recent years has focused on these large organizations and their leaders because we think the lessons from this group have an important story to tell about American culture and religious life. Nevertheless, we are firmly committed to expressions of faith in small churches, midsized churches, house churches, and other new forms of religious organizations. We believe each expression can be valid, life-giving, and healthy for Christianity if it lives out its unique response to the Gospel and to its community.

As you will see, though we believe that megachurches share many characteristics with other churches, we also believe that they organize religious life and worship in ways that make them "a sharply different order of God's creation."[1] There is much wisdom to be gained from examining these very large churches in isolation as well as comparing them with other congregations. Not only do these churches function differently, but also they have responded to the changing reality of American society in ways that religious Americans find appealing. A focus on these churches tells us much about society in general.

What Is a Megachurch?

For the purposes of this book, a megachurch is simply a Protestant church that averages at least two thousand total attendees in their weekend services. We do not take credit for this definition. This size determination has become the standard in much that is written about megachurches. We think this working definition does help make several important distinctions.

First, it is a *Protestant* church. American Protestantism is a diverse family of groups. While each denomination and tradition has its own traits, American Protestant churches as a whole are clearly different from Catholic and Orthodox congregations, large Jewish temples, and other houses of worship.

There are many American Catholic and Orthodox churches, and a few synagogues and mosques, that serve over two thousand attendees in an average week, but we believe these churches are organized and led in distinctively different ways that separate them as unique phenomena from Protestant megachurches. Although Protestant pastors can learn lessons from these traditions and vice versa, the language, the role of the senior leader, and many other characteristics differ among these theological streams, which makes comparisons extremely difficult without lengthy explanation.

We use the term *church* while noting that this term is used in multiple ways by American Protestants. We intend our use of the term *church* to mean simply an organization that sees itself as a distinct group of believers in a particular locale. Some authors use the term *congregation* instead.

There are a few Protestant traditions that see themselves as "one church" with many local congregations. Each local congregation tends to have its own culture and is differentiated from other congregations within the same "church." For example, some United Methodist, Lutheran, and other denominations will stress that they are "one church" but many congregations. From this perspective, our use of the word church would be identical with the use of the term *congregation*, meaning a particular local body of believers.

Large churches often also use the word *congregation* to describe a subgroup within itself that has a distinctive cohesive characteristic. For example, some megachurches refer to their multiple congregations as defined by worship venue, time, or style (our 8:30 A.M. Contemporary service; our Edge venue). Others use the term to describe a subgroup based on what their purpose or function is, such as a large Adult Bible Fellowship, or even a musical group.

Throughout the book, we use the terms *church* and *congregation* interchangeably and to imply each of these meanings. We trust that the context of the passage will make the diverse meanings of these words clear.

The next part of the definition—*averages at least two thousand in weekly worship attendance*—is the key distinction. Size matters. It is, in part, the magnitude of these congregations that is significant to the character of the organization. There is nothing magical about the two thousandth person that transforms a very large church into a megachurch. We see this number as a convenient marker for a Protestant congregation that is large enough to possess many of the characteristics definitive of this religious phenomenon.

But it is not just numbers of people affiliated with a church that makes the difference, but rather those who are actually actively involved in the life of the church. At this point we run into record-keeping issues with some churches. We are speaking and writing about *attendance* and not *membership*. This is a big shift for many observers accustomed to talking about church membership.

Membership means different things in different traditions. For some traditions, little is expected for people to claim membership in a particular church. Likewise, these groups may not have a strong desire to purge their records. These traditions often tend to have a higher number of people on their membership databases than they have attendees in any given week. Other traditions have high expectations for persons who are members, including extensive educational classes, behavioral qualifications, and annual covenantal commitments that include giving and serving guidelines. These churches tend to have membership rolls that are much smaller than their actual number of attendees.

Again, we argue that the key distinction in megachurches, and later we will argue for all churches, is attendance. Attendance is a good barometer of participation. It is the measure most church leaders focus on when they reflect on their church's identity, program, and organization. Finally, attendance provides a consistent standard for comparison among churches within traditions that have radically different ideas about membership.

While some churches count only adults in worship, we include all persons present on a typical weekend in our consideration of megachurch status. Each local church can have a distinctive mix of age groups. There are now a few large churches that have sizeable adult attendance and relatively small attendance from children and teenagers. Alternatively, we have seen some churches in which the total number of children and teenagers exceeds that of adults in a given weekend. Whatever the pattern, all persons within a church must be organized, equipped, and supervised, and their spiritual needs must be addressed in some way. Therefore, all persons, no matter what their age, "count" as organizational and spiritual entities for a church—and so they also count for our consideration in this book.

We often use the phrase "averaging two thousand" to be intentionally vague about the cutoff of what constitutes a megachurch. We will confess that church leaders are not always the best at accurately counting their individual attendees. In their defense, in a church this large, it can be difficult to track people accurately each week. For those churches with highly active Sunday morning Christian education programs, accurate counts are much easier, but many megachurches do not use a traditional Sunday school model, or their education programs are not stressed as essential for all worshippers. Definitive counts get even more difficult when a church has multiple rooms or venues at one location worshipping simultaneously, or multiple locations all considered as one church. Likewise, our experience says that any church averaging two thousand on a typical weekend could have as few as eighteen hundred or as many as twenty-five hundred at any given time.

It should also be noted that the average attendance in a given week is only a percentage of the total group of attendees in contact with a congregation within an entire month. The full number of active participants in megachurches (those coming at least once a month) may well be 50 percent or more higher than the number in any given week. This may be an important realization for churches of all sizes. It is certainly true for megachurches; there is a large constituency in a given community that considers a particular megachurch to be "their church" even though they are not "members" and may only attend once a month or less. We will discuss this phenomenon later in the book.

As we begin this venture to clarify the megachurch phenomenon, it is important to keep in mind that the two thousand average attendance is primarily a baseline indicator of the relative size, character, and complexity of the church. We assume that by the time a church has reached this general size, it will have made changes to its organizational structure, staffing, and leadership patterns; programmatic offerings; worship forms; and physical plant that give it the full range of megachurch characteristics we use as definitive of the phenomenon.

However, as you will note later in this book, the definition of exactly what a megachurch is continues to be pushed by the rapid growth of multisite and multivenue churches that have more than one primary meeting place. Likewise, smaller congregations have learned from megachurches and are adopting their organizational and programmatic ways of behaving—in short they are beginning to look like "mini-megas." Additionally, more churches are offering multiple midweek services that count as part of their attendance, as well as add to the consumer options and distinctive character that shapes a megachurch. Finally, we have begun to hear reports of Catholic churches and Jewish synagogues that are adapting their specific tradition's worship and organization in ways that imitate Protestant megachurches. All these changes are beginning to further complicate the phenomenon and definition of exactly what a megachurch is.

The Data and Their Presentation

The bane of every researcher is the lack of good data gathered in a systematic way. Like most researchers and commentators, we would love to have a complete census of all megachurches using a uniform standard of measurement that is comparable with similar characteristics from the entire set of churches and religious bodies in America. Unfortunately, such is not the case. We do rely on two large national surveys of megachurches done in conjunction with several well-documented scholarly national random studies of U.S. congregations to draw our conclusions. We have also tried to find additional national studies of churches and attendees to extend our perception of this reality. However, much like every consultant, researcher, and scholar, we also bring our own set of eyes, ears, and thoughts to the challenge of understanding megachurches. Of course, we bring, as well, our own biases in drawing conclusions from the best data available. Although we may be accused of defending the phenomenon, we try to present as objective a perspective as possible, while trying to correct what we see as fallacies in the understanding of megachurches.

The data for this task come from different sources with a number of diverse approaches. It will be immediately obvious to the reader that we draw extensively on a number of quantitative surveys of megachurches and other congregations. However, we have also used observational visits, compilations of group discussions and personal interviews, analysis of financial documents and annual reports, as well as excerpts from sermons, speeches, and writings of megachurch leaders both to enrich this book and to formulate our understanding of this phenomenon over the years.

Beyond Megachurch Myths is our attempt to draw together a wide range of informational sources and interviews and yet present our findings in a readable and instructive manner. One of our goals is to provide a holistic perspective that synthesizes many types of material including quantitative surveys, qualitative reports, in-person interviews and conversations, and our many years of experiences with and observations on megachurches throughout the country.

The core resource for our book is the Megachurch Today 2005 study conducted jointly by the Hartford Institute for Religion Research, Hartford Seminary, and Leadership Network. This study, the largest ever conducted, had two primary tasks: first, to identify every megachurch in the United States; and second, to gather basic information from as many of these churches as possible. The data collection was performed in conjunction with a larger national survey for comparative purposes and in order to replicate a similar, but less extensive, survey we did in 2000. In January 2006, we released a preliminary report from this research that highlighted some of the key findings of the study. Part of that information is repeated in this book. Since that time, we have done further analysis that has revealed new findings.

This book is intended to be more than just an expansive report of one research study, however. We have benefited from the research of other scholars and students on megachurches and use those studies to broaden this book's perspective. Throughout the book, we report facts from a number of studies, although we do not offer extensive footnotes in the text unless we are quoting published findings. We want to thank the principal investigators of these studies for giving us permission directly to use this material or indirectly by generously making them available on the Association of Religion Data Archive (www.theARDA.com). In the Appendix to this book, we offer details of each study that we draw upon extensively. The research and data collection are the investigators' work, for which we are quite grateful; however, do not hold them accountable for our use and interpretations of their materials in this book. We take the blame for any unintentional misuse of their fine work.

As we said earlier, we have drawn implicitly and explicitly on other data sources as well for this book. The writings of scholars, consultants, students, and journalists have offered clues about the meaning and importance of the quantitative data. We have examined denominational reports in this effort. Some denominational traditions have large and skillful research offices that receive extensive annual reports from their churches. These groups tend to provide reports rich in data and are important for understanding congregational health as well as information about giving to missions, budgets, worship attendance, and enrollments in Christian Education classes. When such information is compared across denominations, one can get a more complete picture of the religious landscape. Unfortunately, some traditions and independent churches survey irregularly or not at all. And the denominational groups almost never standardize what they ask across traditions. This is problematic for understanding the whole picture when one of the fastest growing areas of American religious life is nondenominational churches or churches that act as if they are not part of a denomination. It is also one of the reasons we have drawn heavily on the Faith Communities Today studies that have tried to get these denominational and nondenominational groups to survey their congregations collaboratively using a common questionnaire. Again, we are very appreciative of the assistance we have received from all these denominational research offices during the development of this book.

On occasion we also have used random poll surveys of Americans. These poll-based reports are often derived from phone interviews to explore individual religious behavior and attitudes. Based on the questions asked, respondents explain their own behavior, including church attendance. This information offers yet another window on the phenomenon.

In addition to these more formal quantitative types of data, we have also gained from other types of reports. We have relied on small focus groups of pastors and members in our work over the years. Specifically, Leadership Network has conducted small-group meetings with large church leaders for over twenty years. In 2006 alone, Leadership Network held twenty-five meetings, each one attended by dozens of pastors. In these private sessions, these leaders are quite willing to share both the high points and low points of their ministry. They share the "story behind the story" that in many cases goes unreported elsewhere. At Leadership Network, we have allowed a select few authors to attend these meetings in the past, but this work represents the first time in which insights from attending over one hundred of these sessions have been recorded in a book. Likewise, both of us have formally and informally talked with hundreds, and perhaps thousands, of persons who attend megachurches, as well as having visited many of these churches over the past fifteen years; although few of these attendee comments are found in this book, they will be present in future volumes.

Along this same line, we have greatly benefited and drawn on the experiential wisdom and insights of consultants to these large churches in this book. The conversations we have had and the books we have read from these consultants have been valuable in forming our perspectives and shaping our thinking. Additionally, we draw on the recent work of academic colleagues and a number of fine graduate students who are beginning to compile a body of excellent work on the subject. We have not directly cited all this work in the text, but we do reference it on the extensive Bibliography that is available on the book's Web site at www.megachurchmyths.com.

Another valuable source of information are media reports. In the past year alone, we have tracked over five hundred media stories about large churches. Many of these stories might have focused on a particular church and its ministry in a local area, but taken together all these articles offer a window on the phenomenon that no individual, no matter how well traveled, could get by himself. In addition, there are numerous magazines and newspapers for church leaders that regularly feature stories about these churches. We are grateful for all these stories and are always willing to cooperate with the authors of these stories that we find both valuable in their breadth and at the same time infuriating in their lack of depth.

What You Can Expect from This Book

This book is designed to help readers better understand megachurches and start to realize what can be learned from them. We do this by framing the chapters around a predominant myth that reflects a statement or a version of a "truth" that has been widely accepted by the general public. We find these statements repeated in media reports, in church circles, in books, and directly to us in conversations. In some ways, these myths have become the "common knowledge" on the subject.

Our task is to take each myth and show what is true and what is false about it. We will do this by using our data, others' research, and stories from megachurches to help draw an accurate picture in that area of church life.

In addition, we have included a small application section in each chapter for church leaders. The purpose of this section is to help the readers consider their own church situations and apply a few of the lessons from the chapter to their own congregations. Some of these sections encourage further discussions and others suggest practical action steps for your church. While this is not a "how-to" book in any way, we did want to provide leaders with ways to make the material practical in their own context.

We are not saying that every church can or should be a megachurch. Every church has a different calling and place within its community. In these application sections we are trying to say that churches can learn from megachurches in order to improve the health and effectiveness of their own ministries. There are many books designed to teach church leaders how to grow, including some written by megachurch pastors. This book is not one of those. The application sections in this book are simple reflections from material in each chapter that highlight lessons for church leaders from that chapter.

We have found reading a book like this and discussing its key points with a group of people to be a profitable investment of time and energy. Perhaps you could use an existing group of leaders within your own church or bring together a group of pastors to read it collectively. In addition to the application sections, additional information, presentations, and discussions can be found at www.megachurchmyths.com to help process the information found in this book.

Our first chapter will lay the groundwork for understanding the scale and scope of megachurches in America. This wide-angle view will help the reader understand the contours of the environment and organizations being discussed.

Chapter Two addresses the myth that megachurches are all alike. If you were to read general news reports and watch television, you would see the same church names and leader names over and over. Our work will show that there is considerably more diversity to this movement than the media portrayal evidences.

Chapter Three responds to the common view that these churches are just too big. Surprisingly, this view comes not only from general commentators, but also from some pastors of smaller churches who believe that increased size does not lead to a healthy congregation. We will address some of the challenges of size in this chapter and explain that for those who attend, they seldom have the perception that their church is "too big."

Chapter Four addresses probably the most common myth: that these churches are personality cults and will fade away. While it is true that these churches rely on strong leadership, we will describe other factors at play in the leadership of these churches.

The view that these churches are selfish and only concerned about their own needs is addressed in Chapter Five. This myth is spread primarily by church leaders and denominational leaders who bemoan some of the methods megachurches use. The idea also comes from critics who believe that megachurches are not involved in enough good works in their communities. Our research shows a different picture.

Chapter Six addresses the myth repeated in numerous places that these churches water down the faith. The assumption is that if a church is that successful, it must be taking out the hard stuff of Christianity. Our research will show that these churches are in fact clear about their views on orthodox Christianity and communicate it directly. They have high standards for committed believers and attempt to create structures that help members become more committed.

Chapter Seven addresses the common perception that megachurches are bad for the overall religious economy. Many people view megachurches as if they were Wal-Marts, swooping into town to steal customers away from smaller stores. We will attempt to show what some of the effects, both good and bad, can be when one has a megachurch in their backyard.

Chapter Eight addresses the common critique of this movement that megachurches tend to have people of the same race, class, and political view massed in one congregation—that they are homogeneous. There is actually a surprising amount of diversity of all sorts within most of these large churches. In recent election cycles, attention to a few outspoken pastors has led many to believe that these places are full of political activists and bastions of Republicanism. In fact, the reality is much more complex than that.

Chapter Nine points to the commonly held belief that megachurches grow because of the show. There are some who suggest that religious consumers are dazzled by entertainment and that megachurches only grow because they rely on this approach to entice new converts and members of other churches with the spectacle. While it is certainly true that the primary worship services are vitally important and entertaining, megachurches have other characteristics that are equally responsible for their success.

Chapter Ten addresses the often-repeated predictions that the mega-church movement is dying and that younger generations will not attend them. We point to the paucity of evidence supporting this view and the abundance of information opposing it and let readers draw their own conclusions.

Chapter Eleven offers our thoughts on the future of the Megachurch movement. We suggest some challenges it may face in the near future and what its possible importance might be.

We see this book as a beginning, a current description of the state of megachurches in the United States. Through our respective roles and organizations, we will continue to work in this area. We hope to complete national studies of megachurches in 2008 and 2010, as well as undertake a comprehensive, representative megachurch attendee study in the near future. Our final chapter alludes to further research and questions we hope to cover in future publications. Please accept this book as our current thinking, not as our final thoughts, on the ever-changing religious reality that is called the megachurch.

May we always have both the information and the courage to challenge our firmly held myths.

I

THE SCALE AND SCOPE OF MEGACHURCHES IN AMERICA

AMERICA HAS SEEN AN EXPLOSION in the number of megachurches over the past three decades. They are growing bigger, faster, and stronger and are thriving in nearly every state in the nation and in much smaller communities than was previously believed possible. A few have grown to hold more people than the town in which they reside. If all the people who are *members* of megachurches were combined, they would be the third largest religious group in the United States. Their combined annual income is well over $7 billion. Yet these megachurches account for only one-half of 1 percent of all the religious congregations in the nation.

In 2007, there were 1,250 megachurches out of a total of 335,000 U.S. congregations of all religious traditions. This relatively small number of very large Protestant Christian churches has the same number of attendees at weekly services (roughly 4.5 million) as the smallest 35 percent of churches in the country. The pastors of these churches wield tremendous power within their denominational groups, in the larger Christian world, and even in the public and political realms. The ministry activities and worship styles of the megachurches affect tens of thousands of smaller churches in the country and, thanks to the Internet, literally millions of pastors around the world. There is nothing insignificant about the megachurch phenomenon. Even the renowned management consultant Peter Drucker observed in 1998, "Consider the pastoral megachurches that have been growing so very fast in the U.S. since 1980 and are surely the most important social phenomenon in American society in the last 30 years."[1]

The megachurch is more than just an ordinary church grown large. The size and approach of a megachurch alters its social dynamics and organizational characteristics, making it bear little resemblance to smaller, more traditional congregations. Although large congregations have certainly existed throughout Christian history, the rapid proliferation of these churches in the past generation is both distinctive and is also fundamentally altering the American Christian landscape.

Beyond the raw number and power of these churches, we believe that megachurches, their practices, and their leaders are the most influential contemporary dynamic in American religion. They have superseded formerly key influences such as denominations, seminaries, and religious presses and publishing. Indeed, a large part of the resistance to megachurches comes from leaders of these organizations who see their own influence waning.

We are convinced that the mistaken impressions about megachurches have arisen, not necessarily due to jealousy, spite, or mean-spiritedness, but because of ignorance. This lack of knowledge is the fault of researchers, scholars, and consultants who watch American religion. The public has not had enough broad representative and reliable data about megachurches, despite the length of time this phenomenon has been around. We are trying to correct this situation. We offer data from two national studies of megachurches and draw extensively on the few quantitative studies of megachurches from the past ten to fifteen years.

We use this information to offer as broad and representative a picture as possible, while also framing it from our perspective and experiences of studying, worshipping at, and interacting with many of the megachurches and their leadership over the last two decades.

There are many myths, misperceptions, and misunderstandings surrounding these churches. These myths are repeated not only by reporters, but also by scholars, consultants, denominational leaders, and pastors. Like any good myth, there are bits of truth mixed into the fiction; that is part of what makes these myths so appealing and believable. We hope our book will sort out the wheat from the chaff regarding megachurches. But these fictional accounts about what megachurches are "really like" have blinded us all (including at times the authors of this book and the megachurch pastors themselves) to the lessons that can be learned from these congregations that have been so successful in appealing to contemporary Americans. These lessons are not just about church growth and relevant ministry; they also offer insightful glimpses into American culture and the psyche and needs of the citizens. We intend our use of the term *myth* to describe these misperceptions and misunderstandings, and hope that our attempts to explain the reality of megachurches will bring readers to a point of greater understanding about the current American religious context.

America: A Religious Nation

Despite claims to the contrary, America is still a very religious nation. Its religious life, as expressed through congregations, remains stronger than its Western counterparts and equal to much of the rest of the world. The breadth and diversity of religious expression is also astounding, making the United States one of the most pluralistic and spiritually oriented nations in the world.

Religious Belief

America has grown over the centuries as a result of strong waves of immigration, much of it for religious reasons. The tapestry of various cultures and religions has thrived in the soil of religious freedom, ease of assembly, voluntary group formation, and friendly tax laws for nonprofit organizations. Americans have also transmitted their faiths to their children down through the generations at surprisingly high levels when compared to other Western countries. Religiosity, even the veneer of such, is still highly valued in American culture. In addition to the general expressions of religion and faith in America, the specific expressions of Christian churches and other religious congregations are vital when viewed as a whole.

That being said, there is some cause for concern. Some commentators view the current state of religion and churches with great alarm and dissatisfaction, others with worry about the future. Mainline church leaders, whose denominations are fragmenting over polarizing issues and whose attendance numbers have taken a dive over the past few decades, are rightly concerned. Leaders of evangelical movements point to numerous attitude and opinion surveys that seem to show the depth and content of religious faith as quite shallow. Some in both camps point to the rising presence of other world religions in the United States and New Age spiritual experimentation as causes for worry. Other social commentators point to a rise in births to unwed parents, increased drug-related arrests, and the rise of media and music celebrity culture as an indication of the substantive loss of influence of religious leaders in American public life. Still others have rightly pointed out that scandals and infighting among church groups are reasons to worry about the positive role of religion in our society.

We are not deaf to any of these concerns, but we try to keep our view of the American religious chalice as simultaneously half empty and half full. Yes, there are definitely aspects of religious life in the United States that give us pause for concern, but as a whole American religion and, specifically, American Christianity can still be seen as thriving and as influential as ever. Bad news makes for a better story for the newspaper and other media, but it is not the whole story.

Numerous surveys have been conducted over the years asking Americans if they consider themselves "Christian" in their religious beliefs. This figure has remained remarkably stable, around 85 percent, for a long period of time.[2] In addition, when phone pollsters ask self-identified Christians, "Have you attended a religious service in the past seven days?" the figure is consistently around 40 percent, with a recent poll showing a quite optimistic figure of 47 percent.[3] Recently, academic researchers Kirk Hadaway and Penny Marler have made very credible claims that this stated behavior doesn't match the reality found in actual congregations around the country.[4] We generally agree with these researchers' findings that show actual attendance on any given week to be around 20 percent of the adult population. Nevertheless, we feel the larger percentage is still a significant measure of those in the population with a strong commitment to Christian religious practice, even if this practice doesn't include worship attendance every week. Further, by some reports, 34 percent of Americans claim to be Christian but are "unchurched," meaning they did not participate in a church service on a regular basis in the past year.[5] Still, 65 percent of all Americans claim some sort of Christian church membership.[6]

Two points here are significant. First, although this percentage has remained relatively constant, the American population has grown from 200 million in the late 1960s to 300 million in 2006. Therefore, the percentage stayed the same, but the gross number grew. Second, while much is made about immigration making the country more diverse religiously, with significant growth in Islam, Hinduism, and other Eastern traditions, this has been counterbalanced by immigration from Central American countries with large Christian constituencies. So while the gross number of religious believers in traditions other than Christianity has grown significantly, the total percentage of Americans confessing a Christian tradition has at least remained constant.

America's Churches

The actual number of churches in the United States is difficult to calculate. Denominational records provide some insight, but the growing numbers of independent and nondenominational churches, the influx of immigrant congregations of all religious traditions, and the ease with which congregations are formed and closed make it difficult to come up with exact numbers. Recent estimates range widely from 300,000 to 400,000, including congregations of all types: Protestant, Catholic, and Jewish, as well as Muslim mosques, Hindu temples, and other religious organizations. For the purposes of our calculations, we use 320,000 as an approximate number of the organized Christian congregations in the United States and 335,000 as the total for all congregations.[7] Most of these 320,000 churches are quite small. According to the National Congregations Study (NCS), the median size of a church (Protestant and Catholic combined) in the United States is seventy-five persons in regular attendance.[8]

We estimate that the number of clergy in the United States is over six hundred thousand.[9] Not all are leaders of congregations. Some serve as staff pastors or chaplains, or in other roles. In addition, as we will discuss in later chapters, the definition of church leader/clergy is somewhat fluid.

The predominance of small churches contributes to the general mental picture of churches in our culture. The assumption is that the "typical" church is a small organization that is fortunate if it has one full-time pastor. This romanticized view of the church has been long held in American history from colonial times to the farmer-preachers of the frontier. In the last century, with increasing urbanization, research has focused more on larger churches and in some ways has shifted the mental image. In many denominations and congregational studies, the mental picture of a representative church is one that has a few staff members in addition to a pastor and has an attendance of around three hundred. These mental images of the "typical church" carry considerable power and influence when one begins to assess the place of the megachurch.

Church Distribution and the Concentration of Attendance

There is yet another seldom-told story regarding the national religious picture that relates directly to megachurches. Attendance is not evenly distributed over different church sizes, and the size distribution has been changing dramatically. In the National Congregations Study, the smallest 50 percent of all the congregations surveyed contained only 11 percent of those who attend worship. At the same time, the NCS project showed that about 45 percent of the persons attending worship did so in churches in the top 10 percent in size.[10] This means that most people worship in relatively few large churches (with over three hundred attendees), but a huge number of small churches are home to relatively few people. The largest 1 percent of U.S. churches contain at least 15 percent of the worshippers, finances, and staff in America. Across the whole of Protestantism, the largest 20 percent of the churches have around 65 percent of the resources. Money, resources, and people are concentrated in the largest churches.

Mark Chaves, the principal investigator of the NCS study, recently analyzed membership data across the last century for numerous denominations and discovered a general trend toward an increasing number of very large churches, especially since 1970.[11] At the same time, in many denominations, there were an increasing number of very small churches as well. We believe that this small, but growing, number of very large churches, when compared to the rest of the landscape of American Christianity, has a big impact on how religion is being practiced in the United States.

Megachurches in Context

Megachurches are not an entirely new phenomenon, in terms of size, charismatic leadership, multiple programs, or the use of small group ministries. But the rapid proliferation of these churches since the 1970s, and especially in the past few decades, is a distinctive social phenomenon. While there are roughly 1,250 megachurches at this time, we estimate that number is increasing by at least fifty churches per year. Until the last ten years, there was not an entirely reliable, accurate count of all the megachurches in the United States. While we have confidence in our own current numbers, we do not presume that our tally is 100 percent accurate.

Previous writers have provided very good overviews of the scale of the movement historically. In 1969, Elmer Towns, a longtime church growth expert and dean of the school of religion at Liberty University, listed sixteen churches with two thousand or more attendees weekly. We think this number may be low, as it did not include some, now well-known, very large African American congregations. By 1984, reports from John Vaughan and other observers claimed about seventy very large churches in the United States. In 1990, reports had the number at 310.[12] In 2000, we found six hundred megachurches that we could verify. We have continued to add megachurches to our list in recent years as our informal tracking showed their numbers continuing to increase, but we had not done any formal systematic research to verify this growth until 2005. That year, our survey efforts and research found that there were

Table 1.1. Megachurches per Million of
Population by Year.

Year	U.S. Population (millions)	Approximate Number of Megachurches	Megachurches per Million Population
1900	76	10	0.13
1970	205	50	0.24
1980	227	150	0.70
1990	250	310	1.20
2000	275	600	2.19
2005	300	1,210	4.00

approximately 1,210 such congregations; our current count shows 1,250 verified megachurches.

It is natural to think that the rapid population growth of the United States in the past century would lead to more megachurches. Table 1.1 shows an interesting finding in this regard. When one examines both the population growth and the number of megachurches per million of population, it is evident that the number of megachurches per million Americans is increasing at an ever faster rate. Not only are there more megachurches, but also there are more megachurches per million Americans now than previously, and they are growing more rapidly than the population. From 1980 onward, the number of megachurches per million of population doubles every ten years and seems to be on track to do so between 2000 and 2010.

In an effort to document this phenomenon, our organizations have conducted two major academic surveys of megachurches. The first in 2000 was a part of a larger study, the Faith Communities Today 2000 survey. This survey was a small part of a larger study and marked our first attempt to survey the phenomenon. It collected information from 153 churches. In our recent Megachurches 2005 study, we were able to obtain data from a larger percentage of churches and have information on 382 churches with attendance of two thousand persons or more. Taking into account this recent study, the 2000 study, and other surveys, we feel we have a good base from which to analyze the megachurch phenomenon. The Appendix at the end of the book provides further details about these studies and others used to help generate this portrait of megachurches. We believe that this data, when combined with our experiences, firsthand stories, and observations, gives a clearer picture of these churches than has previously existed.

Table 1.2. Megachurch Distribution by Size.

Number of Attendees	Percentage of Megachurches
2,000–2,999	53.8
3,000–3,999	19.1
4,000–4,999	11.1
5,000–9,999	12.0
10,000 or more	4.0

Growth Trends in Attendance

In our 2005 megachurch survey, the average attendance each weekend was 3,585 persons, compared to their reported average attendance in 2000 of 2,279, indicating that attendance at these churches grew an average of 57 percent in five years. The median attendance in 2005 was 2,746 persons. (The median is the midpoint in the distribution, so half of the churches had an attendance between 2,000 and 2,746 and half had an attendance over that number.)

Obviously, not all churches fall within this range. In our 2005 survey, they varied in attendance from 2,000 to 20,000. A majority of megachurches fell in the 2,000-to-3,000 attendee range, while there are very few over 10,000 in weekly attendance. Table 1.2 indicates the range in attendance of all the megachurches on our total list of churches.

Location of Megachurches

The location of megachurches in the country can be addressed from a number of perspectives. The first approach has to do with their relationship to national geography. Another approach is to identify where they are within specific regions and states. Yet another looks at their position within major metropolitan areas and in the type of community where they are likely to be found.

Nationally, they are spread across the country. The map in Figure 1.1 shows the percentage of megachurches found in each U.S. census regional division.

In terms of state concentration, California leads the number of megachurches with 178, Texas follows with 157, Florida is next with 85, and then Georgia with 73. These are followed by Illinois, Tennessee, Ohio, and Michigan, each of which has 40-some megachurches. In the past five years, there has been significant growth in the number of these churches in the Northeast and Mid Central states. We have found no

Figure 1.1. Regional Distribution of
Megachurches. Megachurches are now found in
most states; the southern states retain the highest
concentration.

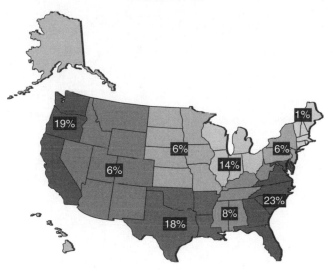

churches in Maine, New Hampshire, Vermont, Rhode Island, South Dakota, or Wyoming. Interestingly, even these states have churches of one thousand or more attendees in a typical weekend. We believe it is only a matter of time until every state has a congregation of megachurch size.

With a few exceptions, we estimate that there is a megachurch within a ninety-minute drive of 80 percent of the population of America. The map in Figure 1.2 shows the location of every megachurch in the country, represented by a small black dot. Notice that the large black masses in certain metropolitan areas actually represent many dozens of churches. We will address this pattern in later chapters, but this map makes it apparent that megachurches cluster around the largest metropolitan cities in the nation.

Within these regions and states, we also explored the megachurch's primary location in the metropolitan area. Figure 1.3 compares the locations of megachurches within a city for the 2000 and 2005 studies.

As Figure 1.3 illustrates, 45 percent of the churches are found in newer suburbs and another 29 percent in older suburbs. The remaining churches are split between being located in downtown and older residential areas. It is apparent from Figure 1.3 that newer suburbs have seen the most recent growth. In many cases, the new churches in this area are not the product of relocation but the result of newly planted churches growing

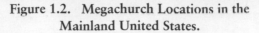

Figure 1.2. Megachurch Locations in the
Mainland United States.

Figure 1.3. Metropolitan Location of
Megachurches, 2000 and 2005.

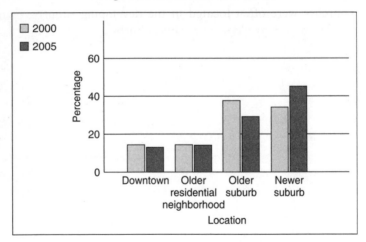

very quickly to the two-thousand-attendee level. At the same time, a
significant number of megachurches continue to reside in more urban
settings.

A brief historical glimpse at the growth of megachurches in the past
few decades shows the location of these churches relates strongly to
when they grew to megasize. Nearly all of the oldest and earliest of these

churches were urban. They were often either the historic, high-status, predominantly white, downtown "First Churches" (such as First Baptist of Dallas, Texas; First Baptist of Atlanta, Georgia; First Presbyterian in Houston, Texas; Riverside Church and Marble Collegiate in New York City; and Mount Olivet Lutheran Church in Minneapolis, Minnesota) or they were the older, established, predominantly African American congregations (including Abyssinian Baptist Church in New York City and Trinity Church in Chicago, Illinois). Due in part to their urban context and condition (such as older facilities, shortages of land, inadequate parking, and unique ministry situations), these groups of churches have adapted distinctive ways of being megachurches that set them apart somewhat from the rest of the phenomenon.

Ten years into the national proliferation of megachurches in the late 1980s, the location pattern of megachurches shifted dramatically, reflecting the country's migration dynamics. While megachurches were still predominantly found in the fastest growing metropolitan areas of the country,[13] over 75 percent of them were now located in suburban Sunbelt states. Nearly half of these were located in the Southeast, around the sprawl cities of Houston, Dallas/Ft. Worth, Atlanta, Oklahoma City, Orlando, and Nashville, although the metropolitan area of Los Angeles and surrounding cities contained the greatest number of megachurches. These churches were often located in the developing suburbs of these cities, areas now seen as older inner-ring suburbs.

Another decade or more of church growth has not substantially altered the areas of greatest concentration of megachurches, but the last ten years have seen an increased dispersal of very large churches throughout the country and widely distributed throughout metropolitan areas. The newest megachurches are predominantly locating in distant suburbs or exurbs, with a few developing in central city, urban locations often by reclaiming abandoned buildings for new spiritual purposes.

It is perhaps too soon to know for sure if this pattern of dispersal indicates that the megachurch phenomenon has become less dependent on population growth patterns, but there is evidence that it might be the case. Certainly there are very few states now that don't have at least one megachurch around their major population centers. As these congregations take on an increasingly regional character, there are very few large urban regions around the country that will be unable to support one or more of these churches.

There are numerous reasons why concentrations of megachurches exist in the most rapidly growing, suburban metropolitan areas of the country. Suburban areas offer larger, less expensive plots of land suitable for the acres of parking lots and auxiliary buildings needed to support a congregation of thousands. In the initial phases of suburban development, zoning regulations are often less restrictive and planning officers less concerned about their tax base. Newly developing suburbs often come complete with easy access to major highways, support institutions such as new restaurants and gas stations, and most important, burgeoning residential housing complexes and their residents who are exactly the type of people most attracted to megachurches: consumer-oriented, willing to commute great distances, highly mobile and often displaced, middle-class, in middle-level management positions, well-educated, and with a traditional nuclear family structure. All of these characteristics point to the new suburban fringes of major cities as fertile soil for megachurches.

The recent founding or current relocation of many megachurches in the outer and newer suburbs hints at other explanations for why they often seem more able to grow, adapt, and remain technologically sophisticated. Research shows that newly established congregations have a considerably greater likelihood of growing.[14] These rapidly expanding congregations can evolve their buildings, leadership, and programmatic structures along with their growth. More established churches, if caught in a time of growth, must undertake the often difficult and painful task of discarding or revising many of their traditions, ingrained organizational habits, and even physical structures. All too often, established congregations end up limiting their potential membership increase by retaining leadership or organizational models that do not work for growth, or at least they are stuck in a building and physical setting that hampers their development.

However, brand-new congregations or churches with new locations and bigger sanctuaries have no existing patterns to revamp. In essence, they can choose to adopt whatever organizational model, or for that matter building structure, that works best for the size they anticipate becoming. It is a dynamic evolutionary strategy of growth versus a re-creationist effort to expand. This lesson is not lost on many national denominational leaders who have recently engaged in concerted efforts at new church development.

Given these factors, it is not surprising that many megachurches started out being housed in temporary structures—school auditoriums, abandoned shopping centers, and even circus tents—before building their own sanctuary in a still-developing suburban area. Perhaps the best-known example of maintaining a fluid congregational form during its most rapid growth period is Rick Warren's Saddleback Community Church. This congregation met in a high school, then in countless satellite locations around the Mission Viejo, California, area before they built their current sanctuary. Many megachurches report that every move to a new structure generated a rapid influx of new members to fill the building to capacity.[15] Our 2000 survey of megachurches echoed this "living at the limits of capacity." Those churches we surveyed had an average seating of over two thousand, with 40 percent of them claiming to have moved into their building since 1980, and 85 percent describing the physical condition of their building as excellent or good. Nevertheless, over half the congregational leaders described their structures as inadequate for their current needs, both because of current and projected future needs.

Financial Resources

Financial resources are imperfect measures of the scale and scope of the megachurch phenomenon. However, some sense of the scale and influence of these megachurches can be derived from their budgets. The average total income reported from the megachurches in the 2005 survey was $6 million per year, compared to our 2000 figure of $4.8 million. In terms of financial health, even adjusting for inflation, the megachurches in this study appear on the surface to be better off than they were five years ago. The average expenditures for the congregations also increased to $5.6 million, reflecting almost the same ratio between income and expenses as the 2000 data. It is worth noting that the combined average income from the approximately 1,200 megachurches in the United States is roughly $7.2 billion a year. Nevertheless, when the churches were asked to describe their financial situation (see Figure 1.4), considerably fewer churches described it as excellent when compared to the 2000

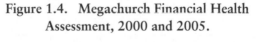

Figure 1.4. Megachurch Financial Health Assessment, 2000 and 2005.

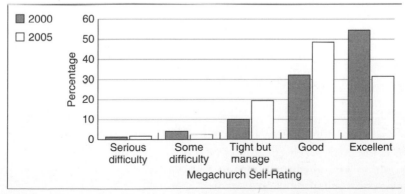

study. Almost 50 percent described their financial situation as good, but almost 20 percent said it was "tight but they manage."

Most of these churches have multiple streams of income that feed these enormous budgets. The largest stream by far is that described as undesignated giving, that is, offerings, tithes, and gifts from attendees that support the overall programs of the church as the leadership sees fit. A second stream would be various forms of designated giving that are directed toward a particular program or ministry. Additionally, some churches gather money for capital campaigns for buildings, land, or debt retirement. Others acquire money for outside projects, including missionaries and church planting, through special project offerings. Another stream includes user fees gathered for programs such as youth camp, books for special studies, and tickets for luncheons. Yet another includes income from operations such as bookstores, television ministries, schools, nurseries, gyms, coffee shops, and cafes, as well as rental fees for the use of the building. This latter approach is a growing stream for many churches that own their own facility. A few of these churches also have endowments, but unlike previous generations of American churches, these numbers are not so significant. Unfortunately, our Megachurches 2005 survey did not ask churches to break their figures down into the various income streams.

Megachurch Growth in Cultural Context

It is our contention that megachurches began to propagate rapidly in the 1970s because of changes taking place in modern American society that made this religious form more appealing to a broad range of contemporary Christians and potential Christians. This is not to deny that God is at work in these ministries or that megachurch pastors are not gifted men and women of God. However, we must ask: What happened to cause this organizational form to gain rapid acceptance in the past few decades when it had not gained such broad acceptance previously even though there were examples of large churches in the past? If one looks at this religious phenomenon in relation to larger cultural changes, then much can be learned about the social needs and spiritual nature of contemporary human beings.

It is absolutely clear that Americans have become more comfortable with large institutional forms. Since the 1950s, hospitals, schools, stores, factories, and entertainment centers have all grown to megaproportions; therefore, why shouldn't churches? Americans have not only grown accustomed to large organizations, but they have even had their character and tastes shaped by them. From the moment of birth, large hospitals, schools, theaters, malls, and amusement parks have been teaching us how to read signs, how to find our path through a maze of hallways, how to wait in lines, how to recall where we parked in a vast lot, how to cope with cavernous indoor spaces, how to watch large video screens, and how to assert ourselves in a crowd if we have a question or need something. The megachurch assumes all these skills of its members. The megachurch takes for granted that those coming to church also work, shop, and play in similar institutional forms.

What seems anomalous and out of place in our contemporary context is when a person downsizes his or her expectations of organizational size to attend a small church once a week. After a week of working in a major corporation, shopping in a food warehouse and megamall, viewing movies at a multiplex theater, and having children who attend a regional high school, it seems incongruous that this family would feel comfortable in a forty-person church. So the force of cultural conditioning is on the side of megachurches.

Another reason for the success of megachurches may be because they unintentionally created forms and features in their churches to handle the size of the organization that in actuality answered the unspoken needs of a contemporary audience. Early megachurches borrowed models of organization and presentation methods from other institutions around them in order to cope with large numbers of attendees. These alterations in response to size created an organizational model of church that fit a new social and cultural context.

The creation of these social and organizational dynamics in megachurches seems to contribute to the vitality of this distinctive religious organization. Several of these dynamics include doing ministry with intentionality, including organizing member interactions; having a clear niche identity; creating professional-quality, contemporary, and entertaining worship; and addressing modern individuals in a way that allows them choice and yet asks them to become serious in their commitments.

Out of necessity because of their size, megachurches have had to overstructure every aspect of member involvement. One cannot expect that natural processes at work in small-scale settings will happen within a massive congregation. As such, megachurches must institutionalize greeting people, ushering them into the sanctuary, incorporating new members into church rules and norms, involving people in the ministries of the church, and the interaction and fellowship of participants with each other during social times between services and week to week. Nothing is left to chance. The assumption is that people in this society do not know each other, nor will they make the effort if left alone. The megachurch assumption is that contemporary individuals do not interact unless forced to and are relative strangers to those they meet. People need the intimacy of small groups, but will not seek them out. There is also the realization that people will remain spectators and marginal participants unless they are strongly encouraged to become involved.

Congregations must have an identity and a clear sense of themselves. This clarity is attractive to outsiders and compelling for insiders. One can choose to commit to something only if the person knows what they are committing to. In a capitalist world of niche marketing, a clear and easily communicated purpose is essential.

Anything done in praise and adoration of God should be done in the best manner possible. Quality denotes professionalism and indicates that the activity has merit and importance. The members of the congregation have been schooled on television, movies, plays, and other professional performances. Religious performances are judged in part by these standards. At the same time, contemporary culture is one that emphasizes informality and relaxed norms of dress and behavior.

These very large churches try hard to convey the Christian message in ways that connote that the faith is relevant to contemporary life. The sermons focus on Scripture but try to make it practical and down to earth, applicable for daily life. The church space and form suggest that it is similar to everyday secular structures, especially for those churches reaching out to persons formerly turned off by traditional church models. The culture of the worship service encourages everyone to "come as you are." There are low, and often almost no, boundaries between where the church's ministries start and the world's influences end. The distinctions between secular and sacred are often minimal at best. Such blurring is easily seen in the use of technology and pop cultural influences in the services. Recent movies are often used as examples in sermons; contemporary Christian music in the service could easily be heard on the radio or at a Grammy Awards show.

Worship is undertaken in part to entertain, to entice, to excite, and to inspire. The congregation is a mix of the committed and the spectator, the saint and the seeker. What happens in worship, however, is only one dimension of the full life of the church, one aspect of their vision of a complete Christian life that also should include education, fellowship, and service.

The religious message must have a relevance to everyday life and contemporary reality. It is not necessary for worship styles and sermon forms to be in contemporary idioms, but for them to touch on daily concerns, issues, and social needs. People have to be able to hear their lives in the message and glean understanding that translates into wise actions throughout the week with their family, coworkers, or spouse. They want to learn about God and grow deeper the faith. They are at church to develop their spiritual lives.

These congregations create a small-town community in a placeless suburbia. Each has its culture and customs, its small groups and programs, its sports leagues and bake sales, and its reconstituted connections and community feel for transplanted and uprooted middle class Americans. In countless interviews, we have heard participants talk in terms of the church's family-like atmosphere, being a home to them, and finding a place there. This is likewise reflected in the names many of the megachurches have adopted. Out of the 1,250 megachurches, roughly a quarter have names that imply a place, whether it is an actual location, a biblical place, or a space such as a crossroads, valley, bayside, or ocean view.

Modern Americans want choice; they want options. In a society where everything is mutable and most identities can be chosen, the act of choosing creates commitment. A church will be able to attract a greater number of diverse persons if it offers a larger number of options for service times and styles, for ministries to meet needs, for places to serve others, and for opportunities to volunteer. Choice enhances commitment. Options allow people to choose exactly what they want to do and be in the congregation. They can interact with the church on their own terms, creating a customized experience of the church to satisfy their spiritual needs as they see fit. But then the church attempts to entice and educate these self-interested new attendees into a more mature Christian walk.

Involvement in the church and in a life of faith is defined by the continual act of personal commitment. The meaning of "being a part of this place" is less defined by a one-time decision—by becoming a member—than it is by active participation—by a continual choice to be involved. This is such a significant switch that many megachurches do not even have a membership category. Likewise, one is intentionally challenged to be involved and deepen their faith commitments—to move from anonymity to engagement.

Finally, the size of the megachurch proclaims the power of religion, exhibiting the prominent place of religion in the modern world. It is powerful in its influence on politics, in the courts, and in the national religious community. The success of the church translates into the success of each individual attendee. It is what they aspire to be. As such, it is a motivational element and inspirational ideal for many within the congregation.

Influence Beyond the Numbers

Because of the characteristics and growth we have discussed, it is apparent that megachurches and their leaders are key influences on American religious practices. To some, this is not a big surprise, but the behavior of certain political, religious, and social leaders would suggest that not everyone agrees with this assessment.

Publishing houses, religious newspapers, and even online blogs certainly play a role in religious leadership as do denominational leaders and seminaries, but our view is that leaders of megachurches are defining what Protestant America looks like for the foreseeable future. It is our contention that church leaders, both clergy and lay, look to megachurches and their pastors for their cues and direction for the future. These churches are the seedbed of innovation, change, and growth in other churches as well as their own. Some are becoming educational institutions and organizations in their own right through the establishment of Bible colleges and seminaries and numerous conferences and training events. There is an ever-growing number of publishing resources coming from these churches, especially in the area of small-group curriculum and worship materials. While a few parachurch organizations, including Leadership Network, seek to build networks of friendship and support among these churches, it is the churches themselves that are the leaders today.

Historically, larger churches in every denomination and tradition have had great influence over the state of affairs in their respective traditions. An examination of the speaker lists for conventions, gatherings, camp meetings, and conferences from previous eras would show that most of the speakers came from larger churches. Those meetings might also have included a professor, a denominational leader, or a popular writer. Now megachurch pastors tend to dominate those platforms.

Megachurches serve as a dominant influence on religious life in local communities as well. Each community has its own contextual system at play, but the largest fish in the pond help to set the agenda for the rest. In some communities, leaders of smaller churches act in opposition to, or distance themselves from, these megachurches. But many times the attendees of these churches have friends in the megachurches and report what these churches are doing, hoping to have similar programs and ministries within their own church, and leaving smaller church pastors more frustrated than ever.

Many of the megachurches are leaders in diverse areas of community life outside the church. With large resources of people, finances, and creativity, they apply themselves to the pressing problems of their communities in the areas of literacy, hunger, and homelessness.

Finally, a small handful of megachurch pastors such as Rick Warren, Joel Osteen, Max Lucado, T. D. Jakes, and Bill Hybels have gained prominence on the national and occasionally on the international stage. This is a continual cycle in American religious life. Each generation has its own prophets, preachers, and popular spokespersons. The most famous tend to sell lots of books, appear on television shows, and conduct regular speaking tours. This is never more than a small handful of pastors, but at present all of them are leaders of megachurches. Yet this is not the entire story regarding these churches or their leaders, and to judge the whole movement by this small group presents a distorted picture of the phenomenon. In the following chapters we hope to clarify that picture.

○

Applying What You Have Read

In this chapter, we want you to consider the religious context for your ministry. Every region has its own culture and contextual factors to consider, but there are some key areas we think it wise to consider.

1. Define the contextual area that your church actually serves right now. If you were to mark on a map where the attendees currently live, what would that map look like? There are some handy Web tools that we mention on our Web site for doing this, but don't overdo it. A crudely drawn map will do just fine. In working with congregations over the years, we find that leaders are often surprised about how large an area the church encompasses.

2. Mark the locations of other churches in and around the same area your church serves. Our Web site includes tips on doing this easily. Include some larger churches that may not be in the area, but might have influence and draw attendees from your area. Remember to mark those in a wide variety of traditions, not just those in your own denominational family. In addition to their locations, write down the suspected weekend attendance of these churches. You can ask around through friends and acquaintances, or even just call the church to inquire. How does your church fit this picture?

3. Obtain key demographic information, which is easily gathered from local officials, real estate sites, or the census bureau for your area. You don't need exact numbers here; just get a sense of the area. On your map, write down the estimated population in the region. Most of the census studies also break down the population by age, income,

and racial groups. Also get some idea of how mobile and transient people are in your area. Mobility refers to the number of people that move into or out of the area in a given time period. A rough percentage is usually available from state and county government Web sites.

Now you can compare the total population of your area to the total attendance church attendance in the region. Most church leaders are astounded to see that the majority of people are not attending church. Additionally, many times we find that the number of highly mobile residents in an area can be equal to half of all the church attendees in that region.

In most areas of the country, there are many people not currently attending church anywhere, even if there are plenty of churches in a given regional locale. Reflect on this mapping and the place of your church within that region in light of the lessons of this chapter.

- How would you describe your map and your place on it?
- What are the largest three age groups (or other demographic characteristics), and how do these relate to your congregation's mission?
- Roughly, how many people are currently not attending any church and what could you do to reach them?

2

"ALL MEGACHURCHES
ARE ALIKE"

_Imagine it: . . . there is an enormous building . . . relatively
modern in design. . . . Inside . . . is stadium seating enough
for 10,000 sometimes 20,000 people. The stage is filled with
various instruments, microphones, cameras, and a huge video
display screen. . . . Now you can grab a meal, find a personal
trainer, or even join an athletic team. It is impossible to grasp
that in the 21st century churches would become corporate
conglomerates, essentially "selling" the word of God to
Christian consumers._[1]

_Part of the problem is what Leith Anderson calls "generic
Christianity." He points out that "today, one can go into a
church (especially a megachurch) of nearly any denomination
. . . and be unable to notice any difference among them. They
all are likely to use the same praise songs and contemporary
worship style. The sermons will tend to be about practical
biblical tips for successful living, and go light on doctrine
and sin."_[2]

THE ABOVE JOURNALISTIC DESCRIPTIONS of the megachurch phenomenon are just one example of the almost daily portrayals that echo a
similar theme: all megachurches look alike. The press and popular media
have painted this religious reality with a broad brush and a monochro-
matic palette. The resulting portrait is impressionistic at best and does
not accurately describe more than a handful of megachurches. The truth
is that although there are many similarities across megachurches, there
are also significant differences among them. While their similarities help
explain why this form of church has been so successful in attracting

members in the past few decades, the diversity among them explains why particular congregations have grown so rapidly.

Where Does the Myth of Sameness Come From?

There are good reasons for the misconception that they all look alike, and it can't all be blamed on the press. The largest megachurches in the country garner the vast majority of attention in the media and with the general public. After reading a dozen news stories about Willow Creek Community Church, Saddleback Church, or Lakewood Church, the reader easily begins to draw the conclusion that all megachurches look and function like these prominent examples. Likewise, researchers and consultants attempt to explain the phenomenon simply and clearly to their audiences—and that works best with one story line. That story line goes something like this: megachurches are huge, nondenominational, seeker-oriented, founded in the past forty years or less; they seldom use traditional symbols of the faith such as crosses and stained glass; they do embrace capitalism, the Republican Party, and evangelical theology; and they are the domains of a strong authoritative leader. In fact, this portrayal accurately fits only about a quarter of all the megachurches, if even that many. These characteristics often cause certain megachurches to stand out from the rest of the religious community in the United States, so their traits get emphasized. A comprehensive and nuanced look at the megachurches in the country shows a tremendous amount of diversity.

Differences Among Megachurches

By definition, all megachurches are large. Their size and the management of such large numbers of attendees mean that most of the megachurches adopt similar organizational forms and leadership structures. These churches scan the religious and secular world to identify and adopt the most successful leadership, organizational, business, and technological models in addressing the needs of their thousands of attendees. This borrowing of "best practices" does create certain commonalities across churches, but if one looks past this similarity, many variations among the 1,200-plus megachurches are evident.

Later in this chapter, we will describe four distinctive streams within this movement of megachurches. The streams all run into the same river of megachurches as a whole, but these tributaries have some characteristics that let us distinguish some of the differences within the movement. The

Figure 2.1. Megachurch Growth Rate, 2000 to 2005.

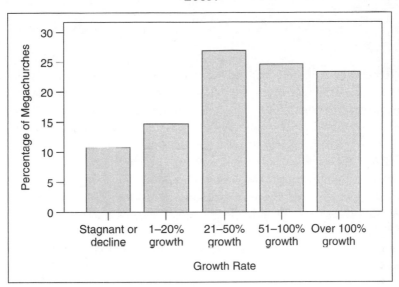

overall diversity within the phenomenon begins with the key definitional characteristic of the megachurch: its size.

Size

Less than 5 percent of all megachurches fit the often-described ten thousand-plus horde of worship attendees. In fact, the vast majority of megachurches average between two and three thousand attendees at weekend services.

The megachurches in our 2005 survey reported an average regular weekly attendance of 3,585 persons, with an average stated increase of 57 percent of their attendance over the previous five-year period. However, not all of these large congregations grew at the same rates; over 10 percent of them did not grow at all, and a few dozen actually declined in attendance (Figure 2.1).

It should be obvious, but it seems often overlooked that if a church has two thousand or twelve thousand in attendance it makes a huge functional difference. Throughout the following chapters, variation in the size of megachurches influences their characteristics, resources, and approaches to ministry in ways that often go unrecognized. Size distinctions are important when thinking about megachurches, not just in setting these churches apart from others, but also in understanding the differences among them.

Founding Date

It should be apparent to anyone with even a modest knowledge of American religious history that throughout the last two centuries there have been a number of large megachurches, often with the contemporary characteristics of charismatic pastors, countless ministries, theatre-style auditoriums, and performance-oriented services. A few such famous historic examples include Henry Ward Beecher's Plymouth Church, Aimee Semple McPherson's Angelus Temple, D. L. Moody's Chicago Street Church, and then the later and larger Moody Church, and finally the Moody Memorial Church, or Charles Mason's Mason Temple.[3]

These examples, however, are nearly always forgotten in discussions of the contemporary megachurch. The assumption is that the megachurch model of the church appeared in the 1960s out of thin air. This is not the case in terms of the large-scale worship sanctuary, entertaining or small-group worship, and multiple ministries. Neither is it the case that all the current megachurches were founded within the last few decades. What is significant about the contemporary growth of the current megachurches in recent years, however, is that the culture at this time has proved to be fertile soil for this form to proliferate at a rapid rate compared with previous times in U.S. history. Likewise, for individual church growth, it is noteworthy that nearly all of the churches founded before 1960 grew to megachurch size only after the mid-1970s. There is something distinctive about the last few decades that has promoted the development of so many megachurches. There is a distinct resonance between what megachurches offer and what many contemporary Americans desire—but that is a story begun in the previous chapter that will continue throughout the book.

In the 2005 Megachurches Today study, the average year that the megachurches were founded was 1951, with roughly 50 percent having begun prior to 1965; but further examination of this allows us to see many variations. The more recent the date of origin, the more rapid the growth was between 2000 and 2005. It is also more likely that a newer megachurch still has the pastor who was in charge when the tremendous growth occurred. Interestingly, they also have higher median weekly attendance rates than megachurches founded in earlier decades. In contrast, the older, established churches in general have larger sanctuaries. Logically, newer megachurches should have rapid growth over a short period, still be in the tenure of their first pastor, and have

Table 2.1. Megachurch Growth, Attendance,
and Sanctuary Size, by Decade of Founding.

Year of Founding	Share of All Megachurches (percentage)	Median Rate of Growth in Five Years (percentage)	Median Attendance	Median Size of Main Sanctuary (number of seats)
Before 1945	29	33	2,600	1,500
1945–1954	7	36	2,650	1,500
1955–1964	12	27	2,900	1,675
1965–1974	8	58	2,556	1,300
1975–1984	20	55	3,100	1,100
1985–1994	16	100	3,350	1,200
1995–2005	8	250	3,430	1,150

smaller buildings, but such characteristics are seldom taken into account when thinking about the overall megachurch reality. Table 2.1 shows the details of these trends by the decade of founding for the megachurches.

New Spring Church in Anderson, South Carolina, for example, began as a ministry to college students that met in the local Baptist College. As increasing numbers of noncollege-age adults started attending, the decision was made to launch New Spring as a church in 2000. From 2000 to early 2006, the church grew to four worship services each Sunday before moving into its first campus in February 2006. The new building seats twenty-five hundred in its auditorium and has extensive spaces for children. It regularly has over seven thousand persons in weekly attendance. This church did not even exist when we did our 2000 survey, and while a rather extreme example, illustrates how fast these younger churches can grow.

Region and Urban Location

A megachurch's location in a region and in a metropolitan area plays an important role in how it functions. Over the past forty years, the distribution of very large churches around the country has been shifting. In part, the growth of megachurches has always paralleled the changing concentrations of population.[4] Early in the megachurch phenomenon, from the period of 1945 until 1970, most large churches were found in the downtowns of major metropolitan areas throughout the country. During the 1970s and 1980s, however, they proliferated in suburbs of rapidly growing sprawl cities of the southern and western regions. By the 1990s, nearly every state in the nation had several megachurches, and significant numbers of megachurches were appearing outside the Sunbelt. The highest concentration of megachurches remains consistently in the southern and western regions. However, the phenomenon has become increasingly evident in the eastern, central, and northwestern states. Examination of the 2005 median growth rates of megachurches shows those in the Northeast and North Central regions are increasing in size more rapidly than in the South and West, even though the southern and western regions are growing faster in population and have higher concentrations of megachurches.

Likewise, a comparison of our 2000 and 2005 megachurch studies shows that the locations of these churches are shifting within metropolitan areas as well. Not only are established congregations moving into the outer, newer suburbs of these cities, but brand-new megachurches are also more likely to be found in these exurban locations. Those churches located in newer suburbs had much higher five-year growth rates than churches in the other parts of those metro areas. Interestingly, megachurches located in the inner city or downtown had the next highest rate of growth.

We are now seeing a rapid rise in the number of churches reaching megachurch proportions that are located in more exurban, formerly rural counties. Many times they are not classified as metropolitan areas, but are fringes of metropolitan areas or transportation corridors that connect metro areas. Some of these outlying rural-oriented counties now have their own homegrown megachurches. The church mentioned previously in this chapter in Anderson, South Carolina, is one example, and Christ the King Church in rural Skagit Valley in Washington is another.

Denominational Affiliation

Although it is often assumed that all megachurches are nondenominational, in reality nearly two-thirds belong to a formal national denomination. However, there are twice as many nondenominational megachurches as there are megachurches from any single denomination (see Table 2.2). Among the roughly 65 percent that are denominationally affiliated, the largest number are associated with the Southern Baptist Convention, which is the largest Protestant denomination in the United States. A relatively new quasi-denominational organization, Calvary Chapel Fellowship of Churches, has the largest percentage of megachurches within a denomination. This loose fellowship of churches began with Chuck Smith's Calvary Chapel in Costa Mesa, California, in 1965 and today includes just over one thousand congregations in the United States. With a total of fifty-five megachurches, nearly 5.5 percent

Table 2.2. Megachurches by Denominational
Affiliation.

Affiliation	Percentage
Nondenominational	34
Southern Baptist	16
Baptist (unspecified)	10
Assemblies of God	6
United Methodist	5
Calvary Chapel	4.4
Christian	4.2
Four Square	1.2
Church of Christ	1.0
Evangelical Lutheran Church	1.0
Vineyard Christian Fellowship	1.0

of its churches have grown to several thousand attendees in just over forty years.

The top ten denominational affiliations listed in Table 2.2 account for roughly 50 percent of all megachurches. However, because many of these churches hide or at least downplay their denominational label, it is not surprising how the perception that most megachurches are nondenominational has arisen.[5] Denominational names carry with them preconceptions about style, theology, and worship formats. Megachurches want to be judged on what they have to offer, not on the latest announcement by a denomination's national office. Megachurches are also quite self-sufficient; they don't need the resources, guidance, or identity that a national body can provide. As such, many of the megachurches are functionally nondenominational; they hold both the national body and the denominational label and identity at arm's length.

Worship Styles

Much is made of the distinctive uniform worship style of megachurches. According to our survey, the vast majority of megachurch worship is characterized by contemporary praise music, led by a worship team, accompanied by orchestra, drums, and electric guitars and augmented by state-of-the-art sound systems and huge projection screens.

However, there are some exceptions. A closer look reveals considerable variation within the worship service. Fifteen percent embrace a relatively high-church, formal liturgical approach to worship complete with Old and New Testament readings, weekly communion, robed preachers, and the like. Almost a third of churches always use choirs, while roughly the same percentage never or seldom use them. Recorded music is both wholeheartedly embraced and rejected by equal numbers of megachurches. Twelve percent of these churches seldom or never celebrate communion, while 20 percent always include it in worship. Speaking in tongues can nearly always be found in roughly 15 percent and absolutely never in 60 percent of megachurches. Creeds are recited often in approximately 20 percent of these churches, never in about 40 percent of them, and used sometimes in the remaining ones. As is evident in these figures, the Megachurch movement is much more diverse in worship styles than most news stories and book authors would lead one to believe.

More than any area within the megachurch phenomenon, worship content and format continue to evolve. In our 2005 study, over twenty percent of megachurches said they changed their worship style a lot in the past five years. A quarter of them reported they had multiple worship services of vastly different styles, and a third of those with multiple sites said their worship styles differed according to location. Far from having a uniform worship format, megachurches are constantly experimenting with various types of worship experiences to appeal to a broad range of potential constituents. For example, Saturday evening may be a service designed for families with young children in mind, where a family can be comfortable attending in a group. Sunday morning might have two worship experiences in the morning, one led by a contemporary praise band and the other by a choir. A separate children's program is offered at both services. The final worship of the weekend may be Sunday evening and target young adults and college students without children. It would have the loudest music and, surprisingly, perhaps the longest sermon also.

Racial Makeup

Because megachurches reflect the racial composition of the overall U.S. population, the majority are Caucasian. But that does not diminish the variety in their racial makeup. Roughly 10 to 12 percent of megachurches are predominantly African American, another 2 percent have mostly Asian attendees, and approximately 2 percent are primarily Hispanic.[6] Perhaps the most interesting characteristic regarding race within the megachurch phenomenon is that of the large percentage of churches with a significant multiracial constituency. We will discuss this aspect in Chapter Eight.

Vision and Audience

Who is your target audience? What is your ministry's vision? These have become commonplace questions thanks to extensive reporting about the marketing and visioning efforts of well-known megachurches such as Saddleback and Willow Creek. Indeed, many of the churches we have studied are highly successful precisely because they have a clear vision of who God is calling them to be and reach with the Gospel. Some define their ministry niche narrowly and others more broadly. Some target an age and life stage demographic such as young adults, young families, or in the case of retirement and resort communities, "active adults." Others target a mind-set that transcends age such as "California leisure" or "black urban professionals." These churches have tailored their interpretation of the Christian message and their presentation of it to appeal to a particular cultural niche audience. These intentional efforts to focus their ministry efforts on a particular target audience shape the character of the church itself, its program, worship style, and makeup of the congregation.

In effect, the carefully crafted, distinctive identities of megachurches help create the diversity found across the phenomenon. This is an often-overlooked reality. Many megachurches think seriously about the type of person God is calling them to minister to and use marketing strategies to define how best to reach this audience, but this process does not create uniformity in the megachurch model. Instead, it results in considerable diversity of focus, architecture, style, and substance among the megachurches. In addition, the clear targeting of a few niches leads to focused ministry, and that intentionality strengthens the ministry. But it also creates great diversity in the overall phenomenon. For example, New Spring Church in Anderson, South Carolina, looks considerably different from New Birth Church near Atlanta; Redeemer Church in New York City looks radically different from North Coast Church in Vista, California. New Spring reaches younger Caucasian adults and has loud music in a fairly rural context, while New Birth reaches upwardly mobile African Americans with forceful preaching and exuberant singing in the growing Atlanta suburbs. Redeemer Church in New York City uses classical music, social outreach, and small groups to reach young married couples and singles in the heart of Manhattan, while North Coast has multiple venues and locations using a variety of music styles to reach the California casual culture of northern San Diego County.

As we look across the more than twelve hundred megachurches, significant distinctions can be seen regarding what generations, cultural groups, or societal styles are being addressed. Often these diverse forms reflect the senior pastor's approach or personal calling, but they may also represent a distinctive context or, on occasion, the dominant characteristics of those who are drawn to a particular ministry.

A story we have heard frequently throughout our years of working with these pastors goes something like this: Many times a younger pastor either starts a church or comes to a church and wants to reach "their generation." The pastor's mannerisms, illustrations, stylistic patterns of speech, and other methods resonate with younger generations in that area. The leader and the church position themselves as an alternative to other churches in the area, providing a different type of ministry and outreach to the community. This ministry emphasis flows from the pastor's person and identity rather than being an intentional idealization of a type of prospective member to be reached. "I want to have a church where I would want to be a member and that my kids could love" often describes the motivation among the younger generations of these pastors. Toby Slough, lead pastor of Cross Timbers Community Church in rural Argyle, Texas, is but one example of this. He had been a member of staff teams at other large churches before, but felt trapped by the expectations to "be perfect" and not be authentic, honest, or transparent with the congregation. Knowing he had some issues in his own life, he started Cross Timbers Church for people like himself, people with "life issues." He made Cross Timbers a place where those issues could be addressed. He told folks when they started the church in 2000 to come as they are and the church would address their problems and sins. Now, five thousand people attend weekly, and the church has a "Care Center" with multiple ministries to help attendees deal with all their "life issues." We will say more about this striving for authenticity and dealing with human needs in a later chapter on leadership.

Four Distinctive Streams of Megachurches

Over the years, there have been many attempts to classify churches in various ways to help understand them better. Congregational scholars usually do this by size. They assign labels to different size categories and then use these categories to identify leadership, program, and organizational distinctions among the churches. In general, these have been good tools. But once a church exceeds two thousand attendees, the variations continue. Size is not the only significant variable. Some religion researchers have used location (urban, suburban, or rural) as a primary classification. Others have focused on worship styles ("traditional," "blended," contemporary," or "emergent") as the primary classification type. While we would agree that size, worship style, and location do lead to some understanding of a church's culture, organization, and mind-set, we have developed four categories or "streams" that attempt to encompass these and other variables in an effort to categorize distinct types within the megachurch phenomenon.

We acknowledge that many readers may not agree with our classifications, including some megachurch pastors. Nevertheless, we find these categories to be a useful tool when trying to describe how large groups of these churches are different from each other. The stream or tributary metaphor indicates that while the collection of churches is a part of the same river system, there are distinct differences within the internal and external perception of these churches. Acknowledgment of these diverse streams helps explains how one megachurch pastor can proclaim success resulted from his "way of doing church," while another asserts that a totally different approach can be equally flourishing. Each stream can articulate some common points of emphasis that have proven successful for them, yet the other streams see little value in those points of emphasis. These streams are in part cultural and stylistic distinctions created to appeal to different audiences. However, these different styles also can reshape a church's organization, format, ministry approach, and entire character of the congregation. We suggest that there are at least four distinctive streams of megachurches, as follows:

1. Old Line/Program-Based
2. Seeker
3. Charismatic/Pastor-Focused
4. New Wave/Re-Envisioned

These are not necessarily exclusive categories, and in some cases the characteristics blend across the types (see Table 2.3); nor are congregations easily placed in one or the other given that they all are continuing to evolve and change. Nevertheless, as a rough percentage we currently see 30 percent in the Old Line/Program-Based approach, 30 percent in the Seeker stream, 25 percent in the Charismatic/Pastor-Focused stream, and 15 percent in the New Wave/Re-Envisioned stream.

Old Line/Program-Based

Megachurches within this stream are often among those with the oldest founding dates. They are usually the established First Churches in their locales and are more likely to be located in the downtown urban and older suburban parts of a city. They often existed long before the pastor under whom the significant growth occurred and are liable to have gone through pastoral transition since that person. These congregations are

Table 2.3. Characteristics of Megachurch Streams

	Old Line/Program-Based	Seeker	Charismatic/Pastor-Focused	New Wave/Re-Envisioned
Percentage of megachurches	30%	30%	25%	15%
Predominant locations	Downtown/tall steeple/"overgrown country churches"	Suburbs	Older and newer suburbs. Some urban.	Older and newer suburbs with a few urban areas where young people are moving in. Most likely to have multiple sites.
Constituency	Usually the most monocultural and monoracial of all types. Predominantly Anglo, or alternatively, predominantly African American.	Mostly Anglo, baby boomer target, at least originally, and now spreading to younger generations.	All races and ages, and the most multiracial; multicultural stream in the movement.	Mostly Anglo with Asians and black mixes. Predominantly very young and young adult families. Second-most multiracial.
Worship styles	Most traditional. More likely to use formal, liturgical, high-church worship. Worship characterized most often as "reverent." Worship leaders are called "Ministers of Music." More communion than any other stream.	Contemporary. Led by "Worship Pastor" and Praise team. Informal, simple format that rarely changes from week to week. Most likely to use drama. Designed for those outside the church. Communion is seldom, given at weekend services.	Exuberant. Designed to energize believers. Longest sermons. More focus on response from the hearers and prayer times than any other stream. Led by worship leader and teams that differ in size; may also have a choir.	Explicitly Christian. Most likely to be driven from the large video screens. More reflective, and more calls for public commitments than the Seeker. More direct preaching styles and direct confrontation of the hot topics of the day.

Music used in worship	Use organ and choir more often than the other streams. Can have some contemporary services as well.	Upbeat music similar to Top 40 pop music. Most likely of all streams to use actual tunes and songs from the popular culture.	Heavily God- and Spirit-focused contemporary. Praise sung with fervor with arms outstretched to God.	Mix of music and various formats. Smaller music ensembles with a mix of music, but usually led by electric guitar.
Role of the senior pastor/leader	Administrator/leader/preacher	Chief evangelist/preacher-teacher/leader	Bishop/preacher/leader/decision maker	Leader/teaching team leader/team leader
Education of senior pastor	Almost always master's-level graduate of accredited seminary.	Most actually have master's-level degrees from a seminary.	Usually less formal education than the other streams.	Least traditional in pastoral education.
Christian education/discipleship methodologies	Sunday school/Sunday-based classes predominate.	Small groups that usually meet in home predominate.	Some cell and small groups, but not a big emphasis.	Small groups that vary in composition and style.
What matters the most	Maintaining the witness in the present location. An evolutionary approach to change. Stewards for the next generation of worshippers in this place.	Reaching those that are seeking God. Making church a place that can reach the unchurched.	Getting persons in to experience the worship of God through the anointing on the pastor and worship leader. Reaching out to the community through empowered worship.	Proclaiming Jesus to their targeted constituency. Influencing and reaching culture in creative ways.

(continued)

Table 2.3. (continued)

	Old Line/Program-Based	Seeker	Charismatic/Pastor-Focused	New Wave/Re-Envisioned
Denominational ties	Strongest of all the streams. Most likely to carry denominational label in name.	Most are tied to a denomination, but hide the fact and do not have it in their name.	Weakest in formal sense, but these churches tend to start their own daughter church networks.	More independent than denominational, but not overtly tied to the denomination.
Architecture	American classic church architecture. Worship spaces that are more plush. More pews than any other stream.	More open atrium, glass, and soaring spaces. Little religious imagery when compared with the other streams.	Larger auditoriums than the other streams.	Smaller buildings, although that may be a reflection of life cycle. Those that own property are eyeing large tracts of land.
Advertising focus	Programs for all ages. A picture of the buildings. Focused more on the long-term history.	"We are different." "A place for those that hate church." Most likely to have photos of families enjoying the ministries.	Focus on the pastor, the family, and the excitement of the church.	Focus on young adults and their families. Most focus on the current month's teaching series and how it connects to daily life.
Outreach focus	More about current members than future members, but still trying to reach others.	Very focused on reaching those seeking God and helping others "find their way back to God."	Focused on reaching all that need the healing touch of God. Deliberately target those under difficult circumstances.	Focused on everyone in the community. Not afraid to be somewhat controversial.

Web use	More minimal than the other streams; more like a brochure.	The site is focused on introducing outsiders to the church. Focused on the basics of the ministry at that church.	Focused on the powerful worship experience, the pastor's messages, and what the pastor is doing in the area.	Most extensive Web sites that often have special sections for members. Broadcast of services and messages via Web and podcast.
Television/ radio usage	Most likely to feature broadcast of worship service or preaching.	Least common of all types as far as broadcast television. Occasional ads via cable TV and radio. Will broadcast messages via Internet in audio and video.	Proclamation focused on pastors preaching. Rapidly growing Internet broadcasts. Also most likely to appear on "chat shows" designed for Christian audiences.	Rarely use broadcasts of worship services but will engage in radio and cable TV advertising.

apt to be part of a denomination, and are most likely to claim a connection to a Methodist, Presbyterian, or other mainline denomination and call themselves "traditional" in religious identity. Given the ties to a denomination, variations within this group are often related to the heritage and style of that denomination. For instance, churches in this stream affiliated with the Evangelical Lutheran Church are likely to reflect distinctiveness in worship, organizational form, and programmatic style similar to the denomination as a whole. Their mission programs and causes, structure of leadership, and rituals within the service will shape and identify many of them as Lutheran in comparison with other megachurches. This same dynamic will, likewise, distinctly characterize megachurches within the Episcopal, Assembly of God, United Methodist, Nazarene, African Methodist Episcopal, and other traditions as they may mirror the larger styles and programs of their denomination.

Churches in this stream are also more likely to use piano, organ, and choirs in their services. Their services are more apt to employ a formal liturgy, and they are likely to characterize their worship as reverent rather than exuberant. They are also more likely to celebrate communion frequently. Those persons attending services are generally somewhat older and more likely to be of one dominant racial group. The African American churches of this type tend to be found in urban inner city areas and are often the stalwart churches of their denominations. They have a distinctive message and ministry of social and economic betterment of the community. While some of the Caucasian churches of this type would share a similar vision of social betterment, their identity is not as focused on this vision nor is it reflected in their programs in the same way as the African American Program-Based megachurches.

Old Line/Program-Based churches are more likely to use Sunday morning Bible classes as the primary "Christian education" experience. These classes are often well attended when compared to their total weekend attendance. In some cases, the attendance at the Sunday school for all ages may be larger than the worship attendance at this type of megachurch.

When promoting or advertising their church, Old Line/Program-Based megachurches focus on the numerous activities and programs that they provide for all age groups from Mothers Morning Out to Senior Adult day care. They often have fitness programs for all ages in their gymnasiums, multiple special interest classes during the week for Bible literacy, and leisure activities such as crafts and nutrition. The senior pastor role tends to be that of the leader and administrator. The staff members are usually charged with running various programs. Such churches may have created some of the programs for their own needs, but many use well-proven denominational programs. If you were to look at a brochure or advertisement for these churches, you would tend to see a photo of the outside of their building, but inside the brochure would contain a long listing of what they have to offer. If an Old Line church has a local radio or local television ministry, it is more likely to have the name of the church in the title and focus on the broadcast of the worship service, as opposed to having a more generic title or being a talk show that features the pastor.

A few of the more famous examples of the Program model type of church would include First Baptist Church of Dallas, Texas; First Baptist Church of Orlando, Florida; First Presbyterian Church of Orlando, Florida; First Presbyterian Church of Houston, Texas; Trinity United Church of Christ in Chicago, Illinois; and Ben Hill United Methodist Church in Atlanta, Georgia. Examples of Old Line/Program-Based nondenominational churches would include The Chapel in Akron, Ohio, and First Baptist in Hammond, Indiana. Much of the writing and research about large churches several decades ago focused on churches like these.

Charismatic/Pastor-Focused

This stream of megachurches is more often nondenominational, although not exclusively. Such churches tend to have a founding date that corresponds to the arrival of its current pastor. Much of the identity of these congregations is formed around the vision and passion of this founding minister, and few have undergone pastoral transitions. They frequently have a founding or rapid growth date from the 1960s to the 1980s and are regularly found in older suburban areas of a city. They are more apt to be within a Pentecostal or charismatic theological tradition. For those unfamiliar with the Pentecostal/charismatic label, it is a form of Christianity centered on "the gifts of the Holy Spirit," including ecstatic tongue speaking, prophesy as direct communication from God, healing of physical and mental conditions, and lively worship including exuberant singing and dancing. In America, it is closely identified with the Azusa Street Revivals in the early 1900s and continuing through a less exuberant although more culturally progressive expression in the 1960s and 1970s known as the "charismatic movement." Historically, the denominations identified with Pentecostalism include the Assemblies of God, The Church of God, Cleveland TN, The Church of God in Christ (COGIC), and others. The label *charismatic* is often used to describe those leaders and believers who practice the gifts of the Spirit but remain independent or are in churches of other non-Pentecostal denominations.

As we use the term *charismatic*, we do not mean to imply that this type of church is exclusively the province of the Pentecostal/charismatic theological traditions. These churches can also be evangelical and non-charismatic, and they can even be from a strong denominational tradition. The key distinctive feature is that the churches rely greatly on personal "charisma," the presence and authority of the senior pastor, for definition and identity. If one were to look at a church brochure, Web site, or television ministry for this type of church, there would be a clear focus on the senior pastor and his or her ministry and family, including what the pastor is doing external to the ongoing ministry of the church, such as preaching tours or the latest book deals.

Megachurches within the Charismatic/Pastor-Focused group are equally likely to have a racial composition of either African American or white. They often have a distinctively multiracial constituency. It is a mark of this stream that it often is a congregation of diverse attendees, not just in terms of racial makeup, but also in terms of age groupings, income levels, and religious backgrounds. These congregations are especially adept at holding together a varied group of members that may have little in common socially except a commitment to the powerful vision and personality of the senior pastor.

Charismatic/Pastor-Focused churches generally are most likely to sponsor television ministries, hold pastors' conferences, and establish schools. They are less program-oriented overall, but they may also have uniquely creative and thriving congregational ministries birthed out of the vision of the senior pastor. These tend to be high-profile programs that garner considerable attention externally. As one digs deeper into these churches, however, there are often many other ministries at work in the life of the church, but few of those receive attention unless the senior leaders are directly involved.

While some pastors in this stream would have an aversion to the characterization of their church as "pastor-focused," others accept it willingly and feel that God has given them gifts in unique ways to lead a large church. A growing trend is to build the focus of the ministry not only around the senior pastor but also around their spouse as well. Examples of this trend include Randy and Paula White of the Church Without Walls based in Tampa, Florida; Creflo and Tafi Dollar of World Changers Ministries in College Park, Georgia; Keith and Deborah Butler of The Word of Faith International Center of Southfield, Michigan; Mac and Lynne Hammond of Living Word Christian Center in Brooklyn Park, Minnesota; and similar ministries. Some of the more prominent examples of this type of charismatic pastor include Joel Osteen of Lakewood Church in Houston and T. D. Jakes of the Potter's House of Dallas, Texas, in addition to those mentioned above.

Seeker

Within the Seeker stream of megachurches are those churches that strongly embrace an unconventional approach to Christianity, explicitly reshaping the presentation of the Gospel message to correspond to a suburban and exurban post-Christian baby boomer cultural style. These churches tend to have a focused mission statement aimed at the evangelization of those who are seeking God. Some have now reformulated this approach and shifted their focus from the individual seekers looking for God and programming that meets their needs to the idea of "God as the seeker" and the church as playing a role in helping connect the person to what God is already trying to do in the person's life. The thrust of the Seeker megachurch is to find ways to connect and reach persons outside the faith. The identity they embrace and language they use to describe their church is that this is "not your typical church." Churches in the Seeker stream attempt to differentiate themselves from older style churches and the traditional baggage of religion as seen by contemporary secular people. Here we see an interesting formulation. The marketing phrase "not your typical church" attempts to counter the mental model that some people hold in their heads of the small white-steepled church, Bible-thumping preaching, and an intense emphasis on money. But many of the people these churches are trying to reach only know that stereotypical image from television and movies or from early personal experiences as a child. Few seekers have recent involvement in a church of any sort.

Churches in this stream tend to be founded during, or to have grown rapidly in, the 1980s and early 1990s and are more likely either to be nondenominational or to be affiliated with an evangelical denomination (although they downplay that connection). The growth of these churches took place during the pastorate of the current senior pastor and few have experienced pastoral succession yet. Unlike the Charismatic/Pastor-Focused stream, this stream has a considerably broader leadership base, with fewer family members on staff and multiple decision-making levels of the organization. They are less likely to use choirs, organs, or pianos in worship. They celebrate the Lord's Supper or communion less frequently. Likewise, their services are more likely to be described as informal, joyful, and exciting. Churches in this stream are likely to have a large percentage of converted new members and to involve a high percentage of their members in recruitment. Seeker congregations may be quite diverse racially depending on their target audiences. They almost always contain larger percentages of younger people than of older persons. While the target audience for many of these churches was originally the baby boomer generation, the Seeker churches have become adept at reaching younger generations of religious seekers as well.

Seeker churches are the churches most strongly influenced by current corporate business practices and values. They have mission and purpose statements and organize much of their staffing according to their functional roles as described in these statements. For example, if their vision or purpose is evangelism, they will have a pastor specifically charged with evangelism duties. If they highly value small group ministry, they will have a pastor who oversees the small groups ministry. If they value generosity, they will have a pastor charged with the administration of generosity in the church's ministry.

These churches, and those of the charismatic pastor model, tend to get both the most press coverage and criticism. These were the leaders and fast-growth churches of the past few decades, and their leaders have become the spokespersons for much of the religious innovation in the contemporary American religious experience. They are the ones who originally discarded much of the traditional language, symbols, and trappings associated with church architecture and worship from the 1950s. Their fantastic growth using radically different methods from the previous generation has led them to the interesting position of being both innovators and targets. While not every pastor in this category would want to accept the characterization of "seeker" as a compliment, churches in this stream share many characteristics. Willow Creek Church in South Barrington, Illinois; Kensington Community Church in Troy, Michigan; Southland Christian in Lexington, Kentucky; Northpoint Church in Alpharetta, Georgia; Saddleback Community Church of Lake Forest, California; or the Lutheran Community Church of Joy in Glendale, Arizona, are examples of megachurches within this stream.

New Wave/Re-Envisioned

Megachurches in this stream were founded since 1990 and have grown to thousands of attendees in a very short time, yet they may well be unfamiliar to the reader. Some of these churches have received press attention, but many of them remain under the public radar. New Wave churches are more likely to be multisite and multileader churches and to offer multiple services on many days of the week. By *multisite*, we mean that these churches can have multiple locations throughout a region, and by *multileader*, we mean that they are more likely to utilize a "teaching team" approach and the multiple lead pastors model. If there is a designated senior minister, he is often under thirty-five years of age and was the leading minister at the time this church grew.

Many of these churches have intentionally rejected a Seeker approach, with its nontraditional language and mind-set. Instead, they embrace overtly traditional, and even ancient, Christian symbols, language, and teaching. It is not uncommon to hear the use of creeds from the first few hundred years of church history. Classes may teach personal spiritual practices such as journaling, fasting, and meditation. Likewise, congregations within this stream embrace an active social ministry and at times a progressive social activism. The church leadership explicitly asks for high commitments from people who desire to join. Yet this reclamation of church history and rituals is not without innovation and adaptation. These churches often utilize cutting-edge technology in terms of lighting, music, and sound while eclectically combining it with ancient practices. They are significantly more high tech than the other streams, employing sophisticated Web and Internet components throughout the life of the church.

It is not surprising that these high-energy megachurches have a large percentage of attendees under the age of thirty-five and from all racial groups. It appears that many of those drawn to these churches have had little experience with Christianity, but unlike the Seeker model, they desire to embrace the established church tradition on their own terms in new ways, rather than reject and eliminate the old practices. These churches use their weekend services to teach a high-commitment Christianity. Many will employ "ancient-future" techniques to make the worshippers aware of historic Christian creeds and practices, while using highly advanced technology to do so.

As these are younger churches in a rapidly growing life-cycle phase, they tend to have physically cramped quarters and much simpler buildings for conducting their ministries. The offices and workstations have a "stacked on top of each other" feeling. Examples of this type of megachurch include Mars Hill Church in Seattle, Washington; Cross Timbers in Argyle, Texas; New Spring in Anderson, South Carolina; Bay Life Church in Brandon, Florida; and The Village Church in Flower Mound, Texas.

Later sections of this book will continue to explore these distinctive streams among megachurches, but the point is how much megachurches differ from one another. We trust that our typology of megachurches highlights the distinctive strains within this phenomenon, while also showing the patterns and similarities among some of them. Even more important, the variations and commonalities among certain groups are responsible for shaping how the worship is done, what ministry styles are employed, and the character of the churches and their members.

○

Applying What You Have Read

We want to address two areas in this application section: audience and vision. Does your church's vision match its audience? Or do you feel that something needs to change at the church? A church cannot really change the date of its founding. A church can change its location, as churches can and do relocate frequently, but this is a difficult transition for most churches. Churches have been known to end their denominational affiliation and choose another, or choose to be independent, but this is often an unnecessary step.

We feel the best step for most churches is to begin by praying and seeking God's will about whom God is calling your congregation to serve, who is your audience. To inform your prayers, go back to the map of your region that you drew in Chapter One. Who are the groups of people in that region who are not served well by existing churches in the area? These might be groups classified by age, language, aspirations, cultural influences, race, and so on. Think about your context as you pray and ask yourself the question, Who is God drawing to us as we look back at those who visited our church in the past year? Perhaps they did not come back, but for some reason, they at least came once. These can be indicators of the types of people God is naturally drawing to your church.

Since most of the people in the United States live in metropolitan areas, the pool of potential attendees can be much more diverse than many church leaders think. We have found that churches often desire to reach the populations in their area who are already well churched, or groups who do not even live locally. As an example, we worked with a church that had the talent for and desire to reach Spanish-speaking immigrants. However, the Spanish-speaking group left the area a few years before and had been replaced by other language groups. The church's Hispanic ministry limped along for several years with only a handful of attendees, with the church wondering why the ministry failed. We are not saying that ministry direction should only be aimed at large populations of people, but be specific about those people in your region on whom you will focus your efforts. Large churches are intentional about the ministries they start, and continue them as long as there is a need. This is one of their key strengths. Intentionality of ministry and a willingness to evaluate ministry directions should be a strength for other sizes of churches as well.

As we describe in the chapter, there is a second piece that we want the reader to reflect on: the church's vision. Without debating the technical aspects of vision, mission, and values, let us state that we feel it is important for the leadership to create an essential story of the church.

This essential story is the bridge that new attendees can use to become connected with the church. This essential story should be simple enough to be understood and communicated by everyone in the church. This story will be aspirational and inspirational enough for believers to connect with at a heart level and for many unbelievers to identify with enough to want to "check it out." All church leaders over a sustained period of time should reaffirm this essential story with regularity in messages, both written and oral. This story is not a restatement of doctrine, but rather is a statement reflecting a unique vision for a church in its context and setting. It alludes to what important work God is calling the congregation to do at this particular moment.

After casting this story or vision for a long period, then the leadership can often develop new ministries that fit both the new audience and the mission to which God is calling the church.

- o Who are the potential audiences that God is asking your church to reach?
- o What is the essential story of God that connects your church to those audiences?
- o How do you convey this essential story, this vision, to the congregation?
- o How does this vision shape the mission and ministries of your church?

3

"THAT CHURCH IS JUST TOO BIG!"

On average, smaller churches are the better churches. To say it in a simplified way: "The larger, the worse." This pattern is so significant that it is difficult to see why no one else has come across this pattern. Instead some authors even proceed from the opposite thesis, namely "The bigger, the better."[1]

From a recent news article about a large church in Connecticut planning to build on an open 100-acre site: "Now that the congregation has voted to proceed with plans for the Easton property, opposition there is growing. Some residents of that leafy community are openly questioning why the church doesn't relocate to Bridgeport, where they believe it would be more suitable and less controversial. 'You're talking about a place the size of Wal-Mart,' said Dolly Curtis, an Easton resident helping to organize the opponents. "'Our main concern is the size and scale of it. It's uncharacteristic for Easton,' said another opponent, Princie Falkenhagen. 'There are already enough churches in town for a community of Easton's size,' said the Rev. Nayiri Karjian, pastor of the Congregational Church of Easton. 'There are five churches in town. That's a lot of churches for a town with 2,700 households,' Karjian said."[2]

ALTHOUGH FEW MEGACHURCHES are the ten thousand to twenty thousand attendee behemoths of the stereotype, it is true that compared with the vast majority of churches in the United States, even those in the two thousand attendance range are giants. As we pointed out earlier, of the approximately 335,000 congregations of all religious groups in the country (roughly 320,000 of which are Christian churches), the median congregation (meaning half are above that figure and half fall below it) has about 75 regular participants.[3] The median attendance based on another recent study is 90 people.[4] Therefore, 60 percent of the all U.S. congregations have fewer than one hundred participating adults and children, and a full 71 percent have fewer than one hundred adult participants.[5]

According to the most representative survey of U.S. congregations, only 11 percent of total worshippers in U.S. congregations are found in 50 percent of churches. On the other hand, just 10 percent of American churches (roughly thirty-three thousand congregations) have more than three hundred fifty regular participants (many of these are large Roman Catholic churches), but those congregations contain almost half of the worship attendees in the country. This means that many people who experience an organized religious service in the United States are in fact experiencing it in a church of three hundred fifty persons or more—essentially, the reality of large church worship. There are good reasons for the perception that megachurches are "too big." The largest of the megachurches, those fifty or so churches with attendance around ten thousand or more receive nearly all the attention from the media and religious leaders. Likewise, these churches have massive financial resources to enable them to fund television programs, sophisticated Web sites, national conferences, elaborate community productions, and noteworthy missions efforts. These also garner considerable numbers of visitors and spectators during a single service, usually on Sunday morning.

Judging by the number of times megachurch Web sites say that "we are not too big," they indeed must be overwhelming to the first-time visitor. Walk into a gathering of fifteen hundred or, even worse, five thousand, and you will feel lost, especially if you are coming from a church of thirty-five or even three hundred fifty.

Seldom do those who claim these churches are too big actually attend more than one or two worship services. The mass gathering in worship can seem "too big," but there is more than this to a megachurch. This organizational form of the church is more like an online conversation in a discussion board than a face-to-face conversation. In a face-to-face encounter, everything happens—in that one contact. In a discussion board, the posted conversation takes place over a week or two with individuals contributing to the interchange as they encounter it across time. Such is the "congregational" life of a megachurch. Church does not just take place between 9:30 and 11:00 A.M. on Sunday. It also happens in smaller informal gatherings throughout the week and month, as well as in ministry settings, group meetings, and other activities sponsored by the church. All these activities result in over 48 percent of megachurches saying that feeling like a close-knit family describes them "very" or "quite" well.

It is a well-established fact that many Americans experience the practice of religion in a free-market, voluntary manner. No one is forced to go to a particular church, or go to church at all. In most U.S. cities, a dozen churches can be found within a mile of each other, so there is no lack of choices. Likewise, the yellow pages and the Web make it possible to contact and even experience a public presentation of churches before you even go to them. It stands to reason, then, that the size and resources of larger church organizations give clear welcoming signals through these forms of outreach and are therefore more appealing. Certainly, these large organizations can offer more programs than churches of other sizes. The reason that megachurches are so large is ultimately because so many people are getting their needs met in them. It is unlikely that attendees and members would say that these churches are too big because they continue to come, although it's unclear whether it is the size they are coming for. Perhaps large gatherings have an appeal to modern Americans.

Too Big for the People?

Apparently, the megachurch reality isn't too big for everyone because nearly 4.5 million people attend megachurches each week. Expand this to those who might call a megachurch their "home church" and consider themselves to be members, and this number could easily reach twelve million people or as many as 10 percent of all participating church members in the United States.

So what do these people who are regular attendees say about these churches being "too big"? Do they feel lost in them? There is too little quality information regarding such questions to provide an adequate answer. However, the information we have does seem to indicate that those who go to megachurches are comfortable there. Scott's earlier in-depth study of a nondenominational megachurch showed in a survey of attendees that 80 percent of the congregation said they have close friends at the church. Additionally, 64 percent of them agreed that they know as many or more people at the megachurch as they did at smaller churches. Almost two-thirds (60 percent) reported they had received pastoral attention for spiritual or personal issues, and a full 80 percent claimed that they felt "cared about" at the church. When attendees were asked if they "were just another number" at the church, over three quarters (78 percent) disagreed. Clearly these figures show that participants do feel connected to the church.

Another study from the 1990s of the mother churches of the Calvary Chapel, Vineyard Fellowship, and Hope Chapel movements showed similar results. The principal researcher, Donald Miller, found that 80 percent of the attendees at these three churches felt satisfied with level of pastoral care they were receiving. Likewise, 75 percent of them claimed to have at least one of their three closest friends at the church. Another interesting finding from this study was that a full 95 percent of the attendees reported that they felt they were free to touch or hug other people while at church.

Finally, the more recent information from attendees of the largest Protestant churches in the U.S. Congregational Life Study indicated a similar connectedness to their churches. Eighty percent of the over six thousand attendees reported that they had a strong sense of belonging, and 75 percent of them said they had some close friends at the church.

Such findings hint at a possible answer regarding how megachurch participants view and interact within their churches. But these are sketchy findings, and much more research needs to be done. This information does seem to imply that strong ties to other members and to the church itself are forged in megachurches, at least for the more highly committed participants.

The results of these studies also suggest that the congregants who remain at megachurches enjoy the worship and ministries and get much from it. The information we have indicates that a large percentage of attendees are involved regularly in ministries, programs, and worship. They feel heard and empowered and are encouraged to use their gifts. And as mentioned above, they have good friends at the churches and have a real sense that they belong there.

These connections and feelings of community and intimacy are both accidental and also intentional. In the early years of the growth of megachurches in the United States, there were few models of what worked to deal with large-scale church life. Pastors and church leadership at first almost completely ignored the need to structure community building and interpersonal interaction into the life of the mushrooming megachurches they led. They had almost no discussion of "cell groups" or intentional small fellowship groups until the idea was imported from the successful model at Yoido Full Gospel Church in Korea. The use of cell groups was one of the primary reasons Yoido and other Korean churches grew extremely large (for instance, Yoido's average attendance was over two hundred thousand at the time) before most American megachurches even existed. Some earlier U.S. megachurches, such as First Baptist, Hammond, Indiana, and others, had strong Sunday school programs that functioned as small groups to unify the congregation. Additionally, many of these churches had strong kinship ties and were composed of families who had lived in the area and been at the church for generations. This is considerably different from later megachurches located in Sunbelt suburban sprawl cities, where attendees had recently moved into the area and had few social ties. Within a few years, amid increasing numbers of these large churches, books were written about them, such as Elmer Towns's *Ten Largest Sunday Schools and What Makes Them Grow* and Robert Schuler's *Your Church Has Real Possibilities*, and conferences were held to make sense of the growth. These churches needed more effective and intentional ways to connect members to each other and to the church. They needed models to follow, and Yoido's use of cell groups was one such way.

The present situation is a different story. Megachurches have learned their lessons well. They do not rely at all on chance interactions or informal networking to create social groups. Rather, they intentionally structure multiple ways for people to interact and form social ties. Exactly how many, and to what extent, megachurches use small groups varies depending on the individual church. Nevertheless, the effort to connect people and gather them into smaller groupings is now universal among megachurches.

These megachurches have organized small groups and other programs that address individual needs and connect people in intimate small groups for multiple purposes. Half the surveyed churches in 2000 said their use of small groups was central to their strategy for Christian nurture and spiritual formation. Another 44 percent had such groups but said these were not central to the church's program. Over 80 percent said they have an organized program for keeping up with members' needs and providing ministry at the neighborhood level. These groups may be formal and highly structured prayer or fellowship cells, or they may be activity-driven, such as small groupings of parking attendants, police officers, lawyers, or businesspersons. These connections might be forged around adult education classes, mission and ministry efforts, or even sports, exercise, or other hobby gatherings in the church. There is no doubt that this intentional organization of social interaction enhances community and fellowship building. However, it is not the groups and cells themselves that are key, but rather the multiple efforts by church leadership to encourage participation and actively promote interpersonal interaction between members that is most effective in creating community and making the megachurch feel small for attendees.

Out of necessity, megachurches have had to overstructure every aspect of member involvement. One cannot expect that social processes at work in small-scale settings will necessarily happen within a massive congregation. As such, megachurches must institutionalize greeting visitors and ushering attendees into the sanctuary. They need classes to school new members in church rules and norms, teach members basic doctrines, and introduce them to the ministries of the church. Megachurches often assign mentors, shepherding deacons, or associate pastors to help facilitate the integration of new members into the congregation. The church also has to plan events and activities to promote informal communication among members between services and throughout the week. Nothing is left to chance or happenstance.

Megachurches assume that people in this society do not know each other, nor will they make the effort if left on their own. They also assume that contemporary individuals do not interact unless forced to and will tend to remain relative strangers to those they meet. People desire the intimacy of small groups but will seldom seek it out. Megachurch leadership also realizes that many people will remain spectators and marginal participants unless they are strongly and intentionally encouraged to become involved.

But just as in smaller churches, there are also informal methods of becoming connected to others at the church that supplement the more intentional efforts. Attendees invite their friends. They bring their family members and relatives to church with them. In this way, friendship networks are created within the church. People are also creatures of habit; we often sit in the same place in the sanctuary week after week. This patterned behavior is yet another way interpersonal connections are made. When researching a megachurch for nearly three years, one of us (Scott) sat in the same section most weeks thinking no one took notice of whether he was there or not. When Scott came back to church after having been away for nearly a month, he was shocked to find that the usher and a number of nearby "regulars" approached him and inquired about his health and the reasons for his absence. Some of this was intentional: the ushers were assigned the responsibility to get to know attendees in that area of the sanctuary. Another part of this, however, was the informal altruism and connectedness that develops naturally during regular interactions even in a mass gathering. Anyone with season tickets to a sports team knows this phenomenon of casual but real relationships that develop.

Involvement within any church is defined by either a conscious or unreflective act of personal commitment. Getting out of bed and coming to church each week is at least a modest recommitment to the value of this congregation and a reaffirmation of wanting to feed one's spirit in this place. The meaning of choosing to be "a part of this place" is less defined by a one-time decision—by becoming a member—than it is by active participation, by a continual choice to be involved. Megachurches are well aware of this. That is why many megachurches do not have a membership category. Rather, they constantly challenge attendees to be involved at ever-increasing levels and to work to deepen their faith commitments—to move from anonymity to engagement.

Attendees at megachurches are free, in some sense, to choose what level of involvement they desire, from anonymous free rider to a forty-plus-hour-a-week volunteer ministry leader. They can choose what hour best suits them to come and may even be able to select a service (whether youth, contemporary, traditional, grunge, or praise) that fits their tastes and style. They can choose to volunteer in diverse ministries, to engage in a multitude of programs, to tackle projects, or to join fellowship groups. Essentially, each individual and family can create their own custom experience in the congregation. They can participate in this place on their own terms. Of course, this freedom is always conditioned by the encouragement of the church leadership and the structures of commitment.

The invitation, even insistence, to increase participation is regularly communicated in the preaching and printed materials at the megachurch. Instead of a call of "we need you to volunteer," the call is for individuals to grow as Christians through service. Participants are then trained and equipped for specific tasks or assignments. At New Hope Christian Fellowship in Honolulu, Hawaii, the engagement begins when a member asks a friend or newcomer to "help me do my job" at church. At this point, the newcomer gets involved in service through their friendship. At New Hope they say that everyone should be a both mentor and an apprentice in different areas of church life. Some churches use "Discovery" classes to help potential members learn more about the church. They then use membership and ministry classes to equip these persons for service. We will say more about this dynamic in a later chapter.

Too Big for the Municipalities?

Size creates other challenges for megachurches in addition to the integration of new persons. There are few communities in the United States where institutions the size of megachurches fit in without considerable difficulty. It is not surprising that megachurches are situated near highways, on the edges of mixed suburban neighborhoods where industrial, commercial, and occasionally residential development is located.

These areas are less desirable for residential development. Few homeowners want a large office-park-type structure with twenty acres of parking lots and gallons of water runoff in their backyards. Likewise, few small towns overtaken by suburban sprawl are interested in giving up the tax revenue that a massive tax-free megachurch on one hundred acres of prime commercial development land represents. Given the geographic patterns developing among newer megachurches in the past ten to fifteen years, these are exactly the situations in which churches and communities find themselves.

Within the past decade, megachurches have appeared in locations where they are quite foreign and somewhat out of scale for the community. Whether megachurches desire to expand into residential or commercial areas, in recent years groups of concerned homeowners and city elected leadership seem quite willing to take them to court to stop the unwanted growth. Much of this litigation has yielded few successes by cities and landowners; however, in 2001, the congressional Religious Land Use and Institutionalized Persons Act (RLUIPA) was passed. This act essentially allows religious groups considerable freedom with regard to land use, even over zoning rules and ecological conservation efforts. It has been used by quite a few megachurches when restrictions threaten to hinder property expansion or relocation seen as necessary for the continuation of their mission and ministry. Nevertheless, this act is yet to be challenged fully in appellate courts. Ultimately it will come before the Supreme Court in order to determine the constitutionality of the Act. Until then, however, the implications of RLUIPA are serious for communities around megachurches.[6]

As we will discuss in Chapter Eleven, property rights are a growing concern for both municipal leaders and churches. Church leaders don't want to be seen as "fighting" for the right to develop their property. Likewise, municipal leaders view their actions at times as a no-win situation politically. On the one hand, they have planning meetings where hundreds of residents near a church are generally opposed to development of any kind. On the other hand, city commissioners may have a church of several thousand likely voters holding the opposite view. Towns and counties don't necessarily want to be seen as repressing religious freedom, but they also have to protect the quality of life and sensitive wilderness areas and also generate an expanding tax base. Behind much of the opposition lies a lack of understanding about megachurches and the usually unspoken idea that a "real church" is one with a modest structure and a hundred members. "True churches" don't have bookstores, coffee shops, gyms, or services and gatherings seven days a week. In many situations, litigation seldom solves the difficulties underlying the case even if a judge does rule in favor of one of the parties. Ill will and bad feelings result no matter who wins. Each case is unique, but many of these conflicts could be resolved by creative compromise rather than holding inflexible demands and an unwillingness to negotiate.

Faced with potential or actual opposition to continued expansion, many megachurches are either delaying or avoiding a conflictual situation by opting for multiple, smaller campuses. Seacoast Church, based in Mount Pleasant, South Carolina, is a good example of the multisite movement within churches in general and megachurches in particular. In 2001, it was a church averaging thirty-five hundred people in multiple services, and the church wanted to build a four-thousand-seat auditorium to expand further. Prevented by the city council from expanding on land it already owned, the church went down the street to start the first of its off-site venues. It now has nine locations across South Carolina and averages around eight thousand people each weekend.[7] We address this recent innovation later in the book.

There is no doubt that megachurches are by definition large, and maybe even too large for many people and certain contexts. They are not the typical or average congregation of one hundred fifty persons. However, just because they are cut from a different cloth does not mean they are dysfunctional when cast at a grand scale. They offer a religious experience that many people find appealing. They work hard to compensate for their size by creating structures that help people become connected and nurtured in the faith. And with compromise and wise planning, they may even be able to fit comfortably in most communities.

○

Applying What You Have Read

In this chapter, we have addressed several issues related to how megachurches, in spite of their size, help attendees find a smaller group of individuals with whom to form a connection. In our experience, one of the challenges of smaller churches, say under a hundred in attendance, is the belief that "everyone needs to stay together." Larger churches do just the opposite. They know that individuals and families can only connect with a limited number of people to have meaningful relationships. What large churches do is help people establish those close relationships with smaller groups and then help them involve others.

We mentioned small groups in the chapter as a way to connect people. At times, this connection is made through formalized Sunday schools, adult Bible fellowships, or in home groups that connect attendees in informal settings to share their lives. Other times, task-oriented groups are started to involve attendees in projects together. Again, the idea is to break people into small, formalized groups for them to make connections and build bonds of friendship, trust, and mutual support. This is a key connection. These groups may need to be "open" so that attendees feel comfortable inviting a friend. By being included in the group, new people are by extension more able to be connected to the church. Large churches often start new groups on a regular basis. The "newness" of a group allows it to start fresh and potentially be more accepting of both new and longer-term attendees.

We also mentioned the tactic of New Hope Church in Honolulu where regular attendees invite nonattendees to help them in a particular service role. Sometimes that "job" is on the weekend during one of the services and sometimes it is during the week. The key is the connection in which an outsider can feel useful, but has the comfort of serving alongside a trusted friend.

Our final suggestion has to do with one of the key roles in any congregation: the teams of people charged with making everyone feel welcome during the worship experience. We suggest that individuals want to remain anonymous when they visit a church. That is true to some extent for certain people. It is our experience, however, that everyone wants to be personally welcomed. They desire a connection without having to reveal too much about themselves at first. They appreciate it when someone remembers their name and makes inquiries if they are missing. In some smaller churches, three or four trained individuals that greet persons at the door or in the worship space can really make a difference. These team members would not just greet new attendees, but also check in with regular attendees and give them a word of encouragement each week. This team can also be trained to listen for pastoral and prayer needs from all attendees and then communicate these to the leadership. This small change makes a huge difference in a newcomer's impressions about whether the church is "open" or "closed" to visitors. Our experience is that most churches err on the side of not being aggressive enough in greeting newcomers.

o What new small groups could your church develop in the next two years?

o Who could serve as leaders of these groups (and are not already overburdened)?

○ Who are the outgoing, but underutilized people in the church who could be trained to serve the congregation by warmly welcoming all who attend worship services?

○ Consider asking acquaintances who do not attend the church to visit and report to you how they were greeted, how many people spoke to them, and whether they considered the church friendly and welcoming?

4

"MEGACHURCHES ARE CULTS OF PERSONALITY"

---

*"You have a kind of cult of personality that confuses the
faith with a particular individual," said Balmer, author of*
Thy Kingdom Come: How the Religious Right Distorts the
Faith and Threatens America. *"I just think it's very difficult
to recover from this sort of thing."*[1]

*Televangelist downfalls and other religious scandals show
the fine line between dynamic leadership and a cult of
personality. A personal failure in a small denominational
church affects far fewer lives than the destruction of a leader
of dozens of employees and thousands of congregants. Even
if a megachurch pastor leaves under good terms, he can be
difficult or impossible to replace, as megachurches so often
stem from one man's vision.*[2]

LEADERSHIP IS A CRITICAL FACTOR in a church of any size. Pastors are
often the center of attention whether the church is large or small. The
reality for all clergy no matter the church size is that the congregation
bestows some degree of personal power on them. When they are chosen
to lead the church spiritually and function as God's spokesperson to the
flock, they are given a significant degree of authority. This power dynamic
varies considerably across religious traditions and leadership structures,
but it is always present, even if it is seldom discussed. The mantle of
congregational leader carries with it a level of power and authority, which
can increase as the size of the church grows. The success of the church
is in part attributed to the skill of the senior minister. With increased
success comes greater power. Success creates a situation where one needs
to meet increasing expectations of continued growth and further success.
If one is both the spiritual leader and the founder of a hugely successful

multimillion dollar enterprise with hundreds of employees and thousands of followers, fame and notoriety are natural developments. This is true whether it is inside a church or in the business world.

Given such a situation, it is not surprising that megachurches are often identified by the names of their senior pastors. Any successful enterprise can come to be characterized by its leader. But it is unfortunate that this reality has led critics to suggest that megachurches are more about a pastor's ego than about God's kingdom. Some commentators further expand their criticism to the attendees of megachurches by portraying them as blindly following their "cultic" pastors anywhere and unquestioningly treating the pastor's word as though it were God's. These critics frequently imply that megachurch attendees will do whatever the pastor instructs them to do in many areas of life. Political observers often implicitly suggest that the duped members of megachurches are conditioned to vote whatever way the pastor dictates. These perceptions don't just cast blame on power-hungry leaders of megachurches, but they paint all the attendees as brainwashed fools with no self-will or spiritual discernment. And, while it is clear that some attendees are enamored with the status of their pastors, many millions who attend these churches have not surrendered their spiritual freedom and personal integrity to some megachurch's omnipotent leader.

It is true that certain megachurch pastors can seem larger than life. One can easily form the impression that these pastors are like rock stars with their hordes of fans, devoted groupies, and protective bodyguards. This perception is most likely if one focuses on the handful of pastors of the largest megachurches who can fill arena-size auditoriums. These popular pastors travel the country hosting citywide rallies in massive venues. Such figures are indeed media celebrities and have come to be treated as such. But the megachurch pastors who attain such status are relatively few.

Being a megachurch pastor does open the door wider for members to relate to the senior leader as a unique and gifted individual. The reality of being seen on television (over a third of pastors have such programs) or heard on a radio program (44 percent) amplifies the power dynamic even among pastors of modestly sized megachurches.[3] In addition, for many people sitting in the sanctuary each week, the senior minister is not just perceived as larger than life, he or she actually is viewed on the huge media screens as a twenty-foot image. The powers of the jumbotron are not to be dismissed easily, nor are the camera-enhanced images and the rich booming effects of a state-of-the-art sound system insignificant. Taken together, the "media ministries" of the megachurches, which may include radio, television, publishing, and extensive Web technologies, can inflate the name and role of the senior pastor beyond that of the church.

In such an image-rich context, the pastor can become the visible symbol of and a potent "brand name" for the church.[4]

Some megachurches have even intentionally marketed the pastor as a media personality in order to increase television or conference exposure. Or similarly, a popular pastor might form a separate organization using his name to brand his preaching, teaching, and writing products. Often this is done as a for-profit venture separate from the church because of tax laws, in an effort to protect the church's nonprofit status. Such extensive marketing efforts are in the minority, but they do happen. Intense media attention on these types of things tends to lead the casual observer to see these situations as the rule rather than the exception.

There is no denying that megachurches are reflections of the leadership abilities of a senior pastor or directional leader. Nearly always, the megachurch pastor is the most prominent and high-profile position in the congregation. The pastor is the center of the staff and the energy hub around which the congregation revolves.

Leadership of a megachurch does take a considerable amount of ego strength. But it must be remembered that leadership of any organization of this size can lead to constant challenges, headaches, and criticism. It takes confidence and resoluteness to continue on in spite of these challenges. Those pastors who have started churches that have grown to megachurch size clearly have leadership gifts that have been demonstrated and proven. They are responsible for piloting the church's development and guiding it successfully through its many phases of growth. As such, it is no surprise that everyone in the congregation looks to these pastors as uniquely gifted leaders.

As a church grows larger, the pastor is much less likely to have direct personal contact with the average person in the pews. The senior minister may have direct personal involvement with two hundred to four hundred people at the church and indirect interaction with several hundred more. But by the time a church grows to several thousand, the senior pastor's time is in such demand that a gulf develops between regular attendees and the top leadership. Layers of associate pastors, ministry leaders, deacons, and administrative assistants protect the senior leader's time by buffering him from the crowd. In this context, the senior minister can become a "public persona" rather than a "real person" for many of those who attend. These naturally occurring dynamics further increase the potential to see the senior pastor as set apart and special.

The dynamics of megachurch leadership increase the possibility that the senior pastor will develop a large group of ardent admirers and followers. These devoted members can become overzealous in the amount of attention and trust they have for the senior pastor. Such a situation can develop into a cult of personality around the pastor, if not guarded against. This potential for the development of a personality cult is most powerful among churches within highly spiritualized theological streams, within nondenominational and independent churches, and in the group of megachurches we identified as Charismatic/Pastor-Focused. These streams of megachurches seem the most prone to emphasize the pastor's spiritual authority and personal ministry as a dominant characteristic of the church. The pastor is featured prominently in visual images of the ministry, and the pastor's personal ministry may take priority in the organization, often downplaying other ministries.

To guard against such dynamics, churches and senior ministers have created oversight boards, encouraged denominational staff involvement, set up rules of conduct for staff and clergy, and discouraged members from developing overly intense relationships with senior leadership. Additionally, a number of pastors of large megachurches have avoided creating a television ministry and have intentionally promoted the church's name over their own. These would include Rick Warren of Saddleback Church, Lake Forest, California, who only recently allowed a televised broadcast of a special Christmas Eve service in 2006, or Bill Hybels of Willow Creek Church of South Barrington, Illinois. Taken together, these two well-known clergy have become the poster boys for megachurch pastors, but neither is a television personality. Likewise, the highly popular Mars Hill Church of Seattle and its pastor Mark Driscoll have avoided the temptation to televise its services. They do this to stress that participation in worship at Mars Hill is meant to be experienced in person in order to fully understand and embrace the church's vision.

Even with these cautions, there have been abuses of power by certain megachurch pastors. Stories can be found of financial misconduct, salary and lifestyle extravagances, and sexual wrongdoing. From our studies of megachurches over the years, we do not believe that megachurch pastors are any more likely to succumb to the temptations to abuse the power with which they are entrusted than pastors of smaller churches. This is in part due to the greater awareness these pastors have of the temptations of power and the intense scrutiny on them. Likewise, our perception is that in recent decades, megachurch pastors have learned valuable lessons from the painful experiences of their earlier predecessors and have instituted multiple levels of checks and balances to guard against potentially compromising situations. However, as we have seen with some prominent examples, such checks do not overcome all sinful temptations or the fallenness of human nature.

Even given the potentially powerful role of the senior pastor in a megachurch, it is a mistake to reduce the significance of the megachurch phenomenon to a "great man" theory of church growth. A close examination of the leadership systems evident in these churches shows much more complexity than this. All megachurches have multiple ministry leaders exercising authority, leadership, and initiative within the organization. These churches usually have strong teams of leaders surrounding the senior minister. These teams are not merely composed of "yes men" taking direction from a strong central authority, but are innovative and creative leaders of successful ministries on their own.

It is clear, though, that in many megachurches the senior pastor is the dominant driver of the vision and mission for the church and often the catalyst for its growth. This is especially the case for those pastors who are the founders of their churches or who are responsible for growing an established congregation to megachurch proportions. But even this situation doesn't mean that the senior pastor is all that attracts people to the church. Attendees from the nondenominational church with a powerful pastor who was also its founder were asked what attracted and kept them at the church. Approximately 5 percent identified the senior minister by name; however, five times as many attendees claimed it was the preaching that brought and kept them there. The senior minister preached most sermons, but it was the message more than the messenger that the participants found attractive. Megachurch pastors tend to lead their churches and drive their teams based on a clear vision and purpose, which is articulated frequently and in various ways to tie the system together, and as such they are its central figure.

Senior Pastor Profile

The most significant finding in the 2005 study concerning megachurch pastors is that 83 percent of the churches grew dramatically during the tenure of the current pastor. This is even more amazing when one realizes that 1992 is the median year that the leader became senior pastor. This means that half these clergy became lead pastor before that date and half in the thirteen years between 1992 and 2005. One-third of these pastors took charge prior to 1989, but 35 percent assumed leadership after 1995. It is also important to note that nearly 20 percent of the megachurches had a transition to a new pastor subsequent to the person who was responsible for the growth. This issue of succession is one we will address at length later.

The average age of the senior pastor was fifty years old in the 2005 survey. In the megachurch study five years earlier, we found the clergy to be slightly older on average at fifty-two years of age. News reports often imply that megachurch pastors tend to be younger than pastors

of other congregations. Indeed, many times the focus of these accounts
leads observers to generalize that these are "young churches" with young
clergy. But the average megachurch pastor's age of fifty is roughly
comparable to mainline and evangelical pastors of churches of all sizes.[5]

In general, the senior pastors are well educated. This may come
as a surprise, since again news accounts often prominently focus on
megachurch pastors who do not have professional theological degrees.
Our 2005 survey found that such pastors are clearly the exception.
Seventy-two percent of senior pastors held either a master's or doctoral
degree with an additional 19 percent holding at least a bachelor's degree,
while fewer than 10 percent had no postsecondary degree. The 2000
megachurch survey specifically asked about ministerial degrees and found
that 22 percent had Bible college degrees, 31 percent had a seminary
Master of Divinity degree, and 42 percent had obtained a post-master's
seminary degree such as a Doctorate of Ministry. Additionally, nearly
all megachurch pastors are male, with less than 1 percent being led by
women. In terms of racial makeup, the senior pastors reflect the racial
distribution of megachurches generally.

Analysis of the 2005 megachurch data reveals some interesting distinctions between the churches that have pastors who were present during the
initial explosive growth compared with those who came after. Where the
senior pastor responsible for the growth was still in place, the churches
grew at a rate seven times greater over the past five years than the
churches led by a pastor who followed the founding pastor. Likewise,
those churches that still have the same senior minister responsible for
the original growth describe their worship services as significantly more
informal, joyful, exciting, thought provoking, and with a greater sense
of God's presence than those churches with a subsequent pastor. Those
churches without a pastoral change describe themselves as significantly
"more like a close-knit family, more spiritually vital and alive, having a
greater sense of mission and purpose, and as being more open to new
challenges and innovation." They also indicated a greater use of electric
guitars and drums in the worship service, had a higher percentage of
new converts, and were more likely to be a multiracial congregation. In
part, these differences could be a result of the number of fast-growing,
brand-new churches that make up a portion of this group because those
churches founded since 1990 have similar strengths. But this does not
entirely explain the dramatic differences between these two groups.

Such data does not bode well for those clergy who follow the senior
pastors who led during the growth-producing phase. The churches
with pastors who came after the church grew large tended to be older
churches, founded on average eighteen years earlier than the other group.

Their services were more likely to be described as reverent and more liturgically formal. They have more full-time ministry staff than the other group, but roughly the same overall number of staff. The 2005 megachurch data indicate that these churches' subsequent pastors report greater levels of conflict in their churches than did those churches led by the same clergy who were leaders during the significant growth period. The reasons for the conflict are not clear from the survey; nevertheless, taken together all these differences between the growth pastors and subsequent clergy are significant and should be kept in mind when we turn to the topic of pastoral succession.

○

Compensation

A question we often hear in any discussion of megachurch pastors concerns their compensation. The widely reported earnings of some big-name television preachers and the handful of pastors who derive significant income from book sales are far from the norm. Likewise, the press accounts listing details of expensive homes, multiple luxury automobiles, and other holdings are true for only a minority of pastors. While it is true that some megachurch pastors do have major income streams in addition to their salaries, in our experience these are rare exceptions to the norm.

The Megachurch 2005 survey did not ask about salaries, but Leadership Network has conducted regular salary surveys among its large church clients for some time. This data set is slightly different from the broader megachurch study, but its findings are instructive. In 2006, Leadership Network found that the average salary and housing compensation for a senior/lead pastor was $130,360.[6] This income figure varies widely regionally and by denominational tradition. In general, the larger the church, the higher the compensation will be. Those pastors in areas with a higher cost of living earn more; those in lower-cost locations tend to earn less. On average, the homes owned by the megachurch pastors are similar to a typical upper-middle-class church member. While headlines lead one to believe that pastors receive other excessive benefits and perks, this is rarely the case. Senior pastors and their staff at megachurches nearly always have health benefits and some type of retirement package. Annual raises for all staff averaged a little over 3 percent according to this salary survey. In our experience, church governing boards tend to be quite prudent with pastoral compensation, often finding a comparable set of leaders in their community from whom to draw comparisons and set salary rates.[7]

It is true that the levels of compensation for megachurch pastors are much higher than average clergy salaries. Our experience is that megachurch senior pastors and their staffs realize they enjoy considerable compensation and benefits when compared with friends and colleagues in smaller churches. For example, a recent book on American clergy reports that in the year 2000, in churches with attendance from 351 to 1,000, mainline Protestant pastors had a median salary of $67,017 and conservative Protestant pastors had a median income of $60,104. Pastors in churches from 100 to 350 in size were paid a third less, and full-time pastors in churches under 100 were paid less than half of the salary of the average megachurch pastors.[8]

○

Gifts and Responsibilities

It is not just the physical characteristics of megachurch pastors that make them successful religious leaders but also their character and leadership gifts. These pastors are visionary leaders who are often passionate about evangelism. They are also practical communicators. They are creative and inquisitive persons who are willing to take risks and make mistakes as they manage the organization and also spiritually lead the congregation.

Vision

As noted earlier in this chapter, the one aspect of megachurch life that is often directly attributable to the senior pastor is the ideological vision of the church. Without a doubt, these churches have a strong and distinctive sense of identity and purpose. In the 2005 survey, 70 percent of respondents claimed to strongly agree that their church has a clear vision and purpose. The language, stories, and messages communicated by the senior pastor profoundly shape this vision. Our experience in meeting with these pastors tells us that they are quite aware of this critical element in their leadership. They are both boldly activist and also sensitively reflective about their role of visionary for the congregation. They embrace a distinctly outward orientation toward the larger cultural, demographic, and community context within their vision. Yet at the same time, they set themselves apart from other churches as they define how God is uniquely calling their congregation to minister in distinctive ways.

The vision of the megachurch usually offers a coherent, meaningful picture of the world to which others are attracted. At the same time, it provides a distinctiveness that can unify a large and often diverse gathering of participants. The vision articulated by the senior minister has a level of excitement and passionate enthusiasm around which members rally and from which they draw encouragement and energy. This vision is cast in easy-to-remember phrases, pictures, analogies, and forms that connect with members. Such devices help members identify their mission while also reinforcing the norms and values of the church. For example, Blackhawk Church in Madison, Wisconsin, has the mission of "Building a loving community that follows Christ in order to reach a community that is lost without Him." The church then uses its Web site to expound on this mission:

> The following values describe the picture we hope that we are moving towards, through the grace of God at work among us.
>
> Following Christ—We dream about building a community where each individual is so passionate about following Jesus Christ that by the power of the Holy Spirit we reorder our lives—our relationships, habits, traditions, and possessions—in order to become more like Him.
>
> Worshipping God—We dream about building a community where our worship of God is so authentic that we are continually overwhelmed with His greatness. We long to be a multigenerational community that is free to celebrate our God by using contemporary styles of musical worship while continuing to reflect our heritage. We envision becoming a community where the hunger for pursuing God in prayer is normative for every believer.

The site goes on to describe several related values to embody the mission through descriptive phrases and photos showing these values in action. The topical headings include: Communicating Truth, Working Together, Reaching Others, Celebrating Life and Serving Others. Under the heading Serving Others, the description reads: "We dream about building a community where Christ's passion to serve others is caught and practiced by everyone. We hold selfless, humble service of the poor and hurting in our city and world as a high ideal. To us, Christ-like service mirrors God's grace."[9]

Churches have personalities or cultures that form over time and reflect both the pastor's vision and the congregation's values and aspirations. As we wrote earlier, churches of all sizes tend to reflect their senior pastor's vision and values in particular. Senior pastors who have grown their churches to megasize often realize their key role in helping to shape these values and aspirations of the church and its people. These visions are cast in the language of their audience, but attempt to draw people toward godly ideals. These visionary ideals describe not only what the church as a whole should be, but also how each member should personally embody the ideals. Rather than an abstract vision of what one ought to be, megachurch pastors often outline specific steps and actions that members can take to actualize this vision. Our experience is that megachurch leaders can connect with their members in ways that resonate deeply in motivating participants to achieve a goal and giving them concrete steps for accomplishing it as well.

Evangelistic Fervor

Our interviews with megachurch leaders show that a majority have a strong gift, desire, and passion for reaching out to those who are not presently churched. Their stated passionate and sincere objective is to turn unbelievers into believers, to enlarge the number of persons who are Christ's disciples. These senior pastors strive to increase the Kingdom of God rather than solely the numbers at their churches. That enthusiasm and drive to reach the lost becomes contagious in a congregation. It is not that these pastors neglect the task of nurturing existing believers; rather, their personal bent and zeal is toward reaching nonbelievers. Those megachurch pastors with the strongest passion for and calling to be evangelists spend considerable time cultivating personal relationships with the unchurched in order to lead them to become followers of Christ. This evangelistic bent is a near obsession for some megachurch leaders.

As an example, one megachurch pastor responded this way when he was asked what numbers he tracked on a weekly basis. "By five o'clock every Sunday afternoon I get a call from our executive pastor with two key numbers: the number of total persons present in worship that day and the number of persons who said yes to Jesus that day." (Their phrase for a significant spiritual decision.) This pastor went on to say that he keeps track in his head of what those numbers are from season to season and how they vary with the current emphases of the church. When he notes a downward trend, he becomes concerned and passionately increases his evangelistic efforts.

This mentality of creating disciples is not only reflected in the senior pastor's preaching and other communication, but is embodied in the leadership of the entire ministry of the church. This value on evangelism becomes one of the prime drivers of the church and can be seen in almost every ministry expression, as well as in the development of new programs.

Practical Preaching

Our experience is that with few exceptions, megachurch senior pastors are not great preachers in the classical, homiletical styles that are taught in seminaries. They are instead gifted communicators who use a variety of styles of teaching and exposition to get across their message. They recognize the value of "packaging" their message with phrases and stories that are easy to understand. For instance, when churches were asked in 2000 how often the sermons contain certain characteristics, the megachurches had higher rates of the use of personal stories or firsthand experiences, illustrations from contemporary media such as magazines, newspapers, television, or movies, and practical advice for daily living than did all other congregations surveyed in the Faith Communities Today 2000 study. Over 75 percent of megachurches said their sermons "always" or "often" exhibited these characteristics (see Figure 4.1).

While much about the megachurch pastors' preaching style draws objections from other clergy, their sermons tend to draw enthusiastic responses from their hearers. Most of these senior pastors recognize and appreciate other styles of preaching, but intentionally use these simpler,

Figure 4.1. Sermon Elements Compared: Megachurch 2000 and Faith Communities Today 2000.

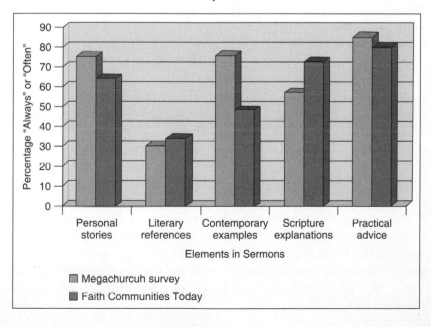

practical styles to connect with a diverse audience. It is clear from our many discussions with megachurch attendees that they find much of value in these sermons. The ability of these pastors to speak directly to the everyday experiences of attendees is amazing. Countless times we have heard departing worshippers exclaim, "The pastor must have overheard our argument at the breakfast table this morning!" or, "How did he know we were going through that problem with the kids?" or most often, "He spoke directly to me this morning." Comments such as these point directly to the power of expressing the Gospel in practical ways. Relating the Christian message through personal stories, everyday experiences, and in response to contemporary cultural situations brings the "old, old story" to life in the modern age. In this way, pastors both model and tie together belief and behavior.

Creativity, Inquisitiveness, Managerial Ability, and Confidence

Megachurch pastors are risk-takers. They tend to be creative in their approaches. We assert this not just to explain their communication, but also to describe their willing adaptation of other churches' and pastors' ideas to their context. They seem to have a strong sense of how to borrow an innovative, new, or fresh idea and reformulate it to fit their situation and purposes. They seldom accept ideas uncritically and instead strive to make them their own. Neither are they afraid to try and fail at something. There is a spirit of experimentation in them that does not disappear after disappointment. They take the lack of success as a challenge to try even more new ventures.

Megachurch senior pastors are likewise inquisitive about a wide variety of subjects, in addition to church leadership. Some have speculated that the leaders of megachurches would have been successful in business, law, or any other vocation they chose. Part of that drive to explore and succeed comes from an innate curiosity to learn and apply ideas from all sorts of contexts to their chosen profession.

Another characteristic of senior megachurch pastors is their management ability. Most of them know how to manage themselves by emphasizing their strengths. In addition, they are comfortable with directing others on their staff as well as collaborating with their boards. Each pastor tends to find a limit on the number of people reporting to them and then devises a system to give leadership to the broader church. They clearly know, or quickly learn, that part of being a megachurch pastor is learning to manage people and systems. These leaders are very aware of their callings, gifts, and strengths. This gives them greater confidence to lead.

In general these pastors are "comfortable in their own skin" as leaders. There are a growing number of younger pastors who have planted or assumed leadership of large megachurches early in their careers and have no hesitation about shouldering this responsibility. In the past, some megachurch pastors have been reluctant or uncomfortable with leading such large organizations. These reluctant leaders often had churches and staff that grew quickly, and they had a difficult time adjusting to the change. Some pastors "hit the wall," burned out, and found other places to serve. Now, however, it seems as if more pastors are comfortable with the role of leading a huge church in part because they are finding help and resources from other pastors and service agencies, particularly in regard to conceptualizing and defining their roles.

Style of Leadership

Several factors influence the style of leadership that a megachurch pastor exhibits. Obviously, the senior pastor's leadership style is shaped by his or her personality, and as such there is a great variety of styles among megachurch pastors. However, the personal characteristics of leadership style are also conditioned by the context, the denominational tradition, and the religious and social norms of the particular area of the country. In part, these factors influence the leadership style of pastors in any size congregation. Perhaps the most profound formative role on a megachurch pastor's leadership style, and what sets the task of guiding these churches apart from other congregations, is the size and complexity of the organization. Additionally, the physical and social distance between the leader and those being led also shapes leadership characteristics in these very large churches. It is beyond the scope of this book to explore all these leadership variables in depth. However, a brief exploration of this latter topic should hint at the leadership complexity and challenges that face megachurch pastors.

Like the CEO of a large complex company with multiple departments and considerable division of labor, the physical and social distance between the leader and those at each level of the organization shapes leadership styles in unique ways. The megachurch pastor's style of leadership with those in close physical and social proximity, such as associate pastors and ministry leaders, may be considerably different from the methods of leadership used with the more distant ministry volunteers or the general congregation. With employees of the church, the leader may be demanding, expecting high performance, instilling confidence, bestowing rewards, and punishing incompetence. The senior pastor with high-quality leadership skills may demand intense commitment, but also encourage freethinking and a diversity of opinions and suggestions from the staff. Alternatively, the leader may use personal charm and relational ties, the authority of his or her office, and bureaucratic rules to accomplish the goals of the organization, especially when dealing with board members, volunteer heads of ministries, and in external negotiations with vendors or governmental officials.

Leadership styles such as those used with staff or significant volunteer leaders seldom work to inspire a congregation or a group of less committed volunteers. When in the pulpit, the leader becomes a charismatic visionary and spiritual authority. This leader verbally manipulates the symbolic identity of the church as the vision is conveyed, reshaped, and communicated in the large public gathering. Storytelling; biblical knowledge; human insightfulness; and expressions of trustworthiness, vulnerability, and genuine self-effacement are the media by which this vision is communicated. At this level of leadership, the organizational and functional methods for accomplishing the tasks of the church are passed to the attendees and volunteers through trusted associate pastors and ministry leaders rather than directly from the senior minister.

Running a multimillion-dollar church organization and hundreds of staff and volunteer leaders, as well as negotiating complex decisions with governmental officials, requires different leadership skills than inspiring attendees and volunteers to become mature Christians and assist in supporting the work of the church. Because these two distinct tasks are seldom found in the same person, even among megachurch pastors, many such churches are moving to a dual leader model or to leadership teams, both of which approaches are described further below.

We trust this example hints at the challenges of leading an organization that is both a church and also a large, complex business enterprise. Too little quality research has been done on the nuances of megachurch leadership. This is partly because it takes a significant investment of time and in-depth participation in the organizational life of these churches to truly see and understand the complex and multifaceted leadership styles of different megachurch pastors. Questions about leadership style cannot fully be answered through a questionnaire or in a brief interview. Leadership can only be observed in action, both in a public inspirational forum and through the daily grind of intimate interactions, with staff and colleagues wrestling over conflicts between functional necessities such as budget and the lofty ideals embodied in the church's vision. It is high-quality leadership skills in both of these arenas that make a truly successful megachurch pastor.

It is possible to see the fruits of such leadership even if the styles that provide the groundwork for that leadership are somewhat obscured.

In the 2000 study, megachurches were far more likely than smaller churches to agree that their congregations welcomed innovation and change, dealt openly with disagreements and conflicts, were excited about the church's future, easily incorporated new people into the church, and had a clear sense of mission and purpose. Nearly half (48 percent) of the attendees of the largest Protestant churches in the U.S. Congregational Life Survey claimed that their leaders encouraged them to use their gifts and skills to a great extent. Roughly the same percentage of worshippers said the church's ministers took their ideas into account to a great extent and an additional 30 percent claimed this to some extent. When the survey respondents in the largest Protestant churches of the U.S. Congregational Life Survey were asked to describe the leadership style of their senior minister, 62 percent chose the description "inspires people to take action," while 17 percent chose "takes charge," and 12 percent said the pastor "acts on goals." This same study asked if worshippers felt there was a good fit between the church and the senior pastor, and 65 percent "strongly agreed" it was a fit, 27 percent "agreed," and only 8 percent "disagreed." Ultimately, however, we still know little about how megachurch pastors inspire, stimulate growth, handle rapid changes in the complexity of their growing churches, and then connect with and stimulate the spiritual development of thousands of attendees. Much more study needs to be undertaken to fully understand the style and dynamics of megachurch leaders that result not just in congregational growth, but also in the inspiration and vitality of members' spiritual development that is evident in the survey results.

Staff Leadership and Roles

Megachurches have large and strong staff teams. In most cases, these ministry assistants could easily serve as senior pastors of their own churches. Frequently, an associate pastor at a megachurch might have responsibility for a ministry area serving five hundred or more people on a regular basis. These duties are often considerably greater than those of a typical pastor at an average-sized one-hundred-person church. These associate and staff pastors often have wide-ranging authority and the autonomy needed to lead their respective areas of ministry within the megachurch. Their duties vary tremendously from church to church and are conditioned not only by the role of the senior minister, but also by a church's organizational structure. These associates run key ministry areas such as youth, children, worship, and missions programs, which can have budgets vastly larger than an average church. In addition to running their respective ministries, in some megachurches a few key staff members form a core team that is asked to offer broader leadership to the church as a whole and advice, guidance, and mutual support to the senior minister. We will say more about this in the following section on leadership teams.

In our 2005 survey, the average megachurch had twenty full-time leadership level staff members and nine part-time leadership staff. This is a significant increase from what we found in the 2000 survey, which reported an average of thirteen full-time and three part-time ministry staff. Additionally, the 2005 study reported an average of twenty-two additional full-time staff and twenty-two part-time staff at these churches.

Some of these full-time leadership staff members are ordained pastors within a denominational tradition. A number of them may formerly have been pastors of their own churches. But many are also "homegrown" staff pastors who began their ministry training by serving as volunteers at the church and have grown into a staff role. In multiple cases, we have seen the entire leadership team come up through the ranks over time. Churches will often promote leaders from within the church who may be experts in secular fields such as media, communications, business, or administration to fill specialized roles in leadership, but who also have a solid grounding in the vision of the church.

In addition to paid staff members, megachurches have an extensive army of volunteers. In some churches, numerous volunteer staff members carry a pastoral title, an office, and are present at staff meetings and retreats. Sixty-three percent of the churches report that they have volunteers spending between twenty and forty hours a week in church ministry. In these churches there are, on average, thirty-five people who volunteer at this near full-time level. Our survey also found that the average number of volunteers who worked over five hours a week at the church was 284 persons. When combined with the number of people on staff, the total average megachurch leadership base is greater than the weekly total attendance at 90 percent of U.S. churches. This broad and deep leadership base is one of the key strengths of the Megachurch movement.

Just as with staff development, these churches are strong in equipping and deploying lay volunteer leaders throughout their churches. While the senior pastor seldom does this, he or she clearly sets the tone with regard to the value of this development and the impetus for cultivating this level of volunteer lay leadership. We know few pastors of any size church who claim they have enough lay leaders, but the pastors of megachurches work to design systems and structured methods to intentionally grow their number of lay leaders. We are not advocating any particular one of these methodologies, but rather assert the critical value of having a system to expand the ranks of lay leadership within a church.

As an aside, these churches are usually very bold in encouraging their best lay leaders to leave secular positions to join the fulltime staff of their churches, regardless of background and training. The emphasis is on observed performance and character, rather than training and education.

The Emergence of Leadership Teams

Although earlier in this chapter we have written extensively about the key role that a single senior pastor plays in the church, other leadership models are coming into being. While clearly a minority at the present time, more senior pastors are adopting the title of "directional leader" to distinguish the role of pastor or preacher from that of the visionary leader. In a growing number of churches, we see a team of "senior pastors" with one directional leader giving overall guidance to the team.

For example, North Coast Church in Vista, California, featured in the Introduction, has four senior pastors who oversee other pastors, staff, and the overall direction of the church. Larry Osborne is known as a senior pastor and has been with the church since 1980. But three other pastors also carry the title of senior pastor, while overseeing different sections of the ministry. One of the other pastors, Chris Brown, also serves as one of the weekend teaching pastors.

In a different model of pastor teams, if you were to go to Fellowship Bible Church in Little Rock, Arkansas, you would find four pastors charged specifically with teaching and administration. A larger team of "shepherding elders," which also includes the four teaching and administrative pastors and other leaders, combine to give direction to the church.

Additionally, while we made much of the senior pastor's key role in guiding the church from the pulpit each week, a growing number of megachurches have begun to use teams of teaching pastors for weekend services. In informal discussions over the past ten years, we have asked senior pastors, "On average, how many weekends a year do you preach/teach?" Ten years ago, the typical answer from a senior pastor would have been between forty and forty-four weekends a year. Today, the answers range between twenty-two and forty weekends a year with the majority of the senior pastors claiming to preach between thirty-five and thirty-eight weekends per year. The emergence of the "teaching pastor" role is significant in assisting the growth of these churches. With the weekend teaching load shared among a team of preacher/teachers, there is more opportunity for pastors to create and develop high-quality messages. In some churches, there are four or more regular teaching pastors who serve the congregation by teaching multiple weekends during the year. Often these teaching pastors have other leadership roles within the church, but by nature of their highly visible teaching role, they are recognized as key leaders in the church.

The exceptions to this estimate of sermons preached per year are in those churches that have media ministries driven by a specific pastor's preaching. For those churches and pastors with weekly television or even daily radio programs, the focus tends to be on one senior pastor as the key preacher/teacher. In these churches the senior pastors tend to carry much more of the preaching and teaching role.

The drop in the number of weekends of teaching/preaching is attributable to several factors. The first is the overall demand for preaching/teaching excellence that requires more planning, preparation, and rest. As was noted in a previous chapter, megachurches have multiple services each weekend. And at least 10 percent of current megachurch pastors are sixty years of age or older and may not have the youthful stamina they once had. A second factor is recognition by some senior or lead pastors that a church needs to hear God's word interpreted through the voices of multiple leaders to receive the maximum benefit. Each preacher/teacher not only has their own preaching style, but also has their own unique understanding and distinctive life experience to bring to the Scriptures. Each pastor can teach and preach using their unique strengths in both scriptural interpretation and style. For example, when there is a series on "the family," it is possible to have a younger pastor teach one weekend and relate to issues faced by young families and have an older pastor on another weekend address issues faced by older generations. This helps the entire congregation better understand the Scriptures and addresses the congregation's needs in these areas. A third factor is a growing desire on the part of some senior pastors to train and equip a group of teaching pastors to develop their own gifts so that these leaders can become senior leaders in other churches. A final factor that affects this shift to multiple preachers is the growing phenomenon of planning for succession in the role of the senior pastor, where one long-time senior pastor first shares the pulpit and then eventually relinquishes the primary mantle of spiritual leadership to a younger pastor.

Succession

We are frequently asked the question that has become its own myth about megachurches: What will happen when these senior pastors retire? Many commentators have predicted that megachurches will decline and fade away once the founder and pastor responsible for the growth retires or dies. This is based on the understanding that the church revolves around the leader and that a retiring charismatic leader's vitality cannot be duplicated by his or her successor. There is some truth to that understanding. As we have said previously, leadership matters. A change in the primary leader, whether it is in businesses, schools, nonprofit arenas, or churches, can be a difficult time. We have seen churches of all sizes significantly grow or decline after a leadership change. Nevertheless, there is a heightened awareness and discussion of leadership succession in megachurches these days, in part due to a large number of megachurch pastors approaching retirement age.

Allow us to relate some anecdotal evidence to address this issue. Ten years ago, Leadership Network held a special gathering of large church pastors to talk about issues of leadership transition. All of the churches had grown very large under their current pastor. We broke the group down by age with three groups of senior pastors. The group of pastors in their sixties was of the generation born prior to 1945. The conversations in this group indicated they were not too concerned about succession. Some claimed they would never retire, others felt the church would figure it out, and most felt any decisions relating to the next pastor would be out of their control and made after they were gone. The second group of pastors in their fifties was cognizant that they would need to develop a plan of succession eventually, but few had initiated any steps toward doing so. Those who had considered retirement were planning a phased transition with a copastor arrangement leading to eventual retirement. The forty-somethings were the clergy who were most aware of the need to begin planning for the church's continued growth and health long before they passed from the scene. Everyone in this group stated they would have a plan in place by the time they approached the age of sixty. These pastors did not indicate a desire for "early retirement" but rather hoped they could make a change in their roles at the church in order to allow new leaders to emerge.

What has happened in the intervening ten years? Almost all of those in the oldest group have either retired or died. About half of the churches they pastored are now larger under new leadership and about half are smaller. For the group of pastors in their fifties, where there was a planned transition, most have successfully navigated the change, and even though there have been conflicts, they have grown or sustained their current size through the transition. If there was no plan, their churches are struggling. The group of pastors in their forties is now in their mid-fifties. Some clearly have a stronger team of teaching pastors around them and have informally said that the future transition should go smoothly, but only time will tell.

From our experience, most of the churches we have observed have handled succession well. For those churches in denominational traditions, there are unique challenges in leader succession. The influence of denominational officials and systems has led to mixed results. At times, the denominational structures and policies have allowed a smooth transition. A bishop or regional overseer has helped select a replacement and nurtured the transition with a minimum of difficulty. At other times, an external selection is made with little consideration of the unique needs of the megachurch. Additionally, in certain traditions churches are forbidden to have a new senior pastor who has previously spent time at the church. A newly selected replacement leader may be completely unaware of the culture of the specific church. In some cases, this has led to significant mismatches between the church and the leader. This is not to say, however, that independent and Free Church traditions have a great advantage in the process. In fact, in the streams of megachurches that are more pastor-centered, this transition has been much harder and riskier. Recent organizations such as ChurchStaffing.com have greatly helped staff replacement by creating an employment service and job bank for large churches to advertise and obtain both pastors and key staff members familiar with and skilled in large church leadership.

In the cases where a pastor on the leadership team is named to be the new lead pastor, he or she has the advantage of knowing the culture and ethos of the church. This is usually a signal by the church's governing board that they desire continuity with the present direction of the church. At other times when an outsider is brought to the church after a nationwide search, it is usually a sign from the governing board that they want a change in direction. Either approach can lead to greater levels of conflict between pastoral direction and church, as was mentioned in our data earlier in this chapter. But there are also times when such a switch proceeds smoothly and successfully.

The First Evangelical Free Church of Fullerton, California, is but one example. From 1971 to 1994, Dr. Charles Swindoll was the senior pastor of this megachurch and found fame through a popular radio program entitled, "Insight for Living," and through his many books. The church thrived under his leadership and formed a cohesive staff team. In 1994, he departed to become a seminary president. Many in the church and outside the church expressed great concern about the next leader having to follow in Charles Swindoll's footsteps. The church asked Dale Burke, a pastor of a much smaller church, to become its new pastor in 1995. The church has continued to thrive since that time. As a side note to the story, after a successful tenure as president of Dallas Theological Seminary,

Dr. Swindoll helped start Stonebriar Community Church in Frisco, Texas, in 1999, which is now a megachurch itself.

Our experience in observing dozens of these transitions is that a key marker leading to the smoothest and healthiest transition is the former senior pastor's willingness to give up power, status, and a prominent public role within the worship life of the church. At times, these "emeritus pastors" find new ministry roles aimed externally or with only a slight connection to the everyday life of the church. In the few cases where, sadly, the senior pastor has had a sudden premature death, nearly all churches have made a healthy transition to a new senior leader. In those examples of leadership change following a clergy scandal or forced pastoral dismissal, the church often suffers, at least for a time, as much as the former minister does.

We are cautiously optimistic that the current crop of senior pastors who lead these organizations will practice the same self-sacrifice they have throughout their ministries by allowing new leadership to emerge and thrive into the future. However, as our survey findings show, any pastor who follows the founding or growth-producing senior minister will have a challenging time making the church's vision correspond to his or her passions and directions and convincing the congregation that their new future will be as bright and prosperous as in the past.

○

Applying What You Have Read

This chapter has dealt with the leadership of the senior pastor, the person giving the prime directional leadership within the church. If you are a senior pastor, there are many things we don't believe you can change about yourself. You can't change your age. You can't change how long you have been a part of your current church, but many times you can commit to making your ministry long-term in this church and adjust your mind-set accordingly.

The leaders that we write about are strong leaders, unafraid to be directive and task-oriented, but also desirous of equipping others to share in the work of ministry. They know their own gifts and strengths and operate from a combination of these gifts and a deep sense of calling. We find that most church leaders are shy when it comes to conflict, whereas megachurch leaders are not afraid to deal with difficult issues. They have a strong interest in those outside the church. If you are a pastoral leader, how do the phrases in this paragraph match up with your sense of yourself?

Our experience is that church leaders are often uncomfortable with many of these characteristics. Their mental model of a pastor is different. They have a different sense of calling. If that is the case, be yourself, not someone God did not make you to be, but don't criticize those who have a different calling or understanding of their ministry.

As we mentioned in the text, one of the key strengths found in megachurch pastors is the equipping and empowering of other leaders. These leaders grant great responsibility to associate pastors within their church. They provide training, mentoring, and resources to get the job done. They spend significant time with staff pastors and key volunteers. Our experience with many pastors of smaller churches is that they tend to do the opposite and spend little time training and nurturing staff and key volunteers. What percentage of time are you currently spending with staff and key volunteers in equipping them for effective service? We feel that 25 percent is a minimum for this type of activity. Many pastors of smaller churches spread themselves too thin and endeavor to do too much of the frontline ministry themselves instead of equipping others.

For those who might say, "I don't have any staff, so what am I to do?" our experience is that even pastors of the smallest churches can often find volunteers to share the ministry journey if they are willing to call forth and nurture the leadership. That person might be young and aspire to become a pastor some day. There could be several retired persons with plenty of free time and gifts and strengths that complement the pastor. There could even be a local retired pastor who would like to continue serving a congregation without any expectation of remuneration. Additionally, we feel that every pastor in any size church can select a small group of people to share in the leadership of the church on an ongoing basis. Some of these people will be formally elected, and others may be chosen because of their spiritual wisdom, influence, or tenure in the church. These informal leaders who are selected do not need titles or specific roles, but they do need attention from the senior pastor in terms of mentoring and direction.

To summarize, megachurch pastors have a sense of being comfortable in their own skin and with the ministry God has given them. Yet they are not without their own insecurities and shortcomings. In all of the aspects of their personality, they are transparent with those around them. They likely use personal stories in their preaching, teaching, and written communication. They communicate not just the triumphs but also their foibles. We feel pastors are at their best when God's story of redemption is told frequently through examples of how God's grace has redeemed them in their life both in the past and present. Our experience is that church attendees know well that their pastors are not perfect, nor do they expect them to be. They do expect that the pastors will share how God's grace is revealed to them through those experiences of failure as well.

Many pastors will claim that they cannot learn to preach in a new way. We know it is hard at times to teach "old dogs new tricks," but not impossible. As pastors know, there is an entire industry of sermon helps, publications, audio recordings, and other tools to help pastors improve their preaching. With an abundance of megachurch pastors' and other good preachers' sermons available free online, there is no reason that every pastor cannot listen and learn from other pastors. We are not recommending that any pastor steal or borrow another's sermon. However, we suggest that clergy listen to a variety of communicators to learn how other pastors craft their message into everyday language to help hearers learn more of God. Many of the megachurches have weekly podcasts that can easily be downloaded into an MP3 player and carried along on your daily routine for review. We would recommend this practice for several months of the year.

Megachurch pastors are also noted for the "freshness" of their messages. They tie their sermon material to issues of the day, television, movies, and other avenues of broad cultural appeal. The preaching and application of ancient Scriptures to contemporary issues give new followers of Christ a beginning place of understanding that is most necessary in today's world.

- How much time are you spending training and mentoring other leaders?
- How can you rearrange your current time commitments to do so?
- If you are a church member, is there a ministry desire or passion you would like to explore with your pastor?
- Look back over your messages for the past four months. In how many did you share how God is at work in your own life?
- Can you find four or five pastors who want to improve their preaching by listening to each other's sermons on a regular basis?

5

"THESE CHURCHES ARE ONLY CONCERNED ABOUT THEMSELVES AND THE NEEDS OF THEIR ATTENDEES"

"Though many of the churches, which are largely in the South and Midwest, are involved in missionary work, their congregants may be able to isolate themselves from the greater community—to engage in a kind of 'Christian cocooning,'" said Dr. Bill J. Leonard, dean and professor of church history at Wake Forest University in Winston-Salem, N.C.[1]

Dr. Wade Clark Roof, a professor of religion and society at the University of California at Santa Barbara, said he worried that full-service churches are "the religious version of the gated community." "It's an attempt to create a world where you're dealing with like-minded people," he said. "You lose the dialogue with the larger culture."[2]

THE INITIAL AND IMMEDIATE CHALLENGE faced by churches who grow to megachurch proportions seemingly overnight is threefold: first, how to nurture, disciple, and mature hundreds of inexperienced Christians; second, how to find the building space to deal with the influx of new people; and finally, how to adequately address the multiple pressing personal needs of a congregation in the thousands. These needs create a situation whereby there is some truth to the image that megachurches spend a great deal of time and energy on the internal growth and care of their members. If they didn't, they would quickly decline, because most people would eventually drift away. All congregations must address their internal needs, but this also has to be balanced with a reciprocal external, contextual focus whether the church is large or small. It has taken time for the megachurches to learn this balance.

Early in the phenomenon (the 1960s through the mid-1980s), much of the energy of megachurches did seem turned inward toward discovering what it was like to worship on such a large scale. While there were notable exceptions of prominent external ministries during that time, the critique that many of these churches were building their kingdoms and catering to their own flocks was somewhat justified. However, over the past two decades, megachurch leaders have also learned that to whom much is given much will be required. They have come to the realization organizationally that they have to structure ways for their members to live out their Christian calling to love, and serve, their neighbor as themselves, and this means ministering to the larger world outside the church's four walls. Additionally, changes have taken place in the culture at large and in Evangelicalism in particular that make social ministry locally and to the world more prominent. Missionary activity is no longer just about saving souls, but also about meeting physical, educational, and economic needs. This revised mission agenda is changing not just how megachurches approach social ministry, but also how the entire evangelical Christian world undertakes mission activity. Megachurches have also discovered that they can tap new audiences who are seeking ways to serve their communities. Asking potential attendees to become involved first with a ministry that serves the poor seems in line with Christ's teachings. This involvement builds both commitment and community, which in turn lead to even more growth in some megachurches.

Many older megachurches have changed their approach to address local, national, and international social needs to a greater degree in the last two decades. Likewise, newer ones have shaped their outreach in significant new ways, which are evident in the recent survey data. Those megachurches founded since 1990 have the highest rates of social ministry in the 2005 megachurch survey.

Most megachurches have begun to conceive of outreach in terms of a diversified ministry portfolio. In the past, these churches defined their outreach by those key activities that were officially sanctioned and directly supported by the church itself, such as starting and supporting a tutoring program; developing a full-scale food and clothing program; or building, supporting, and sending regular workers to churches or orphanages in Central America. The trend in recent years, however, is to continue supporting social ministry at the churchwide level, but also to partner with denominational mission agencies as they had in the past, as well as nondenominational parachurch organizations such as Youth with a Mission or Habitat for Humanity, local women's shelters, homeless shelters, community organizations, and even governmental groups. At times, these efforts are expressed through groups of local churches, usually with a megachurch in the center because it has the staff and financial resources to drive the efforts.

For example, an organization, Sharefest, channels the energies and efforts of over a hundred churches in the Little Rock, Arkansas, area to combine efforts to conduct improvement projects in public schools, fire stations, and other public buildings; to refurbish centers that serve the poor; to conduct heath screenings in targeted neighborhoods; and the like. It has now been duplicated in over seventy-five cities around the country. The foundational church behind the effort is Fellowship Bible Church in Little Rock, Arkansas. Likewise, various churches in New York City focus on particular social needs, but at the core of each of these groups one finds a prominent megachurch such as Redeemer Church. Likewise, in a similar effort in Atlanta, Perimeter Church can be seen as the instigator and sustainer of that movement of churches. Megachurches have also begun to infuse an intentional social ministry emphasis into their small group structure in order to incorporate social outreach in the spiritual development of individual members. For example, at North Coast Church, every "Growth Group" has a regular community-focused ministry outside the church where they contribute their time and resources. This approach has the value of both making these ministries close to those who serve in them and building bonds of relationship between the group members. The effort to think of social ministry in this multifaceted way has given megachurches a robust external ministry, although one that is not always immediately recognized or overtly apparent.

Where Did the Myth Come From?

On the one hand, megachurches have been criticized for being insular and not caring for the community; and on the other hand, as you can see from the above, they are often described as engaged in countless activities. So exactly what do these congregations do that reaches out to the social needs of the larger community, and why is it perceived as somewhat inadequate?

Based on the 2005 megachurch survey, 72 percent of megachurches have partnered with other congregations to do international missions at some time in their history, and almost half had done so in the previous five years (46 percent). Over three quarters (79 percent) of these churches had joined together with other churches on a local community service project, with 54 percent of these having done so in the past five years. Sixty percent of these megachurches said offering support groups, such as self-help, recovery, and counseling-type ministries that are nearly always open to public, are a key activity of the church. Forty percent reported that providing externally focused social service activities such as those mentioned previously in the chapter was a key activity of the church, with 54 percent claiming it was a minor activity. These figures are significantly higher than for smaller congregations in the Faith Communities Today 2005 survey, for which only 16 percent said having support groups was a key activity, and 35 percent claimed providing social service was a key activity. The percentage of megachurches strongly agreeing that their churches were working for social justice was nearly identical to all the Faith Communities Today congregations; 16 percent of the megachurches and 14 percent of all the surveyed congregations asserted this. When asked in the 2005 survey, megachurch leaders estimated that 21 percent of their members volunteered weekly in community service, with almost 10 percent of the megachurches claiming that over half their members were active on a weekly basis.

While these figures indicate a good bit of social service activity is taking place at the megachurch, they don't specify exactly what the churches are doing. In our 2000 survey of megachurches, we asked more specific questions about the type of social ministry programs that the churches supported.[3] Table 5.1 indicates the percentages of megachurches supporting a variety of social ministry programs conducted by their church that focus on persons outside their church.

It is apparent from this table that megachurches support a host of social service efforts. In many ways, this is to be expected. Megachurches

Table 5.1. Megachurch Programs Supported.

Program Supported	Percentage
Programs for youth and teens	99
Counseling services or support groups	95
Cash or vouchers given to families or individuals	91
Prison ministries	91
Substance abuse and twelve-step programs	85
Senior citizen programs	84
Hospitals and nursing homes	80
Temporary or permanent housing/shelter	78
Thrift store or thrift store donations	78

have large numbers of active members, abundant monetary resources, and the physical space to provide a wide range of activities. Size makes a tremendous difference in the numbers of activities a congregation is able to offer. An analysis of the Faith Communities Today 2000 survey of over fourteen thousand churches showed that the larger the church, the greater their engagement in these activities. However, the rates at which megachurches are involved are even greater than those averaging one thousand persons or more (which also includes large Catholic congregations).

This analysis makes it clear that the megachurches are anything but inactive in their engagement with their communities and the needs of the world outside their walls. In almost every case, the largest-sized churches are more likely to have various externally focused ministries than smaller-sized churches are. What, then, drives the critique that they don't engage in social ministry? We posit that part of this perception is fueled by the distinctive role megachurches play in the city as a regional church. They draw people from a broad area of a city. Forty-two percent of megachurches say that 40 percent or more of their members travel over fifteen minutes to get to church, while only 29 percent of smaller Protestant FACT 2000 churches say their members travel that far. In a study of the members of one megachurch, nearly 50 percent drove over fifteen minutes to get to the church, and 10 percent traveled more than thirty minutes to church. Figure 5.1 shows the distribution of ZIP codes of members for one Atlanta-area church, the location of which is marked by a star. Clearly, if this church's data are representative, megachurches are regional phenomena, drawing attendees from a very broad area.

Because their membership is spread across an expansive region and over multiple communities, megachurch social ministry activity may also be dispersed over a large area. These churches have come to realize that they cannot expect all of their members to travel from home to church several times a week. Therefore, social ministry efforts must take place near where their members reside, if a substantial number of them are going to be expected to participate.

There is also a larger demographic factor driving where the ministry takes place, and that is the location of the greatest social needs. As we said before, the vast majority of these churches is found in areas of middle-class affluence, and while certain kinds of social ministry can and should be targeted at the needs of this population, much of what "counts" as social outreach is directed at the economically impoverished and often inner-city residents.[4]

The reality of these churches being located at a distance from the greatest need means that megachurches have to be creative in the ways

Figure 5.1. Typical Megachurch Member
Residence Distribution.

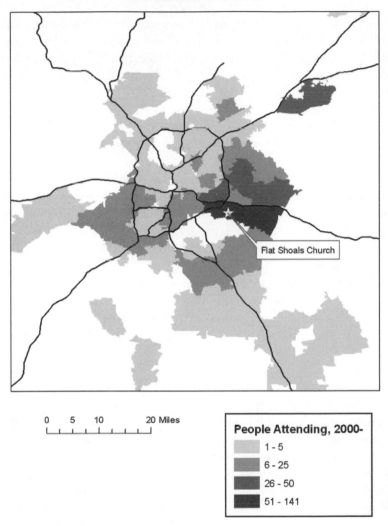

| 0 | 5 | 10 | 20 Miles |

People Attending, 2000-

	1 - 5
	6 - 25
	26 - 50
	51 - 141

they perform social ministry. In the 1980s, Chapel Hill Harvester Church, in Atlanta, adopted a crime-ridden city housing project that was nearly twelve miles away from the church to assist residents through tutoring, job placement, career planning, food and clothing support, neighborhood cleanup, and so on. They ran shuttle buses and caravans to help members get to the ministry site and worked in teams for safety and mutual support. For these efforts, the church was given a Thousand Points of Light award by President George H. W. Bush. Mariners Church, located in Newport Beach, California, has a Lighthouse Ministries division that seeks to serve inner-city poor, the homeless, foster children, and other at-risk youth through a variety of programs. They have started learning centers, mentoring programs, transitional apartment complexes, house rebuilding teams and dozens of other ministries to serve the poor in their region. In 2002 alone, Mariners Church had nearly five thousand attendees involved in regular ministry to the poor through their ministries and partnerships.[5] These are only a few of the many examples that could be cited here.

We would also note that megachurches rarely feature their social ministry involvements prominently in their advertisements and promotion. These ministries to the poor are not so visible or well known among church attendees. Part of the reason is the decentralization of these ministries into small teams of people. Another aspect of the visibility issue relates to the location of the ministry in relation to the church campus. As mentioned earlier, sometimes teams are sent to ministry centers away from the highly visible worship centers in order to be closer to those being served by the ministry.

Megachurches have, in some cases, been hampered in performing social ministry by their desire to do it on their own. While this pattern has improved in the last two decades, often these churches have chosen to create their own outreach efforts within a city based on their own vision for the area rather than to participate in already established ministry projects.

A number of recent megachurches have fully embraced a vision of social ministry to the city as one of their key organizing principles. A noteworthy example of this trend is the Dream Center of Los Angeles. This megachurch began in 1994, but within a few years had purchased the abandoned Queen of Angels Hospital in Los Angeles and began offering a multitude of social services, including health care, a soup kitchen, and a shelter. The church has since grown to over ten thousand attendees; purchased the old Angelus Temple, the former home of the founder of the Foursquare Gospel denomination, Aimee Semple McPherson; and continued to offer over one hundred ministries that serve the poor and homeless. The former hospital building houses a health clinic, a homeless shelter for families, and education and tutoring classes for kids, just to name a few ministries. In addition, this church's model has been duplicated in over a hundred and fifty smaller churches and new church plantings around the world that are imitating the Dream Center style of social ministry to the poor.

When these churches do participate in ongoing projects, the magnitude of their involvement often overwhelms existing structures and other congregations' participation. Occasionally, megachurch leaders garner the ire and animosity of longtime social ministry leaders in the city when they are perceived as taking over because of the scale of participation they can contribute. A number of years ago at an Atlanta citywide social ministry event, one megachurch brought about one thousand participants, which was ten to twenty times more than any other congregation. Naturally, the media focused on this congregation's efforts. Later, other church leaders accused the megachurch's pastor of dominating the event, when in fact the attention was due to the size of the congregation's participation, not the attitude of their leadership.

This example is illustrative of the many stories we have heard where there was a community call for volunteers for a local, needy nonprofit or school. When the megachurch got involved, the response from the church included hundreds of volunteers, and the receiving organizational system in the nonprofit could not handle that amount of participation. There were hard feelings on both sides from the encounter.

As an alternative example, Granger Community Church of South Bend, Indiana, celebrated its twentieth anniversary as a church in December 2006. In celebration of this event, the church held "Twenty Days of Giving," in which it found creative ways to invest in the community over the twenty-day period. On each day, a different group within the church found a way to give back to the community. For example, the college-age ministry did an extreme makeover on the Center for the Homeless. On another day, the church purchased food for eight thousand hungry families to be distributed by their local Feed the Children branch. In addition to the gifts of time by the attendees, the church gave over $500,000 to outside community groups during that twenty-day period.

Another example comes from Omaha, Nebraska, where three of the largest churches (Christ Community, Trinity Interdenominational, and King of Kings Lutheran) began the "Embrace Teachers" movement. The members of these three churches found regular ways to express their appreciation for the servants in the public schools and to work together to serve the community.

On the national level, many megachurches have not been viewed as great participants in denominational mission efforts, especially in the area of finances. They are accused of giving less to these programs, which is partly true. Recently, such charges were made against several candidates for the presidency of the Southern Baptist Convention in 2006. Research on the largest churches in the Evangelical Lutheran Church of America did show that these thousand-plus attendee churches gave a smaller percentage to the denomination's mission programs than did Lutheran churches with fewer attendees. However, the actual amount these forty-three churches gave for these projects was a vastly larger sum than hundreds of smaller congregations. Likewise, when the additional amounts these churches gave to projects outside the denomination were factored in the total giving, the very large churches were contributing a slightly larger percentage of their income to external ministry than the smaller churches were. They just happened to be funding their own programs and those of nondenominational parachurch organizations rather than participating exclusively in the denomination's projects.[6]

This dynamic can currently be seen on the global stage with such well-publicized efforts as Rick Warren's efforts to rally interest in addressing the international AIDS epidemic. In addition to the high-profile efforts of Saddleback Church and its network, we find numerous other churches involved in nation-building activities in other countries. These efforts are multifaceted, with health, education, nutrition, and other components in addition to church planting and theological training. At the time of the writing of this book, prominent attention was given to a recent declaration by the National Association of Evangelicals regarding the care of the earth and global warming. Such media prominence regarding the ministry actions of these key megachurch pastors and religious leaders is having an influence on the understanding of missionary efforts around the world. Likewise, it is blurring the decades-long, perhaps false, distinction that mainline denominational missions addressed physical and educational needs, while evangelical denominational missions focused exclusively on spiritual needs. At the least, this assumption is being seriously challenged by these highly publicized activities of megachurch pastors.

The best mission efforts and social ministry accomplished by megachurches seldom come from the leadership or the church's organized ministry programs. Our experiences in the everyday activities of many of these churches indicate that far more social ministry is accomplished in small group and person-to-person acts than by the churches' intentional efforts. The most vital outreach accomplished by these twelve hundred or more megachurches happens through their efforts to broaden attendees' understanding that a mature Christian walk includes outreach to other people. Nearly all the megachurches include intentional preaching and educational classes in which the necessity of a life of service to others is integral to the definition of being a "good Christian." They teach that it isn't just the church's role to do good in the world, but also that each Christian should strive to change the world, to engage in service to others. Whether this is described as Rick Warren outlined in his Forty Days of Service program or in the Sharefest idea, the result is that many active participants in megachurches are doing ministry in ways and at levels that are different from their previous church involvement. Such ministry happens both in small groups and also at the individual member level.

As we have discussed at numerous points, megachurches use intentional small groups, whether around Bible study and fellowship or hobby and lifestyle groups, to intentionally structure involvement in the church and interaction between attendees. Many of these gatherings of participants are purposefully challenged and even required to have a service or social ministry component. One of us once belonged to a small fellowship group at a megachurch that had as its external ministry focus the adoption of a nursing home. We would visit persons in this home, offer hymn-sings, take residents grocery shopping, and help clean up the grounds. Additionally, our gatherings in homes were full of stories of individual acts of charity and service to others. None of these stories of "doing good" by individuals acting out their faith ever reached the leadership of the megachurch. Neither did these individual and collective acts of service get factored into accounts of how much social ministry was done by the megachurch. Yet it was the church's preaching and requirements for belonging to the small group that encouraged and facilitated this ministry.

An accounting of what individuals within megachurches do in terms of social ministry both through and independent of the church adds yet another, often invisible, dimension of these congregations' outreach to an area. When the attendees of the largest Protestant churches in the U.S. Congregational Life Survey were asked if they participated in church service activities, 20 percent said they were involved in community service activities, 24 percent in social service or charity groups, and 4 percent participated in advocacy groups.

However, when these same persons were asked what specific social ministry actions they had done personally, one finds a considerably greater engagement with the world. Individually, 72 percent gave money, 51 percent donated food, 29 percent loaned money outside of family, 24 percent helped others find a job, and 21 percent of megachurch attendees cared for others. When these people were asked if their congregation is strongly focused on serving the wider community, 54 percent of them "strongly agreed" with the statement.

When the entire portrait of the social ministry and service to those outside the congregation is taken into account, it is impossible to say that megachurches are inactive and not involved in the needs of non-members. It is apparent how such impressions arose and remain an issue of contention, and there was even a time in which there was some truth to the critique. However, such is no longer the case in the majority of megachurches. These congregations not only inspire their members to think of a full Christian life as having a social ministry component, they are also infusing their fellowship and small-group ministry structures with this focus. The megachurches are engaged in acting in their local communities alone and with others. They participate in larger mission efforts both through their denominational organizations and nondenominational parachurch groups. And increasingly, they are acting nationally and globally—alone and in coordination with other megachurches and smaller ministries—to accomplish God's will in the world to care for all God's people.

○

Applying What You Have Read

This chapter has described some of the ministries that megachurches offer to their communities and how they conduct those ministries. Even the smallest congregation can have a ministry focused on a need within its community. Many existing older congregations have long-term external ministries to serve individuals within their community. In some cases, these ministries may have lost their energy and connection to some in the congregation. What began as a passionate experience many years ago is a routine that few individuals hold dear to their hearts. Similarly, we know of many smaller churches with strong commitments to missions and service projects in other parts of the country and the world, but the primary connection is financial. All church ministries need regular reflection and renewal. Each new generation of leaders and attendees must commit to the goals, aims, and vision of that ministry for it to have ongoing effectiveness and relevance to the congregation.

In our experience, megachurches are adept at tying hands-on involvement to greater financial support for causes, whether locally or in distant lands. These churches create small local projects that individuals or the entire congregation can adopt and feel a part of, and where the results of these actions can be seen. Then after doing many of these smaller projects, the church will tackle larger and more demanding distant ministries.

Several chapters ago, we encouraged readers to describe the essential story of your church. We suggest that church leaders tie elements of this visionary story into externally focused ministry activities. This will encourage attendees to get involved in serving as a way to reach out to potential new attendees. Consider undertaking an initial activity that is of limited scope, but will involve a broad cross section of your congregation. For example, your church could help serve during a Special Olympics day or a walk for juvenile diabetes. First steps should be one-day experiences where those involved can feel connected to those being served. Additionally, they should be able to invite their friends to serve alongside them and share the experience. We know of relatively small churches that found a receptive public school principal who needed volunteers to help with a project on the grounds that made a big difference in peoples' attitudes toward social ministry. Even a small group of church members can do such projects in a short time with careful planning and group passion.

We mentioned in this chapter how many megachurches and other churches build partnerships in certain ministry areas. You could work with a megachurch on a joint project in the community. We would encourage you to find a way to partner with them in a focused way, not only to learn from their experience, but also to work together with other churches in your community to share Christ's mission of redemption.

Some will object to these ideas because "they will not have a long-term impact on those who really need help." Our response is twofold. Many "small projects" never get done because organizations bypass them in order to work only on long-term ones. Secondly, a start in a "small project" helps to engage individuals and families to connect to larger visions and larger projects both locally and in other places. Many times, it is from these small engagements that individuals can develop ongoing relationships and projects with those being served. It is often the case that once one's hands are involved with small service projects, their hearts are engaged to tackle larger areas of needed ministry in the community.

We would also encourage the structuring of regular externally focused projects as a part of the small groups within the church. These can be groups formed specifically for social outreach or as an extension activity of an existing group. We would urge you to ensure that the groups are open enough to invite nonattendees to join them in the project. From these types of experiences partnerships can grow between the church group and those being served. For example, many smaller churches find open arms to work with existing community nonprofits that serve families in poverty. These organizations have their own ongoing activities that need teams of volunteers to accept regular assignments. The right church small group can get connected and do great outreach for their church and for the community.

We also know that travel plus service can be a transformative experience in a church attendee's spiritual journey. Churches of all sizes can conduct "mission trips" to travel together and serve in a distant locale. Participants regularly describe these trips as "high points" of their spiritual journeys. The focus and intensity of these trips in terms of service, personal sharing, and bonding with fellow participants results in a sense of mission and calling not found in regular worship. Leaders are wise to build on these experiences "back home" by finding practical ways for the same group to become involved in a regular, ongoing ministry.

- Who are the existing groups in your community, be they churches or other nonprofits, doing God's work in the world?

- Which three or four of these are closest to the vision of your congregation?

- Who in your congregation may have a potential relationship with or passion to work with these organizations?

- Is there an underserved population or community need that fits with the essential story and vision of your congregation to which your church could devote a one-day service project?

- Which of your existing small groups could have a meaningful regular service project with an existing organization, or could be encouraged to start a regular ministry outside your church?

- How can you as a leader magnify and amplify these ministries to the larger congregation to reinforce the essential story and vision for the future?

6

"MEGACHURCHES WATER DOWN THE FAITH"

This week, the head of the World Council of Churches, Samuel Kobia, warned [that] the megachurch movement was dangerously shallow: "It has no depth, in most cases, theologically speaking, and has no appeal for any commitment. It's a church being organized on corporate logic. That can be quite dangerous if we are not very careful, because this may become a Christianity which I describe as 'two miles long and one inch deep.'"[1]

I think the whole megachurch phenomenon is premised upon the idea that we can't do anything with people unless we get them to church first, so the priority is to get them in there. But to get them in there, you downplay the Christian symbolism, you take the crosses off the church, you make the pews as comfortable as you possibly can, you put McDonald's franchises in the lobby. Sometimes you don't even know you're in church when you go to church, because the church doesn't look like a church.[2]

Some conservative Evangelicals denounce megacongregations as devotion lite, delivering plenty of entertainment but asking for little commitment.[3]

THESE THREE QUOTES ARE ILLUSTRATIVE of one of the most disparaging misperceptions regarding megachurches—that they are growing explicitly because they preach an easy form of the Christian message. We could have used many similar quotes as examples, as this is one of the most pervasive critiques of the movement. Many of those raising these criticisms are Christian leaders who feel that megachurches do not transmit an orthodox faith to their attendees. The quotes illuminate the commentators' confusion in distinguishing between what a church looks like versus what a church actually does in a believer's heart. In contrast to detractors, our view is that these churches actually call many believers to higher levels of commitment and, once committed, to a serious life of faith.

As we have stressed in earlier chapters, the modern megachurch is a different style of church. It has little in common with the churches that most of us were familiar with from our childhood. The "church" mental mind-set of critics, as well as most Americans, remains a version of the English country parish model or its American equivalent, a white clapboard New England–style church served by a humble solo pastor. In reality, church observers have noted that this congregational form has not been in the majority for over half a century, but mental models and cultural images die very slow deaths.

Sources of the "Dumbing Down" Charge

The "dumbing down" charge often starts with the rapid growth of a church. When compared to what they think of as "typical," people are amazed that a church can grow to two thousand in attendance. The assumption is that a "serious" church usually does not grow, or if it does, it happens gradually over a long period of time. Because serious churches don't grow, then if one is growing rapidly something about it must be false. In essence, the church that grows is not an authentic church. This charge comes in different versions from liberal or conservative theological critics. For those in the liberal camp, the church is not being prophetic enough if it is growing at such a rapid rate. For those from a conservative orientation, the charge becomes a question of fidelity to the Bible or lax moral standards.

Rapid growth to megachurch proportions does not necessarily mean, however, that the message conveyed in this modern format is any less theologically orthodox or potent. The orthodoxy of the expressed, preached, and practiced megachurch theology are discussed below. The ways people live out their theological convictions formed in these churches are the best tests of how theologically sound the megachurches are. Biblical orthodoxy can be based on diverse criteria, such as what messages are embodied in the religious artifacts around the church and those beliefs expressed in worship, what the clergy preach and teach, and what fundamental beliefs are subscribed to, but we contend that the best way to judge the theological potency of the megachurches' message is to examine how those attendees live it out.

Physical Appearance

Often worries about the religious orthodoxy of megachurches are based on the church's physical appearance. For some persons, the contemporary church architecture and décor are indications that the megachurches have erred. The charge is that the buildings themselves "don't look like a church." They lack crosses, stained glass windows, pews, and hymnals; therefore, these churches have sold out the true faith. The facilities, with their high-end graphics, glass entrances, multiple video screens, and even their high-tech spaces for the children lead critics to charge that they cannot be God's true church. The ambiance and feel of the physical and worship space is so unfamiliar that the megachurch form is rejected as illegitimate.

In fact, the architecture of megachurches is diverse, reflecting various regional, theological, and cultural influences. It is true that most of the newer megachurches don't look like the churches of the past. They use expensive sound systems and orchestras instead of pipe organs. Rather than a high wooden pulpit, they employ twenty-foot video screens so the congregation can see the pastor. These churches have massive walls of clear glass rather than stained-glass panels. They use individual chairs and padded theater seats rather than hard wooden pews. Many of the contemporary megachurches have building designs that are much simpler and more flexible than in the past. The same "sanctuary" in which worship takes place can the next day become a gym and a dining hall. This same multipurpose design theory has had an impact on smaller churches as well. For many megachurches, the buildings are rather ordinary looking, duplicating everyday structures such as office complexes, schools, and warehouses. For them, the architecture "communicates a message that religion is not a thing apart from daily life."[4]

The stream of Seeker megachurches significantly downplays much of the Christian symbolism found in traditional churches. But these churches have developed other symbols such as banners announcing their vision, art that communicates the church's purpose statements, baptismal spaces, and onscreen images that have a deep resonance for the Christian tradition, expressed as those congregations practice it. At the same time, some megachurches in the Old Line/Program-Based stream closely resemble smaller churches of their denominational traditions, but on a much larger scale. None of these architectural changes, however, diminish the message; they just reshape the sacred space to appeal to a new and different audience.

There is a growing wave of megachurch construction of children's buildings that have theater auditoriums, indoor playgrounds, aquariums, and other amenities heretofore not seen in church buildings. Such structures are decorated with vibrant cartoon characters straight from Disney and Nickelodeon. This trend is seen as the ultimate indicator of catering to parental consumerist desires for children's spaces. For the megachurch leader, however, this is a natural extension of church facilities of an earlier era (1960s to 1970s) that touted "modern facilities," which included sinks, arts and craft areas, and extensive nursery space. Church leaders understand that to attract and keep parents and children engaged, these spaces need to reflect the prevailing social norms.

Likewise, a megachurch's use of high-tech security systems, such as bar code scanners, parent call boards or beepers, and camera monitoring, used to check children in and out of nurseries, Sunday school rooms, and youth programs as well as observe the leaders of these programs are perceived as intrusive and secular. Megachurch leaders, however, see these amenities as necessary safety precautions to help guarantee and assure parents that children are cared for in appropriate and professional ways while at church. The sheer size of having four hundred or more children in these programs necessitates the use of these kinds of technologies.

Worship Services

Another frequent target of megachurch detractors is the form and content of worship services. For anyone who grew up in or familiar with a traditional worship style, megachurch worship with its exuberant singing, video projection, praise teams, and lack of creeds, hymnals, and responsive readings can be disorienting, especially with the intense energy level in some megachurches. For certain critics, "worship" means quietness, reflection, and solemn recitation of liturgies. It must be said that many of the megachurches have times of quietness and reflection in their worship services. The recitation, or singing, of a creed enjoys some resurgence, although it is not widespread.

There is indeed less reliance on choirs and less celebration of communion in the megachurch compared to smaller congregations. In addition, these large churches are less likely to describe their worship as creedal and formal than small churches, as Table 6.1 shows.

It is important to remember that the use of creeds and recited prayers (such as the Lord's Prayer) are as teaching and modeling tools to instruct congregants in the facts of the faith. Today's megachurches use other methods, such as video slides, the Apostles' Creed set to music and sung, and multiple displays of the church's vision and values expressed in contemporary slogans, to teach those principles in ways that connect better with today's attendees. Megachurches have recast worship forms

Table 6.1. Megachurch Worship Characteristics Compared with Churches of All Sizes.

"Always" or "Often" Responses to the Question "How Often Does the Worship at Your Church Have . . ."	2005 Megachurch Study (percentage)	2005 Faith Communities Today Study (percentage)
Choirs	53	56
Communion	40	62
Creeds	24*	31*
A formal liturgy or ritual	7	33

Data on the use of creeds is drawn from the Faith Communities Today 2000 and Megachurches Today 2000 surveys.

to appeal to a new generation for whom the traditional models no longer resonate.

Vision statements and slogans are meant to educate, inspire, and motivate members to act out their faith convictions in different but no less effective ways than the repetition of creeds and group recitation of prayers in a service.

Preaching Style

The preaching style and content of megachurch pastors also draws considerable attention from critics, particularly the practical nature of these sermons. For some, such preaching distorts the orthodox message of the Gospel; these preachers are perceived as watering down the true faith. We touched on this charge in Chapter Four and will address it further in Chapter Nine. The conversational style and high energy of these preachers is seen as inappropriate for the sermon, which ought to be delivered in a grave, reverent, and thoughtful manner. In most megachurch sermons, there is an element of humor with frequent laughter from the congregation. Occasionally, there are also visuals, such as bringing a motorcycle on stage, watching a video clip of a popular commercial, or even enacting a short drama in the midst of the service to spark the imagination of the cynical, information-saturated, high-tech, video-conditioned modern consumer sitting in the pew.

These criticisms reflect a difference of opinion about what "church worship" is or should be and what lengths one should go to reach a media-jaded congregation. For megachurch leaders, it is perfectly natural to have laughter; energetic, practical sermons; and exuberant singing that

Table 6.2. Megachurch Sermon Focus
Compared with Churches of All Sizes.

Does the Sermon in Your Worship *Always* Focus On:	2000 Megachurch Study (percentage)	2000 Faith Communities Today Study (percentage)
God's love and care	44	48
Practical advice for daily living	34	29
Personal spiritual growth	38	37
Does the Sermon *Always* or *Often* Include a Lot of:		
Personal stories or firsthand experiences	75	64
Literary or scholarly references	30	33
Illustrations from contemporary media (such as magazines, newspapers, television, and films)	76	48
Detailed explanations of Scripture or doctrine	57	73

engage the hearers' hearts and minds during a worship service. For others, church needs a traditional look and feel that is reverent in a quiet and thoughtful way, so that God can work in a person's heart. In an informal conversation, one smaller church pastor once reflected, "There may have been laughter once in one of my services, but if there was, it was a mistake . . . this is serious business." Truly, worship and the proclamation of the Gospel is serious business; however, the seriousness of the message is not dependent entirely on the forms by which it is presented. Our impression after attending hundreds of megachurch services around the country is that the pastors and attendees are doing serious business with God in worship regardless of what the critics say. This shows up in attendees actions and commitments to the faith, as we have discussed in earlier chapters and will explore further later in this chapter.

One of the significant troubling factors for some persons is the sheer size of the worship services and the countless ministries of the megachurch. The worship service, being the most visible expression of this, has been soundly criticized for being "anonymous" and "spectator" oriented. There is an element of truth to this charge in the largest, stadium-sized auditoriums of some megachurches, such as Lakewood Church in Houston, WorldChangers in Atlanta, and Faithful Central Church, in Los Angeles. Likewise, for the Seeker stream of megachurches, there is an intentional ministerial philosophy that argues that seekers desire anonymity and want to blend in with the crowd in order to check out the claims of Christianity with little fanfare. In this stream, it is preferable to have a large crowd in which people can attend and not be recognized as newcomers. As the Web site of the soon-to-be megachurch Quest Community Church states, "Quest is a safe place. You can be anonymous if you want to. You can be known if you want to. You'll find that people are friendly but not overbearing. We'll be so glad you stopped by, but we won't hound you. As far as we're concerned, you are a treasured guest!"[5] Even within this one stream of Seeker megachurches, in the last ten years, changes in this approach can be seen. Many of the newer waves of megachurches place a high value on congregational praise, participatory singing, and collective prayers. These churches have introduced or increased their congregational fellowship and greeting times within the worship service. Many megachurches have special rooms or locations for people to go and pray, to receive counseling, to share with a pastor, or to learn more about the faith. Additionally, there are kiosks of ministry opportunities for volunteers, cafeterias and coffee shops for informal conversation, bookstores and tape libraries to gather additional spiritual resources, and walls of literature about every activity of the church.

This intentional multiplicity of ways to respond to a worship service is a key difference between these churches and smaller churches. For many small churches, attendees file by the pastor and have an opportunity to speak if they desire. Occasionally, a few members in a smaller church can cluster around a coffee urn or in the nursery or parking lot for conversation. Megachurches strategically deploy many leaders, deacons, ushers, and counselors to encourage people to interact with each other and church personnel. In addition, response cards are often customized to the content of the message that week, where hearers can make immediate commitments as a result of that day's worship experience. We will address these issues in more detail in Chapter Nine.

A pastor at Seacoast Church, located in Mount Pleasant, South Carolina, explains the range of response options they offer worshippers: "As the music plays for the last ten minutes of a service, people can sit quietly in prayer. Or they can go to various stations. At one, get communion. At another, they can be prayed for. At another, confess sins. And at another, they can light a candle in prayer for others who need it." This church has intentionally designed a multitude of ways for worshippers to experience and respond to the presence of God within their worship service. None of this looks like a dumbing down of faith or commitment, but neither does it look like worship as traditional churches do it.

Focus on the Individual

This last example helps to drive home a key point about the worship approach of megachurches. Megachurches take the desires, wishes, and interests of the individual seriously as a valid starting point for the whole of their ministry. Megachurches believe that people make choices based on their experience in the church. How they respond to and are drawn into all areas of the church, its worship, its discipleship processes, and its other programs are key points in their planning. Critics would call this a "consumer mentality," meaning they begin with the individual and not with God and are thus are accused of inverting the faith. For the fans of megachurches, to begin with the hearer and understand how they will react to God's message is an enhancement of the Gospel rather than a detriment to it.

However, the effort to cater to the market interests of attendees can be seen in pastors of all sized churches. These clergy carefully consider their congregations' point of view and needs and work hard to craft interesting sermon titles and illustrations designed to pique a listener's interest. Likewise, leaders of churches of all sizes have always sought to make their programs for children and youth attractive, inviting, and interesting. Megachurches do the same for their entire ministry. It becomes a matter of degree more than anything else.

In the end, for most megachurch leaders, their ultimate goal is the same as their critics, to present the clear Gospel message, but the forms that this presentation takes are adapted to the needs of contemporary people. They desire to see human lives transformed as a result of involvement with Christ and the church. Most megachurch leaders begin with the person or family in need of transformation and design a ministry that helps make that happen.

Theology

Critics of megachurches often accuse the leadership of watering down their theology to appeal to a broad, low-commitment, casual attendee. Far from espousing a weak theological position, most megachurches present a serious, high-commitment Christian message. We don't mean this as a blanket statement that every megachurch pastor's theology is orthodox to all observers. It is abundantly clear that some churches preach a prosperity gospel or kingdom theology or the acceptance of lifestyles and political positions with which many critics from different theological positions would find fault. However, the vast majority of megachurches have belief statements on paper and in practice that are clearly in line with orthodox

Christian doctrines. Even more important, these churches' organized programs and the values instilled into committed attendees show that this theology is promoted and lived out.

○

Core Theological Beliefs

Almost all megachurches are very upfront about their basic beliefs and values. If the reader visits a Web site for a megachurch, there is usually a section that outlines the central beliefs of the church. The following are snippets of core theological statements of various megachurches around the country.

○ "We firmly believe the great doctrines of historic Christianity as they are revealed in the Bible." (Emmanuel Faith Church, Escondido California)

○ "We believe that God became man in the person of Jesus Christ and that Jesus Christ is both completely divine and completely human." (Grace Chapel, Lexington, Massachusetts)

○ "Man is made in the spiritual image of God, to be like Him in character. He is the supreme object of God's creation. Although man has tremendous potential for good, he is marred by an attitude of disobedience toward God called 'sin.' This attitude separates man from God." (New Spring Church, Anderson, South Carolina)

○ "We believe that the Lord Jesus Christ died for our sins according to the Scriptures, as a representative and substitutionary sacrifice. We believe that each person who by faith receives Him as personal Savior is justified on the basis of Jesus Christ's shed blood on Calvary. Each person who receives Christ as personal Savior is born again of the Holy Spirit and thereby becomes eternally secure as a child of God." (Harvest Bible Chapel, Rolling Meadows, Illinois)

Obviously, these statements illustrate core beliefs of megachurches that are in line with traditional Christian orthodoxy. In addition, many of these churches have annual vision weekends to remind and reinforce their core beliefs among the attendees. These churches place their annual vision statements on their Web sites in both recorded and text message form. Visit the site of New York City's Redeemer Church at www.redeemer2.com/about/values/index.cfm to see not only text and audio but also a video clip outlining the church's beliefs and vision.

○

The confusion around the preached theology often results from an assessment of the presentation of the message. As we said earlier, megachurches express the message in forms that use conversational language, images, and examples that resonate with contemporary culture. A pastor may quote from a historical figure or serious theological literature, but it is much more likely attendees will hear quotes from current news, movies, and television to appeal to a broad contemporary audience.

The strategy assumes that the congregation is not full of theological students, but rather people who want a word from God that is applicable to their everyday lives. The goal is to draw listeners toward a personal experience of God's love and salvation in order to motivate them to grow spiritually and live out their faith. While some criticize this approach as being consumer oriented, most megachurch pastors see this effort as nothing more than presenting the Gospel in a culturally sensitive and relevant way.

The Facts About Commitments, Practices, and Beliefs

The Megachurches Today 2005 survey asked about the practices and beliefs of the congregation. Over three-quarters of the megachurches (78 percent) strongly agreed that their church "holds strong beliefs and values." This figure is nearly identical to that of all the congregations in the 2005 Faith Communities Today study. A full 88 percent of these megachurches emphasized the practice of personal Scripture study "quite a bit" or "a lot," and 86 percent said the same thing about personal prayer, meditation, or devotions. Over three-quarters (78 percent) of the churches said they stress tithing and sacrificial giving. Fifty-three percent said they emphasize family devotions (usually described as a regular time when everyone in the household gathers to read Scripture and pray together), and 40 percent stress the command of "keeping the Sabbath or other worship day holy." When compared with congregations of all sizes in the 2005 Faith Communities Today study (FACT 2005), at the highest level of emphasis ("a lot") of these practices one can see an interesting pattern in Table 6.3.

At the least, this comparison in Table 6.3 shows that megachurches emphasize these practices as much, if not slightly more, than all other congregations. The only exception to this is that megachurches are half as likely to treat the Sabbath as unique. This may be due in part to having worship services on many days of the week, but it also could reflect the informal approach to worship as well as a Seeker mentality in certain streams of megachurches. When compared to a random sample of

Table 6.3. Megachurch Religious Practice Emphasis Compared with All Churches.

Congregations Emphasizing These Practices *a Lot* in Their Worship and Education	2005 Megachurch Study (percentage)	2005 Faith Communities Today Study (percentage)
Personal prayer, meditation, or devotions	51	42
Personal Scripture study	54	47
Tithing or sacrificial giving	47	39
Keeping the Sabbath or worship day holy	18	38

smaller Protestant churches, the 2000 megachurches study found that the larger churches were significantly more likely to hold strong beliefs, stress personal prayer and Scripture study, and promote family devotions.[6]

From our informal interviews with megachurch attendees, it is not uncommon to hear how the Bible is being made clear to them for the first time within this church. The attendees are drawn both to the clear presentation of the Gospel and to the instructions regarding its practical application to their everyday lives. They report being challenged in their faith in a deep and significant way. Many of these churches hold a series of worship services and campaigns intentionally designed to deepen the faith and the commitments of the members and attendees. These campaigns can take the form of meetings and services on consecutive nights, but are more likely to be series of consecutive weekends to improve the learning process and accommodate busy schedules. This flexibility is enhanced by their use of the extensive Web sites with both live streaming media presentations of the services and the archived collection of sermons. Some megachurches even create elaborate sections of their sites to extend the impact of the sermon series. One such example is LifeChurch.tv, which developed a site supporting its sermon series on confessing personal secrets that became such a popular destination that the *New York Times* featured it in a story.[7]

These campaigns often include both worship services and small group meetings where as many of the church attendees as possible are immersed in the same materials and interactions for a period of time. The most prominent in recent years is the "40 Days of Purpose" based on the book by Pastor Rick Warren, *The Purpose Driven Life*. This campaign method has been used successfully in a variety of topics and ways by megachurches to lead members to deepen their faith commitments.

The findings from attendees of the largest Protestant churches of the U.S. Congregational Life Study show these general perceptions about what participants get out of the megachurch services to be accurate. Over 80 percent engage in devotional acts at least weekly, with 55 percent saying they do this daily. Sixty percent of large church attendees said the worship service helped them to a great extent with everyday life, and an additional 33 percent said this was true to some extent. Thirty-four percent claimed they participated more since coming to their current church, while the majority participated at the same level, and only 13 percent were less engaged than before. Sixty percent of attendees reported their faith had grown much in the past year. An additional 37 percent said they experienced some growth in faith in the past year. Only four percent claimed their faith did not grow at all.

In addition to the teaching and preaching in worship services, these churches have a multifaceted program of communicating the Gospel. Large percentages of these churches have programs to encourage attendees to interact with each other and with the Gospel. Seventy-nine percent of the megachurches report that study and discussion groups are a key activity in their church. Two-thirds (66 percent) claim prayer and faith-sharing groups are key activities within their church. Religious education classes are described as a core activity in 71 percent of the churches, although this is considerably less than the churches in the Faith Communities Today 2005 survey. A comparison of the megachurches and this FACT 2005 group in Table 6.4 shows that the largest churches are at least as likely or, in many cases, more inclined to have these programs as key activities of their congregational life together.

Moving People from Crowd to Core

Most of the megachurch pastors have a mental model that classifies the attendees by commitment level. These pastors understand that some attendees are on the fringes. Rick Warren, the pastor of Saddleback Church, calls this "the crowd." The innermost grouping, labeled "the core" by Warren, contains leaders, volunteers and staff, and highly committed disciples. Each gradation has its own set of expectations toward which attendees are called and a corresponding level of commitment intensity by these members.

Based on our research experiences, interactions with, and survey data from megachurches, our congregational member divisions are slightly different from Warren's. We see five basic groupings of the total number of active participants within the life of a megachurch. Each member grouping has a different level of involvement and characteristics of

Table 6.4. Megachurch Key Activities
Compared with Churches of All Sizes.

Congregations Reporting that these Programs were *a Key Activity* of the Church	2005 Megachurch Study (percentage)	2005 Faith Communities Today Study (percentage)
Religious education classes	71	90
Prayer, meditation, or faith-sharing groups	66	59
Study or discussion groups	79	69
Fellowships, clubs, or other social activities	51	53
Support groups (twelve-step, wellness, parenting, and so on)	60	16
Evangelism or recruitment activities	58	39
Community/social service activities	40	35
Choirs or other music programs	54	52
Fundraising activities	39	22

commitment. These groupings are as follows, with the approximate percentage of them within the weekly attendance: the core (5 percent), the committed (15 percent), moderate members (40 percent), marginal persons (30 percent), and infrequent attendees, visitors, and spectators (10 percent). It is important to note, however, that while roughly 40 percent of attendees on any given week may well be marginally committed to the church in terms of serious giving, attendance, and participation in groups outside of worship, these more marginal members still probably consider this congregation "their church home." It is equally important to realize that those participants evident in services on any given week are roughly half of the total number of regular attendees at that church. We estimate that in an average megachurch, there are 80 to 100 percent more persons in the marginal and infrequent attendee categories who do participate with some regularity and see the church as their spiritual home. It is likely that these less than ideal participants even attend other churches throughout the month. They can in many ways be seen as free riders, those who are gaining considerable benefit from the church without offering much in return in terms of volunteer time or monetary resources. However, as seen later, these persons do play a vital role in the church, just not in the typical model of a "good member."

To exemplify the commitment levels and practices of each adherence group, imagine a typical megachurch with an average weekly worship attendance of twenty-two hundred adults (the median adult attendance of megachurches in the 2005 study; the child and youth figures are also median figures from the study). This congregation would also have roughly five hundred fifty children from birth to eleven years old and around three hundred youth in the twelve-to-seventeen age range, but for this exercise we will not consider their participation levels because they are often based on those of their parents. Let's assume that this megachurch just completed the construction of a new sanctuary and has seating for twenty-five hundred and offers only one service.

A visitor to a Sunday service would observe nineteen hundred to two thousand people in the congregation, with the remaining 10 percent or so in the choirs, bands, leadership teams, television ministry, nurseries, and youth and teen ministries or serving as ushers, parking lot attendants, and bookstore and cafeteria workers. The majority of these persons are trained volunteers and often rotate from week to week in these responsibilities in order to be a part of the worship service at least a few times each month. Many of these people are core and committed members, but such volunteers are also drawn from the ranks of the moderate members as well.

Within this observable congregation of twenty-two hundred, one would find that roughly one hundred ten persons, or 5 percent of the attendees, who are core members. These people are in the leadership elite of the church. They are often the founding families, occasionally members of the clergy's extended family, and ministry leaders. Many within this group are also full-time staff at the church. They have the greatest level of involvement and sense of loyalty to the church, as well as an intense commitment to Christian life. Many of these people are at church or in ministry forty to sixty hours a week, contribute well over 10 percent of their income to the church or other charities, and are church leaders or staff or related to these leaders. For many of these people, their entire lives are intertwined with the daily life of the church.

Another 15 percent of this congregation, or roughly three hundred thirty people in this example, can be identified as committed members. These persons, too, are highly involved in the church and are sincere in their devotion to a Christian life. They tithe 10 percent or more, attend worship events several times a week, volunteer in the church's ministries, participate in small groups, and have most or all of their close friends from the church.

This is roughly the same pattern one would expect in many smaller congregations. It is a common observation by clergy and consultants alike that 20 percent of the church does 80 percent of the work of keeping the building and worship services functioning. This guideline appears true of the megachurches except for one important difference. This group is not responsible for the bulk of the work. The burden and responsibility of the church's countless ministries and activities by necessity demand that a larger proportion of the congregation be involved. Few megachurches would survive, although there are some that try, with just 20 percent of participants involved.

The vibrant success of megachurches also demands another larger group of attendees, here labeled the moderate members, who account for approximately 40 percent of the weekly worshippers. This group of solid participants is active and involved in the life of the church and their faith journey. They usually attend services every week; volunteer their time on occasion; participate in fellowships, clubs, and educational groups; contribute 5 to 10 percent of their income; and have at least some of their best friends and relatives at the church. These people would be viewed by any church leadership as strong members, if slightly less involved than they could be.

Within this imagined megachurch, the group identified as marginal members is perhaps the most intriguing segment. Marginal members make up roughly 30 percent of the weekly attending congregation but constitute a much larger pool of the regular participant members. Based on their level of attendance, participation, giving, and ties with others in the church, this group may account for twice as many people as the average weekly adult attendance. Given that a characteristic of marginal participant members is attendance once or twice a month, the number of such persons is easily two or four times the amount evident in church on any given week. These people enjoy attending the church and often think of it as "their church." They attend when they can and give a few dollars (almost always cash rather than by check) when the offering is taken. These persons are seldom involved in church ministries and may know a number of folks in the church but have few good friends there.

By most accounts, these people are truly marginal, and few churches would appreciate their continued involvement in the congregation. They receive sustenance from the service and the church, but give back little in return; they are classic freeloaders, the quintessential free riders. These attendees participate in the excellent worship services and the distinction of the church while doing little to support its ministry. Yet these marginal members as a group—often larger than any single worship attendance figure—contribute several critical characteristics of the megachurch on which its success is based. These marginal participants are the "crowd" in Warren's terminology. They fill the pews; they create the impression of a "packed house." Without them, a megachurch would be significantly smaller and less dynamic. These participants balance the intense commitment of the core and committed members, as well as playing another necessary role in the megachurch.

These marginal participants are the church's internal mission field. The megachurch opens its doors to all marginal, anonymous participants, both seekers and spectators, in order to bring the mission field inside the walls of the church. The inspirational sermons, ministries, and fellowship groups to create and solidify interpersonal relationships are aimed directly at this audience. They are tolerated within the congregation of moderate and committed members precisely because they represent those in need of spiritual maturity. This crowd of marginal participants, even if only occasionally present, is critical to the success of megachurches and a key component of the congregation, as unorthodox as that may sound.

The final grouping of persons within our typical megachurch are the approximately 10 percent who are infrequent attendees. This group consists of a large number of people who "drop in" a few times a year to check on how the church is doing or what it is "up to" now. It also is comprised of visitors from other churches, tourists on vacation, first-time participants, those just beginning a relationship with the church, or those at the end of a more committed stance within the church and on their way out. This very fluid group, numbering several hundred people, is almost never the same from week to week, and represents both the fringe of the marginal attendees and the entry point for future solid participants. As such, many megachurches focus their programming intently on these people in terms of choice parking spaces, greeters, welcome receptions, and first-timer gifts.

Our example has generalized the complexity and diversity found among the weekly worshippers and the larger group of regular participants at most megachurches. Yet we feel this description parallels the divisions and member dynamics in most of these churches, with the realization that no one megachurch may fit this illustration exactly.

○

Breakdown of Megachurch Participants (Percentages are based on 100 percent of participants.)

CORE AND COMMITTED: 20 PERCENT OF WEEKLY
ATTENDEES

8 percent assist in or lead worship

10 percent are leaders of a group

16 percent hold other positions in the church

20 percent engage in community/evangelism congregational acts

MODERATE: 40 PERCENT OF WEEKLY ATTENDEES

23 percent said "All my close friends are at the church"

24 percent are involved in a social service group

26 percent attend more than once a week

30 percent participate in fellowships or clubs

37 percent participate in prayer or Bible study groups

47 percent give 10 percent or more of their income to the church

48 percent feel their personal gifts are being developed to a great extent

52 percent have some close friends at the church

55 percent participate in Sunday school or educational groups

60 percent attend usually every week

MARGINAL: 30 PERCENT OF WEEKLY ATTENDEES

77 percent say they are a "member"

47 percent hold no position in church

37 percent say they give more than a small amount of money, up to 9 percent of their income

23 percent are not regularly involved in groups

17 percent give small amounts when at church or don't give any money

13 percent are not members, but participate regularly

11 percent have little contact with others from congregation

INFREQUENT ATTENDEES: (NEW PEOPLE, FIRST-TIMERS, AND SPECTATORS): 10 PERCENT OF WEEKLY ATTENDEES

7 percent say they participate in no group activity

7 percent say they have no sense of belonging to the church and are OK with that

6 percent are new to the church

3 percent say they attend once a month or less

2.4 percent claim to be first-time attendees

Source: Percentages come from the U.S. Congregational Life Survey and are a subset of 6,349 attendees of the ten largest Protestant churches (1,000 attendees or more) in that survey. These figures may have a slight bias toward the most active and committed of the weekly attendees, but they approximate the commitment dynamics at each level of attendee involvement.

○

We believe the conscious segmentation and diversity of attendees sketched earlier actually work to strengthen megachurches when compared with churches of other sizes. While pastors of other churches know implicitly that they have different levels of commitment in their congregation, they tend to speak primarily to the experiences of either the core group or the unbelievers they hope and pray are attending. They treat the worship participants as a club of the saved, holding up expectations and challenges to help them mature further in their commitments, using language best suited for longtime Christians. Seldom are services or sermons intended to convince or inspire those with the potential to grow in the faith beyond just worship attendance. Many megachurch pastors, however, are well aware of this group in their midst and target the service, the sermon, and the ministries to *all* those present in the congregation, whether core and highly committed members or marginal members, occasional seekers, and first-time inquirers.

Commitment expectations for long-time attendees and participating members are higher than for newcomers. Most megachurch pastors understand that people may increase their commitments over time as they grow in their understanding and involvements, but only with intentional encouragement and inspiration from the church and the Holy Spirit. Even after an attendee has made a conscious decision to become a follower of Christ, the church works hard to create deliberate paths that lead these people into deeper commitments and move them from being worship spectators to being full congregational and ministry participants.

As such, megachurches can be seen as very strict and at the same time not strict at all, depending on the level of interest and commitment of the attendee. The church's demand for maturity in one's Christian walk increases as a person's level of commitment increases. The organization encourages, but does not demand, tempts but does not require, the adherence of the masses. The individual is the consumer. The motto is, "Preach the ideal, accept the minimum."

Everyone who attends is allowed and encouraged to participate in megachurches as they are. The benefit of the openness to all marginal participants is considerable, They contribute to the overall worship experience, making it a mass gathering. Their voices add to the "heavenly host." They create a pool of potential "active participants" and are the targets for evangelism by more committed members. These less involved members also contribute in terms of the successful reputation of the church in the community. They are the most numerous group in the public arena and in some ways the best evangelists for the church in that they are more "in the world" than core church members.

As one becomes more involved, spending more time at church, demands become all-consuming, so the interaction with people outside the church decreases. The most committed congregants might have a greater interest in evangelism, for example, but their efforts are hampered because they have few good relationships outside the church. On the other hand, marginal attendees love the church or they wouldn't keep coming; they get a lot of great worship for very little cost. They consider "their church" a great spiritual deal, and they want others to know it. And they are happy to tell others they are a part of such a successful, well-known congregation.

Strict and significant demands on the individual drastically increase as commitment does—as one desires to rise in leadership, in involvement, in Christian maturity by following the intentionally prescribed steps toward being a "good" Christian. But if these levels of strictness, these demands, were required initially of all participants, megachurches would not exist. In some ways, the individual is in control of the commitments he or she wants to shoulder in a megachurch. The level and type of responsibility one accepts is of one's own choosing. It is an individualized, customizable experience, but it isn't a choice that is made without significant intentional programmatic support and the verbal encouragement of the church leadership.

These organizational and educational processes for moving people from having no commitment to becoming high-commitment leaders are distinguishing features of many megachurches. While these processes are not universal, they are widespread. Sometimes these paths are a series of formal classes or groups that help people grow in their faith. On some occasions, interviews with pastors or coaches or other mentors help guide an individual into the most appropriate small group or class. North Ridge Church in Troy, Michigan, describes its introductory discipleship ministry on its Web site in this way: "A guide who is an established Christian here at church that will meet with you, answer your questions, and help you put the pieces together. They will share with you the foundations of our faith and how to get connected here at the Ridge." The mentor process can be individual-to-individual or couple-to-couple according to the attendee's preference.

Many of the megachurch pastors proclaim a few simple expectations of "good participants." For leaders, these expectations become requirements and contain at least three elements: regular participation in worship services, accountability through a small group of believers of some type, and service in a ministry to help others. To this core of three, some churches will add a variety of other elements, such as giving, prayer, or the explicit sharing of faith with friends and neighbors, although there are rarely over four or five targeted requirements.

Admittedly, being a part of the small group may require additional commitments from participants. Some groups have membership covenants as a measure of accountability, renewed regularly, that ask members to live their lives according to the church's beliefs. Even in churches that do not have a formal covenant or membership, more committed participants and all leaders are usually expected to live up to high standards of behavior and belief.

○

The Second-Chance Church

After all of our writing about high commitments in this chapter, we wanted to balance that with an observation about the majority of these churches. Most of these churches, while holding fast to their articulation of high moral standards of behavior and of orthodox belief, will also clearly articulate the vision of "a place of redemption" or "a church of the second chance."

The majority of megachurches are clear in articulating both very conservative religious beliefs and very liberal messages of God's love and grace that triumph over one's past. For this reason, many first time observers are surprised to find a large number of persons who have struggled with the pain of addiction, broken family situations, and other difficult life experiences. While the image portrayed by many commentators is that these churches are islands of clean-living, well-scrubbed, family-values suburbanites, the reality is much more complex. A certain proportion of attendees do fit that profile, but there are just as many cases of people with a broken past who have now found God's love and direction through this church.

These churches focus not only on brokenness and repentance, but also on hope and healing. These churches are strong on second, third, and fourth chances to set life right for their participants. As an example, significantly more megachurches claimed recovery and support were key activities than smaller churches in our surveys did.

In a tour of an Old Line/Program-Based Southern Baptist megachurch, I met one of the key leaders and asked for his story. Here's what he said:

> I came to this church as a homeless alcoholic. I stayed in the Rescue
> Mission of the church and found Jesus there. I had lost my marriage, my
> family, my job, really my whole life. But this church had an intensive
> six-month program for men with addictions that allowed me to get
> cleaned up. They helped me find a job and a place to stay after I

graduated from the program. I came back several nights a week to help other men like me. They let me be a Bible study leader in the program. Although the majority of persons in this church are white and I am black, they elected me a deacon a few years ago. I never got my wife or family back. They moved on, and I can't say that I blame them. But I have been redeemed by God through the ministry of this church. I owe them my life.

This reality is one of the key reasons for the growth of the Megachurch movement. These churches meet "seekers," "the unchurched," and even churched folks that have hard pasts where they are and help connect them to God.

For some critics, this is a sure sign of watering down the clear commands of Scripture for how one should live one's life. For some megachurches in more conservative denominations and traditions, life begins at conversion and the sinful behaviors and lifestyles of the past are left behind. For some others, even past failures in their lives as believers are dealt with by the church leadership, and these people can go on to become significant leaders in the church.

Our observation is that these churches do an excellent job of communicating "the gospel of the second chance" when compared with other churches and acting on it to provide ministry, hope, and healing. While many other church pastors in smaller churches proclaim the gospel of the second chance, they provide little leadership in expressing it in practical ways and seem less willing to provide ministries to meet those needs.

O

Helping Attendees Make Deeper Commitments

As already discussed, many megachurches put great emphasis not only on worship, but also on the power of supportive small groups. For some churches, this translates into adult Christian education classes such as Sunday school where the Bible is taught in a deeper way. Such groups may also offer a place for sharing prayer needs and concerns, fellowship, and care of one another. Other churches use small groups that meet in homes or external locations for similar purposes. Some churches use small groups for care giving, but have less formal Bible teaching within those groups. Certain congregations even use their small groups as evangelistic tools, and intentionally allow them to be open to nonmembers.

Our 2000 megachurch survey focused on these ways of integrating persons into the life of the church. Eighty-one percent of churches said they had an organized program for keeping up with members' needs and providing ministry such as assigning a shepherding deacon/elder, care group, or area pastor to members. Half the churches said small groups were central to their strategy for Christian nurture and spiritual formation, while another 44 percent claimed to have these, but they were not central to the church's program. Only 7 percent said they did not use small groups at all. Three quarters of the megachurches required new members to take an informational class prior to or after becoming a member. Nearly all the churches (96 percent) strongly encouraged new people to volunteer in the church's ministries as a way of becoming more deeply involved. Over half made special efforts such as providing special parking or seating to welcome visitors to the church. Just over a third (38 percent) acknowledged new persons in a demonstrative way such as asking them to stand, raise their hand, or wear a visitor's name tag.

Many of the megachurches offer special classes, groups, and gatherings for those who are simply inquiring about faith in Christ. These targeted classes are places to ask the hard questions and receive non-judgmental answers. Additionally, many churches offer a series of classes dealing with topics relating to Scripture or theology that would be taught at a college level. A few offer graduate-level courses complete with required textbooks, and some have partnerships with seminaries for lay students. An even smaller segment of megachurches have started formal educational training paths for those interested in entering ministry roles.

In addition, there are often special classes on relationships, recovery, grief and divorce support, child rearing, caring for older parents and adults—the list continues as far as the imagination can run. In promoting these courses, churches tend to mix practical living with biblical teaching on the subjects. The church's size makes it possible to offer these courses multiple times a year. We have seen a few churches implement "personal life development plans" that help members and attendees grow in their faith. These systems use paper-and-pencil or computer-based assessments to help attendees determine their point in their spiritual journey and then use that information to help design a plan to help them grow in their faith. Additionally, according to our 2000 survey, a third of the churches pair a mentor with the attendee to help coach them to a deeper level of faith. Some of the churches using personal life plans are now experimenting with Web-based, online systems that offer basic instruction with audio, video, and text-based classes to help believers grow based on the individual's needs. An example of this is the online spiritual health assessment of Seacoast Church in South Carolina at www.learning.seacoast.org/personalgrowth/assessment. We will confess that participation in such programs does not necessarily mean that attendees have deeper commitments to the faith. However, the availability and breadth of such classes allows believers to nurture and deepen their faith in a multiplicity of ways, allowing a choice of forms that fit them best.

Some churches use a more intentional and structured discipleship system composed of several people who work together during a year to mature their faith. While this system has a set curriculum, the essence of the process is based on informal prayer for mutual concerns, confession of sin, and the reading of Scripture. These "life on life" systems are covenant groups designed to connect believers to each other and to the Scriptures during a specified period. Such methods have proven very powerful.

Finally, some megachurches use weekend retreat settings to help their adult members mature in the faith. These churches function on the premise that life has become so hectic for most adults that one must withdraw for a time of intense reflection and teaching periodically to develop ones faith. While only a minority of church participants (often only the most committed) will be a part of any given weekend session, these retreats are scheduled regularly for different age groups as another avenue for attendees to nurture their faith.

Pastoral Care

A common observation from those who have never attended a megachurch is that if they attended a large church, they would never get to know the pastor. At times, critics of megachurches note that the senior pastor rarely visits a hospital room or members' homes. Indeed, certain megachurch pastors themselves encourage this impression with their public statements to that effect. Whether there is truth to these observations or not, it is important to see that the pastoral care of congregational members is done differently in a megachurch.

Megachurches have multiple associate pastors whose job it is to provide care for congregational attendees. Often church staffs also include well-trained specialized pastors or certified laypersons who focus on care and crisis situations. Additionally, congregational members are often identified, encouraged, and trained to provide care and ministry to one another both formally and informally. In a smaller church, these duties would fall to a pastoral staff member or most likely to the solitary pastor. Finally, many megachurches handle member care and personal issues through their small group systems, with group leaders reporting issues to their oversight pastors.

For those few megachurch pastors who claim to never visit a sick member, when pressed in personal interviews they readily admit to providing personal ministry on many occasions. Additionally, it is worth remembering that the day of the clergy coming into a home for a pastoral visit is almost gone even among smaller churches. Indeed, there may be some communities in our nation where it still happens, but the expectations of younger families and of pastors have changed considerably in this regard. These private and intimate home visits are being replaced by more public pastoral visits that take place in coffee shops, restaurants, golf courses, and other locations, which allow pastors to get up close and personal in informal ways.

Pastoral care in a large church necessitates a change in expectation by attendees compared to persons within smaller churches. Those in smaller churches still expect the senior pastor to be available at all times for any need they have. Large church attendees realize they have to look to the whole church and often trained staff—not just the senior pastor—to address their needs in a multitude of ways.

Money and Wealth

In American culture, wealth can be a prickly topic for any setting, including churches. Megachurches are no exception here. Some churches are known for their focus on a "prosperity gospel." This theology teaches that God wants his followers to be prosperous and healthy. While a relatively small segment of megachurches hold this position, many of these have extensive media programs, which lead one to assume that most megachurches embrace this theology. At the opposite end of the spectrum, many Seeker-oriented megachurches previously refrained from talking about money at all. This reticence was driven by their response to Seekers' perceptions that churches spoke too much about money. If financial stewardship was addressed in these Seeker congregations, it was usually through small groups and gatherings outside of weekend services. However, this is changing as Seeker church pastors and other clergy realize that people desire to hear a godly perspective on money, finances, and stewardship of time, talent, and treasure. These pastors have become much bolder in addressing financial issues.

Our experience with megachurches shows that they actually address money in diverse and mostly constructive ways. There is no doubt that megachurch pastors preach on these topics more often than do smaller churches. Additionally, these churches have regular classes and counseling groups for members who struggle with debt and family budgeting or for those who want to develop a greater level of generosity in their giving. Because of their rapid growth, many megachurches use capital campaigns to support the church's ministry and encourage attendees to make sacrificial financial commitments. Megachurches make Jesus' statement about one's heart and wallet being intertwined explicit in their insistence that members increase their spiritual commitment to being generous. Megachurches always seem to have "the next hill to climb" in their ministries that require additional financial and personnel resources, and as such strongly encourage attendees to make commitments to help the churches reach these goals.

In our conversations with megachurch attendees, one finds many people who can recall deeply spiritual experiences in making a financial commitment to a church. At the same time, few people we have talked to complained that they left because the senior minister talked too much about money. This shows both in the resources available to the church and in the ministries they are able to fund. It is also demonstrated in the cheerfulness of those giving to the church.

Whether it is their principles regarding money, participation, or the practices of an authentic Christian life, megachurches do not appear to water down the Gospel message or requirements necessary to be a "good and faithful" believer. These churches have altered the mode of presentation and the forms in which such values are presented, but little of the substance has changed. For the vast majority of moderate, committed, and core participants, their levels of involvement in the church and dedication to the Christian lifestyle are at least the same as those of believers in smaller churches, if not greater. Much of the misconception about the message that megachurches teach comes from judging the depth of the Christian ideal based on a few visits to the Sunday worship service. No matter what type of megachurch (Seeker or otherwise), the worship service is often intentionally pitched to a broader, nominally Christian audience than to the devoted saints. The experience is more like wading into the shallow end of a pool and gradually getting into deeper water than it is always demanding that people jump into the deep end in order to learn how to swim. The weekend service is understood as an initial entrance into the Christian life, with small groups, ministries, educational activities, and other weekly encounters with the church as the place where discipleship, sanctification, and a maturation of the Christian life take place. This gradual and continual encounter with the faith seems ideally suited for a culture less grounded in a Christian worldview and with many competing interests and perspectives. At times, dumbing down a message initially means the person being instructed can receive the knowledge faster and be more likely to build on that foundation with more complex lessons over time.

○

Applying What You Have Read

This chapter has focused on how megachurches reinforce basic faith commitments and beliefs at multiple levels from the preaching, to small groups, to special classes. We have shown how megachurches are intentional about finding ways to help attendees gradually make deeper commitments and gain a better understanding of faith over time. Our experience is that smaller churches expect too many attendees to do this on their own without giving them an intentional process or path to follow.

We recommend that all church leaders start with the perspective and mindset of a new participant or outsider to the faith. For most leaders, this is a difficult thing to do. Putting the concepts of faith in everyday language and offering clear steps about how to follow Christ make it easier for those seeking to do so. While we would agree that developing our Christian commitments is not necessarily a linear, step-by-step process, we would say that a regular, systematic explanation of aspects of Christianity provides an opportunity for all members to develop their faith.

The first area for reflection is how challenging the preaching and teaching is for the entire congregation. Megachurches are not shy about calling individuals to make significant spiritual commitments on a regular basis in the preaching and teaching message. We know that many smaller churches do the same. Megachurches have ways for individuals to respond immediately to the commitment, either publicly or through a response card. Then they offer tools, literature, activities, and classes to help that individual in keeping those commitments. Megachurches emphasize basic faith understandings on a regular basis, often in small groups. These are taught regularly in order for new attendees to grasp the faith basics and reinforce to longer-term attendees the importance of these basics.

A second area for reflection is the selection or development of tools, materials, and small group experiences to help attendees develop those commitments as heart habits to grow deeper in the Christian faith. Luckily for most pastors, these tools, courses, and materials have been developed by others and can be purchased for use by congregations of all sizes. We would encourage church leaders to think through a two- or three-year cycle of preaching/teaching combined with a complimentary emphasis on the tools and materials and small group experiences that can help reinforce this teaching. This can also be combined with the community service experiences we mentioned in the last chapter to help individuals grow through service and not just intellectual knowledge.

We would encourage pastors to specifically address issues related to money, wealth, and stewardship from a biblical perspective on a regular basis. We believe that the grip of materialism is one of the biggest hurdles to spiritual life in this country, and many pastors rarely address it directly. Megachurches clearly preach more about money than do smaller churches. In part, this is because of frequent capital campaigns for new buildings and ministries. But we have found in our conversations with both pastors and attendees of these churches that significant spiritual breakthroughs occurred during the times of these campaigns. Many megachurches also have regular classes relating to practical matters of investment, debt, retirement, savings and stewardship of money and wealth, time and talents. In our society these need to be taught on a regular basis.

- List the sermon topics and themes from the past several months. What commitments have these messages called for? How has the congregation responded?
- Would a new attendee, a new Christian, understand the basic message of these sermons?
- What types of commitments are asked of all members of the church?
- What is the overall level of commitment required, based on giving, volunteering, attendance, and the personal actions of attendees at the church?
- What tools, materials, or classes are offered, or could be offered, to help deepen attendees' commitments?
- How many times were the issues of money, wealth, and stewardship addressed?
- Now answer the same questions as if you were planning a preaching and teaching series over the next three years. How do these lists compare?

7

"THESE CHURCHES ARE BAD FOR OTHER CHURCHES"

You can't avoid at times thinking, "What's wrong with me?" admits Dave Huff, who pastors a small Baptist congregation in Naperville. Though you look back to your call to ministry with varying degrees of confidence, the sense of inadequacy is overwhelming at times. Your significance is reduced in your own eyes by the mass migration of believers flocking to what is, in their minds, a more fulfilling ministry.

I found myself dealing with the same inner doubts. I knew I wasn't as gifted as Bob Schmidgall. He was an All-American quarterback. I wasn't even third string, let alone on the varsity squad. What I felt was akin to those days in grade school when we had to do the 600-yard run or walk. While my classmates, more athletically inclined, sprinted the whole way, I was winded after 200 yards. My face was red as much from embarrassment as it was from being chubby and slow. As I struggled to catch my breath, I gave in to feelings of inadequacy and failure.

In addition to an inferiority complex, I dealt with covetous feelings. I wasn't focusing on the Lord and His sufficiency to accomplish a fruitful ministry through me in a church where the pews were few. Instead, my eyes looked longingly at Calvary Church and their multimillion-dollar budget. The weeds of envy flourish in the shade of dissatisfaction (especially if you water them with drools of desire). I had read articles that Bob Schmidgall had written for Christian magazines. To say I was impressed would be an

understatement. What he had already experienced was the
very thing I'd dreamed of doing.[1]

WHY DOES IT SO OFTEN SEEM that the discontent over megachurches comes from other pastors, denominational leaders, and seminary professors? Partially, it might be because these people care most about the state of religious life in the United States and have the biggest stake in protecting the health of American Christianity. But perhaps it is also because the rise in the number of megachurches has resulted in the loss of power and influence of these groups in particular. Individuals will always have disagreements with the actions and theology of certain megachurches and their pastors, but do smaller churches have reason to fear a megachurch the way a mom-and-pop general store might when rumors of Wal-Mart arise? Some of their concern might be justified, but we suggest that the benefits these congregations bring to other churches can outweigh the challenging situations they create.

The Challenge of Comparisons

Some pastors might feel like David Huff in the quote earlier. Who ever liked being compared to a big brother or older sister? In a nation that measures success by size, it is difficult not to feel inferior when compared to more prosperous neighbors, businesses, or even churches. Many pastors we have talked to feel their churches have lost members and opportunities because of the rise of a megachurch in their area. "Sheep stealing" is a well-known phrase to describe this wooing of members from one church to another. When active members leave a church for any reason, it is disconcerting for clergy who care about their congregation, but it must be worse when they leave for another, seemingly more successful, church.

For denominational leaders, the megachurches in their fold present the challenge of an adolescent who has outgrown his parents' discipline. These leaders are well aware that megachurch pastors don't really need the denomination to play the same role that it does for smaller churches. National leaders are faced with the task of trying to convince large churches to participate with little compensation for involvement. At the same time, seminaries watch hoards of people flock to conferences and network associational gatherings rather than their events. They see individual megachurches ordain pastors from within their ranks, only to watch these young leaders plant new churches and in five years' time become megachurches in their own right. Megachurch pastors write books that are significantly more successful and influential than any seminary professor. Additionally, these clergy are sought out for their opinions and consulted more than seminary or denominational leaders. Perhaps at the core of much of this criticism is a nostalgic desire on the part of these leaders to set the clock back to a day when they played a more prominent role in American religious life.

Without going into a long debate about the change in the American religious landscape, let us state that we believe this landscape has always been very flexible and adaptable. New churches, methodologies, denominations, and resource providers are constantly being born to serve the needs of believers. The American religious context has been described by many as a competitive, consumer-driven free-market reality. Many would claim that accepting this reality and participating in it runs counter to the Gospel. We see their point, but this situation is unavoidable; there has never been a time when new movements were not being born to serve the religious needs of people, and older faiths that no longer had a "market" were in decline or dying. We believe that these cycles of birth, growth, maturity, and decline help keep churches and religion in America strong and vital, connected to the real needs of those that seek to be connected to God.[2]

A few years ago, we spoke with a denominational leader in a regional area just on the cusp of moving from rural to suburban. He related a story about a young man, raised in the area, who had returned from his education with the desire to plant a church that reached his generation. This church planter felt that many of his high school friends and other young people were not attending any church, and he wanted to start one for them. The denominational leader encouraged him and went to several other pastors in his tradition asking for support. Their response was near unanimous, saying, in effect, "Everyone who wants to go to church is already going; this area cannot support a new church."

At that time the denominational leader knew that at least 60 percent of the population had some connection to a church of any denomination, but only about 30 percent regularly attended any church. Indeed, the denominational leader also saw a dearth of young people attending the existing churches. The two largest churches in the area of his tradition had just over five hundred in attendance, and the county seat mainline church drew three hundred people weekly.

Unfazed, the young church planter began the process of starting a new church. He had one young couple move with him from the city and quickly connected to several other young families who had grown up in church, but drifted away after high school. After a few months of meeting with this core group, they held their first public worship service with over two hundred in attendance. After the first year, they were well above three hundred, and by the third year they were above six hundred. Today, that church has well over three thousand people. The attendance at the other churches is up slightly but not appreciably since the new church began.

As one could guess, the other churches did not see this young pastor of the new church as a hero, but as an anomaly and perhaps worse. The big rub was the fact that many of the younger people who were officially connected, but not regular attendees, at the other churches, began to participate in the contemporary worship service of the new church. Their parents, who were comfortable in their existing churches, were torn. On the one hand, they knew that their children infrequently worshipped at the churches of their birth, but they expected them to return someday. On the other hand, they were happy that their children and grandchildren had found a place of vital Christian sustenance and nurture.

The overwhelming majority of the attendees at the new church were people who had not been regular churchgoers in some years, but had some prior church experience. The second largest group of attendees could be labeled as "nevers." This group had never been a regular part of any church. Living in the Bible Belt, they had a passing understanding of what a church was, but no real involvement. The third largest group was the most controversial. About forty people had left another evangelical church because of a long-running controversy within the church over the role of a few key lay leaders. A pastor had been terminated during that controversy, and this group of forty appeared to leave en masse and move to the new church. The reality was a little different in that at first two families came, and then over a year the total reached forty. When the new pastor came to the troubled church, the story she heard was that "those traitors had left for the new church." This same feeling, not always articulated as harshly by other religious leaders in the community, was widely shared. On the one hand, the new church was admired for its growth, but on the other hand, most church leaders saw this new church as competition and not helping their cause. While the young pastor of the new church felt like an outcast in his relations with other pastors, he did not let that resistance hinder his leadership of the new church. The church continues to grow and is now running over four thousand; it has helped plant nine churches in the past year.

Senior pastors of large churches across the country have shared similar stories with us many times.[3] This dynamic can be observed in any area where a megachurch comes into existence. The church-planting pastor in the above example saw an underserved market, whereas the other pastors saw an overserved market. The established church pastors figured that all those folks not coming to their church did not want to come; the new church planter saw that the style of church could be changed in the hope of reaching new people. The established church pastors felt there were too many churches already; the new church planter realized that a new approach was needed. The denominational leader realized that the addition of a new church might mean more total people worshipping each week.

Dominant Churches

Join with us for a moment in thinking of a regional area with numerous overlapping institutions. A diverse education system of public and private schools, colleges and universities, technical schools, and training schools intends to meet a variety of educational needs in specific ways. So too, there are private and public healthcare and hospital systems, walk-in clinics, and general practitioners. There are business systems with manufacturing plants, office complexes, corporate headquarters, and the numerous other companies that interact and compete within this economic system. All of these institutional spheres can be seen as interdependent "ecological systems." Each interaction and initiative by one organization can have an effect on the others within that system and across other ecological spheres. The same can be said of religious and church entities within a region; together the religious players in a community can be described as a complex religious ecology.[4]

Within a well-defined suburban area or exurban town, the presence of a megachurch is like the proverbial eight-hundred-pound gorilla—it has to be reckoned with because it is not going away. A megachurch in the religious ecological context of a community has to be both acknowledged and responded to if the other churches are to survive. The response doesn't need to be competitive efforts to match the megachurch's programs and offerings, but to do nothing, to pretend the megachurch doesn't exist and function as if everything is as it always was, will end in disaster. What megachurches can offer is different from other size churches, but it does not have to be seen as better. What is helpful about an ecological perspective of an area's religious community is that each player has a role in the matrix and a reason for existing if the environment is to be healthy and well balanced in meeting the full set of community needs. It is important to remember that these large churches represent less than half of one percent of all churches, and most surveys indicate that in any community between 20 and 50 percent of the population are unaffiliated with a religious community. There are more than enough churches and potential members to go around. Both religiously observant and unchurched people require all types of churches, not just those within the megachurch model.

The megachurch in a religious environment becomes the dominant player, the big kid on the block, a measure against which other religious activities are judged, and other churches in that context well know it. Of the twenty-one churches in the small area Nancy Eiesland studied, sixteen pastors named the megachurch in their community as most influential.[5] There is no escaping it. What matters is how individual local congregations respond to the megachurch in their midst.

Unfortunately, many respond with disdain, animosity, or even hostility. We have heard stories from pastors and members of smaller churches of sheep stealing, wooing away youth and teen members to elaborate events and programs, accusations of misconduct or heresy, complaints about their refusal to share the ministerial spotlight, and rumors about how and where the vast sums of megachurch money is spent. In areas of rapid change, the megachurch can even come to symbolize unconsciously the menace of new ways of doing things and new strangers flooding into an area. At certain times and in some megachurches, there might be truth to any of these claims, but generally speaking, many of these allegations are in fact attempts to diminish the importance of the megachurch rather than offer a constructive response from the smaller church's perspective.

Occasionally, megachurch pastors add fuel to this tension intentionally or accidentally. Door-to-door witness teams seldom discriminate between the unchurched and those already attending elsewhere. Plans to expand are done without sensitivity to the neighborhood affected. Communitywide events for the general public held at a megachurch often only highlight its own ministries and encourage those who attend the community event to attend its services. The megachurch's leadership often doesn't participate in the local ministerial alliance or area church councils. Megachurch pastors even use small churches as scapegoats or sermon illustrations, such as, "I'm glad we're not one of those little churches by the side of the road." In advertising and public statements, megachurch pastors frequently represent their church as, "We're not your normal church." This effort to distinguish themselves from other religious approaches often unintentionally results in other churches feeling put down by such statements.

Sheep Stealing

One of the most common allegations is that megachurches grow from "transfer" membership—at the expense of other local churches. How much truth is there to this contention? There is no single answer.

Figure 7.1. Percentage of New Members Who
Are New Converts Within Megachurches.

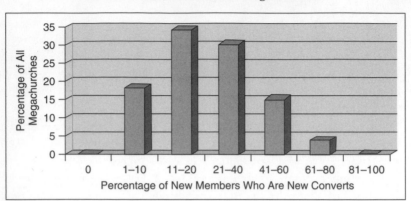

The megachurches we have questioned respond across a continuum with claims that "80 percent of new members are converts" to "most new persons are in fact coming from local congregations of all sizes." This is exemplified in the 2005 megachurch data when leaders were asked what percentage of their new members were new converts. In Figure 7.1, the results show considerable diversity across megachurches stretching from most to hardly any of the new members being converts.

In thinking about this question, it is also important to keep in mind that many scholars have argued that nearly all churches—large or small, conservative or liberal—grow either from more births and good retention rates or from "circulating saints" who go from one church to another.[6] A part of the challenge is due to the religiosity of Americans. It is a challenge to find a person who has never been affiliated with any church. A recent survey by the Baylor Institute for Religion claims that only 10.8 percent of Americans are "unaffiliated" with a congregation, denomination, or religious group.[7] If this is truly the case, then most people circulate across religious groups at some time in their lives.

Hard data to adequately address this question are limited. Most of the reported facts come from a congregation's own survey or analysis of data collected from new members' classes. Without implying any dishonesty on the part of the churches, this information, nevertheless, is somewhat suspect given the different ways of defining a new convert, determining who is truly unchurched, and accounting for those who have dropped out and then returned, or those who have been church shopping after relocating. Americans are very mobile, and a change of address often means a change of church as well.

Few independent studies of members have been undertaken, and the existing data is variable. Eiesland reported that the Southern Baptist megachurch she studied had equal numbers of persons joining through "baptism" and "transfer of membership" in one year of the megachurch's growth.[8] Thumma and Petersen's investigation of very large Evangelical Lutheran (ELCA) churches showed that a third of the new members were youth and adult conversions, a third transferred from other Lutheran churches, and a third came from a denomination outside the Lutheran tradition.[9] Thumma's study of a charismatic nondenominational megachurch showed that 27 percent claimed to be new Christians since coming to the megachurch, but only 7 percent stated that they grew up without a church or in a non-Christian faith.[10]

Finally, as shown in Figure 7.1, our 2005 megachurch study found 82 percent of the churches claimed that new converts accounted for 40 percent or less of their new members. So there is clearly a one-way circulation of the saints at work to some extent, but it is not necessarily an intentional theft of the flock. Megachurch pastors rarely like to see transfers into their churches from another church. Most of the leaders we talk with express no desire to attract disgruntled members from any other church. They will take them and nurture them, but their strong preference is to reach those that have no church experience or those that have fallen away from the church over the past few years. Their stated wish, which is nearly always reflected in the church's vision, is to reach the lost, the unchurched, and for some, the spiritual seekers. That members of other churches find the offerings of megachurches appealing enough to switch allegiances is not the intention of the megachurch's leadership and, in many ways, is beyond their control.

So it is partly true that some people are drawn into large churches and that some megachurches aren't the best playground partners. They challenge other churches to compete with the megachurch's increased programming, different style of worship, and considerable resources. However, it must be remembered that these churches also started out small and attracted their considerable number of attendees on a level playing field. If the religious ecology of an area is also like a spiritual marketplace, the megachurch product is selling well.

Interchurch Cooperation

Another common accusation is that the megachurch doesn't interact with other local churches. This was discussed in Chapter Three, but it is worth repeating here. From the 2000 megachurch study, 15 percent said they allowed other churches to use their facilities to hold services. When asked if they engaged in joint worship, programs, social services, or church councils with other congregations inside or outside their tradition, nearly a third of the megachurches said they hadn't done these activities with other churches. Those that did engage with others were more likely to interact with churches outside their own denominational tradition. Whether interacting with churches in their own or other denominations, 60 percent of megachurches had held joint worship services in the previous year. Likewise, 56 percent engaged in celebrations or other nonworship programs with area churches and 66 percent participated in joint social service projects in the preceding twelve months. Slightly over half were involved in councils of churches or ministerial associations the previous year.

Five years later, the 2005 megachurch survey showed that almost half (46 percent) partnered with other churches in the previous five years for international missions, and three-quarters (72 percent) had done this at some point in their history. In terms of local community service projects, 54 percent had teamed up with other churches in the past five years and 79 percent had done this at some time.

These figures, while not demonstrating the level of sharing and robust involvement that most church councils or ministerial alliances would wish for from their largest and most resource-rich churches, nevertheless are far from indicating a complete lack of involvement and an isolationist stance. Some of the examples for this type of work are mentioned in Chapter Five.

Bigness Benefits

Having a megachurch in their community poses a challenge for many churches, but how does it benefit them, if at all? And if so, does the gain outweigh the negatives? The presence of a megachurch may or may not require a church to alter how it runs its ministries or conducts worship, but it demands that the church define who it is in relation to the mammoth church down the street. This means that congregations within the orbit of a megachurch will have to clarify their distinct purpose, vision, and mission as it relates to their community. Will they attempt to be a clone, be better than the megachurch, ignore the megachurch, run away, fight, become a specialized niche congregation, or offer an alternative expression of spirituality? Nancy Eiesland's work showed how some churches learned to thrive in the shadow of the megachurch by emphasizing their denominational heritage, historic role in the city, distinctive ministry efforts, or unique expression of the Christian faith. Other congregations were less focused and intentional about the identity they crafted. Those that continued to operate as if nothing were different, clung to a sense of entitlement, or remained in their old model of ministry struggled.[11] Our experience is that those congregations who actively and intentionally reassessed their ministry and identity in relation to the megachurch would probably have a vital future.

The key is to determine what the mission focus of the church will be within the ecological system. Making the effort to understand what God is calling that church to be is important. Creating a distinctive identity based on a sense of God's role for each congregation in the religious ecology allows churches of all sizes to feel needed and necessary in the context. If a megachurch in the neighborhood ultimately results in a church coming to a better understanding of itself, its God-given mission and purpose, this is a great benefit.

Just Passing Through

Churches near a megachurch also benefit as the recipients of those who eventually tire of being part of such a large organization. It may seem like a megachurch continually draws in new people and is ever expanding, but that is not the case. Those who have been around megachurches know that these churches have revolving doors in the front and out the back. Hundreds and thousands of new people visit each year, and often nearly that many depart annually. This attrition occurs from burnout and frustration, from the novelty having worn off, and from a desire to worship in a smaller-scale congregation where you get to shake the senior pastor's hand each week. While it is seldom discussed, the migration out of a megachurch can directly benefit those smaller churches in the immediate vicinity. Among the large Evangelical Lutheran (ELCA) churches studied by Thumma and Petersen, roughly half as many members were lost to other ELCA churches as they received from these smaller Lutheran churches. More specifically, of the forty-three very large churches, an average of 101 people transferred in from other ELCA churches, but the same year on average fifty-six persons transferred out to other Evangelical Lutheran congregations.[12]

We have seen multiple examples of a large megachurch with over five thousand in regular attendance seemingly paired with a smaller megachurch of two thousand and several churches of from two hundred to five hundred attendees in very near physical proximity. In these cases, the church of five thousand tends to focus on evangelism and bring in new converts, but is not adept at nurturing long-term spiritual development. Many people in the smaller churches have passed through the larger church. These "smaller" churches have positioned themselves as teaching centers with serious Bible study and extensive group ministries where individuals find a greater sense of connection.

A Resting Place

Much is made of the evils of individual anonymity in worship at a megachurch. While we agree that there are difficulties inherent in this approach, there is also a flip side to this reality. The ability of overworked small church leaders to temporarily attend worship at a megachurch and "hide" can function as a much-needed respite. We have heard many stories of burned-out attendees from smaller churches needing to "drop out" and rest at the megachurch. Chuck Smith Sr. once commented that many people came to Calvary Chapel because they were "burned out on the intense structure of their former church"[13]

This is frequently the case when there has been conflict at a nearby church. At times, the conflict is intergenerational, where younger and older members are squabbling over things such as worship and other programming. Other times the struggle is over a senior pastor's style or performance. Whatever the case, there are times when long-time leaders will leave their church and gravitate into the orbit of the local megachurch. With marginal commitment, these leaders are allowed a respite from the past conflict and a time to rejuvenate their spiritual energy.

Additionally, we know of many clergy from churches of all sizes who were embroiled in a church conflict and then became participants at a megachurch. Some of these eventually took secular jobs and now consider themselves "out of the ministry." Others recharged their spirit and sought another place of ministry service. Most often one finds disillusioned clergy spending several years participating as a volunteer leader at the megachurch and then joining its staff in a specific ministry role. In our experience, megachurch leaders are adept at finding disheartened former senior pastors and dispirited lay volunteers, challenging them with small roles, and eventually nurturing them into more demanding staff roles as they prove themselves.

Further, megachurches can be places of rest and reorientation for believers who have suffered a recent life change such as divorce or loss of a child. The intimate social structure of a caring church is often painful for those who raised their family there and then lost a child to an untimely or traumatic death. While the grief is unresolved, the parents may seek another place of worship to escape those memories. Additionally, those who have been through a divorce are likely to leave the church they attended as a couple and find a new church that only knows them as a single person. Megachurches usually have an abundance of people in every life situation, whether single, divorced, or grieving a loss in some other way. Those who are attracted to the megachurch may not seek out the specialized ministry targeting those needs, but often find normalcy in connecting with others like them.

Resource Churches

In certain ways, megachurches have become quasi-denominational entities, having taken on certain roles and functions previously held by national denominational agencies. Some megachurches have significant ministries to other churches and pastors in their local communities. The largest churches in a area become hubs of like-minded congregations or sponsors of collective activities. Additionally, megachurches have national networks of churches often focused around teaching, training, and resource development. These churches have even created alternative training schools that have developed into accredited colleges and seminaries as well as Bible institutes. In these and other ways, the megachurches have become resources that vie with clergy councils, denominations, and seminaries for participants.

Local Networks

A growing number of megachurches have created local resource networks to serve other churches in their community. These networks involve, for example, hosting pastor luncheons with special speakers, the "loan" of music teams to other churches to help with special events, or youth ministry events that use the megachurch's building for a joint citywide event with other churches. Some of these churches speak of the desire to "raise the spiritual temperature" of the entire community and feel that can only be done in league with other pastors and churches in their region.

In early 2005, Dave had an opportunity to visit Healing Place Church in Baton Rouge, Louisiana. This evangelical-charismatic church, less than twelve years old, had over six thousand worshippers at the time, as well as having started several branch locations and independent churches in the area. Pastor Dino Rizzo stated the church's commitment as "whatever God puts in our hand, we must hold it open. If we are not generous with what God has blessed us with, God will not continue to bless us." In his view, and as evidenced by their church's actions in their community, the congregation was founded on the premise of always being generous to other churches. Three examples best describe this commitment.

In a small, personal way, Pastor Rizzo sends letters of encouragement to area pastors each month. Enclosed with the letter is usually a gift card to a local restaurant with a note that says: "Treat your family to dinner on us this month. We appreciate your service to our community."

A broader act of generosity was evident in the church's interactions with a team from a nearby, newer Presbyterian (USA) church. When Pastor Rizzo heard about the new church, he asked how Healing Place could help. After determining its needs, Healing Place sent worship teams and other volunteers to help the new church for a six-month period. They sent youth volunteers to help pass out flyers and water bottles to advertise the new church. The Presbyterian Church group reported that Healing Place stood by them and helped whenever asked, even more than many churches in their own tradition. Both Healing Place and the Presbyterian Church leaders acknowledged that their worship and beliefs were somewhat different, but they loved and served each other regardless. This Presbyterian community of five hundred worshippers reported they would always be indebted to the generosity of Healing Place.

An even more far-reaching example of the church's generosity was evident when Hurricane Katrina hit in Louisiana and Mississippi. Healing Place was ready to respond. Through its previously formed "Pastors Resource Council," the church immediately was able to collect and distribute resources to affected individuals through the network of area churches. While Healing Place had room for a large shelter and warehousing, it also had a network of partner churches to move quickly in a broad response. This was a natural extension of the church's value of generosity and the preexisting network they had formed in calmer times.

Teaching Networks

In addition to these local networks, megachurches are rapidly replacing denominational offices as the trainers of other churches in areas of innovative worship and congregational practices. This process begins informally as a church begins to grow rapidly into a megachurch and other church leaders call to ask for time to talk with the pastor and staff to understand what they are doing to grow. Early in their existence, many megachurches share what they learn with these other churches via informal meetings and meals. Eventually, the small trickle becomes a flood of inquirers. We like to say that a church then begins to play defense. In order to give an appropriate amount of time to this educational activity, it sets up informal and inexpensive "visitors' weekends" or introductory conferences that help a small group of other pastors understand and learn from what they are doing. The next stage becomes a full-blown conference. This usually results in a formal ministry to and networking with other churches that desire to share the same ministry outlook in their own community.

For some of these megachurches, the next phase is participation in a larger conference that shares the platform with other speakers and leaders. For others, a deliberate choice is made to focus on small groups of churches that desire coaching and consulting. Still others combine these two approaches with the production of literature and video resources and form a full-blown "association" or national network of churches. These associations can be formal and informal, but do usually require some form of monetary payments to help support this ministry of the megachurch. Some even use satellite broadcasting to sites across the country. The Willow Creek Association, probably the largest of these types of organizations, reports over seventy thousand paid participants in the 2006 Leadership Summit distributed by satellite. The Purpose Driven Association, a ministry of Saddleback Church, estimates that over twenty-five thousand churches conducted a Purpose Driven Life campaign over the last three years.

Focusing on the largest of these associations misses the whole story, which is that there are now hundreds of churches holding conferences and practicums and using residencies to teach other church leaders their methods and practices. For every high-profile church conference, there are dozens of smaller ones. For example, Ginghamsburg United Methodist Church of Tipp City, Ohio, has a long history of "Change Conferences" that focus primarily on mainline church leaders. In addition to their conferences, they also publish curriculum and books. New Hope Christian Fellowship in Oahu, Hawaii, features its "Doing Church as a Team" conference and multiple Senior Pastor Practicums each year. Publishers and resource providers are now seeking ways to partner with these churches in order to reach former customers that have left the denominational and publishing-driven conferences to attend those at a teaching megachurch.

Bible Colleges, Seminaries, and Training Institutes

Observers of American history know that many institutions of higher learning have been created by religious groups. Schools such as Yale University, Emory University, Southern Methodist University, and Baylor University began as denomination-based institutions, some of which have now left their affiliations behind while others retain their ties, but in more informal ways.

Roughly 30 percent of megachurches have continued the custom of starting their own training and education institutions attached to their church, based on information from our 2000 study. For some, the

Bible college or training institute is an unaccredited series of courses in ministry-focused areas. The classes are targeted at church members and those living near the church for both personal enrichment or to gain a ministry credential. A few have grown into full-fledged colleges offering multiple majors and degrees. Many of these began as fundamentalist colleges in previous generations, and now have grown large and prosperous and accredited. Examples include Criswell College (with roots in the First Baptist Church of Dallas, Texas) and Liberty University (founded by Thomas Road Baptist Church of Lynchburg, Virginia).

Additionally, some megachurches start or partner with seminaries to offer classes both in practical ministry and in traditional Bible and theology to local students. The goal is to provide more affordable and local theological training. This helps to train their staffs and potential staff members. New Birth Missionary Baptist in Lithonia, Georgia, has operating partnerships with two local seminaries to offer classes to members. Wooddale Church in Eden Prairie, Minnesota, is typical of some churches that offer courses such as New Testament Greek, Theology, The Apocrypha, and New Testament Introduction, in addition to many practical life application courses through its education ministry. Some prominent teaching churches establish partnerships with existing seminaries in order to teach praxis ministry along with the theological concepts.

All of the above types of educational vehicles are not just offered for church members, but also for others interested in ministry. With the growth of internships, pastoral residencies, and church planting programs that are created, established, nurtured, and run by the megachurches, we see them as a big player for future ministry training.

The presence of a megachurch, whether it is within a neighborhood, a city, or a denomination, requires adjustments from all other entities. Their size and influence has an effect on the religious ecology no matter how broadly or narrowly it is defined. Indeed, there are drawbacks to having a megachurch nearby, but it can be of considerable benefit also. The size and structure of the megachurch allows it to act in ways unlike other churches. It functions in ways that make it in part a local church, but also having characteristics of a seminary and denomination.

○

Applying What You Have Read

Return to your context map that we asked you to draw in Chapter One. Look again at the relationships between the numbers of people that do attend church versus those not attending. Many areas of the country are experiencing net immigration, meaning more people are coming into an area than are leaving. Who are these people? What are their characteristics? Where do they seem to be coming from? If you are in an area losing residents, why are they going and where are they moving to? Who in your community is still here?

Examine the following list. It is written to describe two groups of individuals: those that are likely to seek a new church (high potential) and those that are not (low potential). Use the characteristics to identify potential new attendees for your church and those likely not to be prospects.

HIGHER POTENTIAL

- If a person is new to the community in the past year and if they have moved over ten miles from their previous residence.
- If the person has had a major life change, such as in marital status, the death of a spouse, having a child, or losing a child to death.
- If the person is a part of a church that has gone through a major dispute or strife in the past year.
- If the person has not been an active part of any church in over a year.

LOWER POTENTIAL

- If a person has been a member and active participant of the same congregation for more than ten years.
- If a person gives through service and through their financial gifts to that same congregation.
- If a person agrees with the direction and vision of the congregation and denomination.
- If a person is satisfied with their spiritual growth.
- If a person's children and grandchildren all attend that same congregation.

Most people who become involved in a new church after a period of inactivity from involvement in a previous church switch for specific reasons. The most likely reason is that when they became inactive, no one sought them out to reinvolve them. There is little reason that they cannot reconnect with their "old" church if they are encouraged to do so. This should be done through their natural relationships with someone already attending their former church, although careful thought should be given to identifying and selecting those who will encourage the non-attending member.

As you will read in a later chapter, most people who come to a megachurch, or any other church, are not connected by advertising or programs, but through personal contact with someone they already know.

We want to repeat that some of the megachurches use interns, residents, and others who are in training for ministry. Megachurches may have an overabundance of interns and actually seek partners to help find places of meaningful service outside their own congregation. We have even seen them lend interns to other churches for up to a year.

If this sounds promising to you, we would encourage the reader to make an appointment with the person in charge of the intern or resident program within the megachurch and inquire as to the possibilities of having a few interns assist your church. It will take some relationship-building time and you may have to approach several megachurches to find the right fit for your church, but these relationships can yield great fruit for both parties. Many times, the leaders of the programs know that an individual would fit best in a smaller church setting, but have no outlet to place them. On the other side, many pastors of smaller churches could benefit from mentoring and training an aspirant for ministry who is found through a megachurch intern program.

8

"THESE CHURCHES ARE FULL OF PEOPLE OF THE SAME RACE, CLASS, AND POLITICAL PREFERENCES"

---

*These churches . . . are typically suburban, overwhelmingly
white, middle-class, and deliberately shaped for well-off,
well-educated Boomers, though some churches are now
moving on to the niche occupied by the Xers. These are the
birds that are flocking together.*[1]

*To some urban progressives, megachurches represent not
only an alien phenomenon, but a large, threatening citadel of
conservative cultural and political views.*[2]

HOW MANY TIMES HAVE WE HEARD, "Sunday morning is the most
segregated hour of the week?" Indeed, every time the demographic
characteristics of congregations are analyzed nationally, the truth of this
statement is confirmed. Since the civil rights legislation of the 1960s, our
nation has legislated racial inclusion everywhere except in the church. But
it isn't just race that separates congregations. Even with the considerable
progress and leveling of education, income, class, and status in the
United States, studies still show significant divisions among churches and
denominations around these demographic variables.[3]

Therefore, it should be no surprise that megachurches have been characterized as reflecting the same kinds of patterns. Early in the growth of
the Megachurch movement, the churches were pictured as large nondenominational congregations with worship composed of praise choruses

based in the Charismatic movement and the "Jesus people" experiences of the 1970s. This idea was reinforced as a result of considerable journalistic focus on the immensely popular Willow Creek and Saddleback Churches and their claims to target a certain kind of person—white middle-class baby boomer, upwardly mobile residents of the suburban sprawl cities. It should be obvious to the reader that this partially correct portrayal overlooked many large churches in order to focus on those most distinctive at that time: the Seeker types. Left out were the inner-city black megachurches, the intentionally racially mixed churches, and the denominationally grounded megachurches firmly embedded in a Southern Baptist, Assemblies of God, Presbyterian, Lutheran, and Methodist worship style. The megachurch phenomenon has always presented significant exceptions to these broad characterizations, but few people have paid much attention to the diversity across the phenomenon or within individual congregations.

If one looks at these churches from a general big picture perspective, the characterization of homogeneity for a certain type of megachurch was, and somewhat continues to be, an accurate representation. However, the more detailed information we learn about megachurches, the easier it is to see that the social makeup of these congregations is far more complex than expected. Both in the detailed analysis and at the broad national level, this entire phenomenon varies dramatically in terms of social constituency. This is happening for a variety of reasons. In part, it is due to the nature of large organizations. In addition, many of these churches have adopted a vision that states that the church is for all people no matter what race, income, or educational status. Likewise, the worship forms and styles of these churches both reinforce this vision and find great resonance with a generic American pop cultural model imbedded in contemporary society and spread by television, malls, and franchising throughout the country. In other words, they are worshipping in the common language of many people. Finally, the increasing heterogeneity of the megachurches is in part due to more diversified programs specific to particular subgroups attracted to the churches.

The Nature of Large Organizations

It is easy to hide in a crowd. Within a large group, pockets of diversity are easily overlooked. It was this characteristic that first drew one of us into the study of megachurches. While studying a ministry to persons trying to leave the gay lifestyle at a megachurch, Scott realized that there were openly gay men who attended the church. After talking with two of them, he found he was mistaken in assuming that they were infrequent members of the ex-gay group. These men acknowledged knowing about the group but had absolutely no interest in it; they thought its members had a mistaken understanding of sexuality because they were willing to attend such a group. The men also knew the church's pastor was outspoken on the sinfulness of the gay lifestyle. Yet they had attended the church faithfully for several years. When asked why they came, they claimed that the preaching was "anointed," the music "heavenly," and they "believed in the vision of the church." It didn't matter that they did not wholeheartedly agree with the church on every point. What mattered was that the spiritual benefits they received greatly outweighed the occasional reminder that the church's doctrine didn't affirm their lifestyle. They further related that they had numerous friends in the church who knew they were gay, were happy that they attended, and accepted them as part of the congregation. This experience, and others, propelled this author on an almost twenty-year quest to understand how this religious form could hold together such a divergence of opinion within a common worship experience.

While this story is dramatic, especially given the overt actions of some megachurches in 2004 and following years in support of anti–gay marriage initiatives in several states, it exemplifies the ability of a large congregation to support pockets of difference. This is a positive feature of anonymity within the congregation. It allows those who don't fit the majority perspective the freedom to slip in and worship, and perhaps to be convinced of the need for conversion or maturation in the faith. This is the cornerstone of a Seeker-type service, but such a ministry strategy is greatly enhanced by the increased size of the congregation.

Obviously, this characteristic has immediate disadvantages for anyone concerned with doctrinal purity or who sees the worship service as functioning to ensure personal accountability. In a large-scale gathering, it is virtually impossible to impose homogeneity around any issue or characteristic even if the church's leadership wanted it. There is simply too much personal freedom and too many places to hide. This reality is apparent when one looks at the theological and moral differences evident in surveys of megachurch members.

Diversity on Many Levels

Members of the nondenominational megachurch mentioned above engaged in a high level of personal religious practices and showed considerable adherence to the vision and mission of the church. Yet each of the doctrinal questions, such as belief in Jesus being the only way to salvation or the devil literally existing, showed 5 to 15 percent of the

Figure 8.1. Attendee Perspectives on "Wives as
Homemakers and Husbands as Providers."

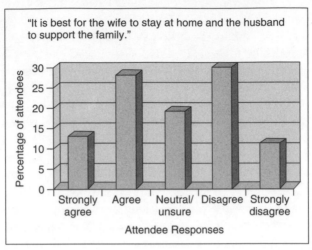

members disagreeing with the often-reinforced orthodox beliefs of the
church. On other more subjective questions, such as whether the Rapture
is coming soon, whether believers should vote for Christian candidates,
or that success indicates God's blessing, the congregation was clearly
divided. And on some questions of moral and social issues, for example,
"It is best for the wife to stay at home and the husband to support
the family," there was no consensus at all within the congregation, as
Figure 8.1 shows.

This church was not an anomaly. Information from a study by Donald
Miller on the three founding megachurches of the Calvary Chapel,
Hope Chapel, and Vineyard Fellowship movements showed a similar
wide range of opinions. The survey findings appendix in Miller's book,
Reinventing American Protestantism, indicates that there is considerable
diversity within the three megachurches he studied, particularly with
regard to members' social beliefs.[4]

Another factor in promoting this diversity is that many megachurches
have intentionally adopted an inclusivist vision that the church is for all
people no matter what race or socioeconomic group. The leadership of
these churches has a strong desire to cultivate an atmosphere of inclusion
and embrace a wide diversity of people. This message is translated to
the people in the pews. When the members of the nondenominational
megachurch were asked if they liked being in a diverse community, 90
percent agreed or strongly agreed with the statement. Eighty-eight percent

agreed that they had become more tolerant since coming to the church. Likewise, the Calvary Chapel, Hope Chapel, and Vineyard Fellowship survey showed their members to be very accepting of racial diversity both within the church and in the larger society.

Not only are these churches firmly committed to this vision, but they are also willing to recreate themselves to demonstrate their commitment to this inclusive perspective. According to our 2005 survey, in the past five years 85 percent of these megachurches had changed their worship format or style somewhat with 23 percent saying they had changed the worship "a lot," 36 percent reporting they had changed it "some," and 26 percent saying they had shifted their worship style "a little." These figures showed a greater willingness to change and adapt than did those megachurches from our 2000 study. Often this adaptation comes in the form of new and diverse worship and musical styles. Within the large nondenominational charismatic megachurch studied, only 6 percent of members said that mixing musical styles in the service made worship difficult. The idea is not to have a diversity of styles for its own sake, but to embrace a vision that crosses many interest groups, and then reflect that vision within worship forms that are contemporary and less tied to a particular racial group, socioeconomic class, or denominational tradition.

Every study of the individuals who attend megachurches shows a considerable mix of economic groups spanning a range of household incomes from lower class, just above poverty, to the comfortable middle class, to those firmly embedded in the upper class making well over $150,000 a year. Additionally, attendees may appear on average well educated, but in most cases 15 percent or more have a high school degree or less, while 15 to 25 percent have at least some graduate education. The same range of diversity is also seen in terms of occupation. While the largest percentage of attendees is usually employed in professional vocations, this characteristic too shows wide variation.

In many ways, the diversity of people encountered within a megachurch should not be surprising. While the majority of churches in the United States draw from a greater distance than they have in the past, in most cases they still have a smaller catchment area than do the regionally oriented megachurches. These smaller churches function either as local congregational expressions of their community, where in many cases the community is characterized by a specific socioeconomic and racial profile, or they are niche churches intentionally appealing to a particular cultural subgroup that is often homogeneous in social makeup. However, megachurches cast their nets wide across a region. The diversity of an entire city can potentially be represented within a large church, especially when that church is making an intentional attempt to embrace that diversity.

There is no characteristic of the megachurch phenomenon where this is more clearly seen than in terms of the racial makeup of the congregation. Much research has recently examined the prevalence of multiracial congregations. In a major national study, Michael Emerson and his colleagues found that multiracial churches, those having no more than 80 percent of any one racial group, represented 7 percent of American congregations. About 15 percent of Catholic churches were multiracial, while only about 5 percent of Protestant churches were.[5]

The 2005 megachurch research specifically explored this issue and found that 31 percent of megachurches claimed to have a 20 percent or more minority presence in their congregations. The average megachurch had 14 percent of the congregation not representing the majority race. Fifty-five percent of megachurches stated that their congregations were making specific efforts to become intentionally multiethnic. The vast majority of these efforts centered on diversifying the racial makeup of staff and clergy, while also giving them more prominent roles in leadership. Additional efforts included creating services in other languages, most often Spanish and Chinese, Korean, or other Asian languages; developing outreach programs to meet the needs of persons from other races, specifically inviting those outside the majority racial group; reshaping the worship services to appeal to a larger variety of ethnic and cultural groups; and strongly encouraging an attitude of racial acceptance within the entire congregation. Judging from the survey findings, these efforts have been quite effective.

It is important to understand that this racial diversity is not necessarily a new emphasis of the megachurches. Thumma's study of a nondenominational charismatic megachurch in the late 1980s showed the number of blacks and whites in the church to be nearly equal.[6] Likewise, Donald Miller's study in early 1990s found that two of the three megachurches he examined had over 20 percent racial diversity, and in the third church, 12 percent of the congregation was comprised of nonwhite members.[7] There is no doubt from these studies that to characterize the megachurch as a homogeneous entity of only white, middle-class suburbanites is inaccurate. A close look at the actual characteristics of attendees shows a diversity that more closely reflects the country as a whole than represented by the vast majority of smaller individual churches.

It is partly this broad appeal that contributes to the ability of megachurches to attract and hold such diversity. The worship forms and styles used within these churches are shaped by the larger secular culture. One of the most obvious characteristics of megachurch worship, which is often soundly criticized, is its resonance with pop culture images and icons. Megachurches take worldly movies, music, television programs, commercials, and pop trends and baptize them into the service of the kingdom. These forms are used to convey the Gospel, to teach a truth about God, or to make the church more appealing to modern cynics. As such, the message of these megachurches appeals to a larger and more diverse audience than traditional churches.

Congregations within a traditional model of church must either convert contemporary persons to an archaic and outdated style of music, language, and presentation, or they are limited in their outreach to those who are familiar with the cultural style embodied in this antiquated worship form. On the other hand, the megachurches, and other congregations who seek to embed the Gospel in various contemporary forms, find greater resonance with overarching generic cultural models in contemporary society, which is spread throughout American society by television, malls, and commercial franchises. Indeed, megachurches intend to reach the same audiences that Disney, Starbucks, and McDonald's do. That audience is diverse, but it is also large, young, and future oriented. Megachurches want their message and the medium by which that message is carried to resonate and be embraced by the assorted listeners of top-40 songs on successful commercial radio stations. Their audience is not the narrow audience that prefers classical or jazz programming on public radio.

A Structured Diversity

It isn't enough that a megachurch appeals to and brings together a diverse congregation, it must also provide a way for the diversity to integrate into the life of the church. The primary way attendees are connected to the church is through worship. The challenge comes when there is a single worship service. Whose cultural style will prevail, or will the congregation be tolerant and endure a multitude of styles mixed into one service? The megachurch has long been able to handle diversity in relation to worship formats and style simply because it grew too fast. The immediate reaction to growth is to begin another service at a different time, but as soon as this happens so does the sorting by social groups. An early Sunday morning service meets the needs of one type of person, while a Saturday evening service appeals to another kind of member. Even without altering the worship style, different constituencies within the church are better served. This is readily apparent in the multiple masses held by most Catholic churches, as it is in the megachurches, where over 50 percent of the churches hold four or more services each week.

The megachurch uses these multiple services to cater to distinctive cultural groups. It creates a structured diversity of musical styles, sermon interests, perhaps even theological perspectives based on when a service is held and to whom it is intended to appeal. The 2005 survey found that nearly 50 percent of megachurches offer services that exhibit distinctively different styles. This process has developed an even greater sophistication with the introduction of simultaneous venues for worship. In multiple rooms on a single church campus, attendees might have the choice of four or five different styles of worship, distinctive music and instruments, leadership appropriate to the format, and even culturally relevant refreshments. This worship specialization around subgroups within a church has even become more apparent with the increasingly common strategy of creating multiple sites for worship physically removed from the church's main campus. This innovation allows not only for the development of venues within one campus, but also for off-site locations tailored to the style of a constituency on the other side of the city or even across the country. Some multisite churches have a vision and calling to reach their entire city by starting culturally indigenous services within each section of their city.[8]

Any megachurch that assumes the worship event alone, even one tailored to a particular subgroup, is sufficient to sustain a Christian's walk is mistaken. Therefore, these churches must also embed diversity within their weekly programmatic structures. This effort is accomplished in part as a result of the internal diversification of programs specific to particular subgroups. And the small fellowship groups are key here. Not only are the small group ministries, programs, and mission efforts divided by age groups, but many times they are also arranged around interest and lifestyle cohorts. Additionally, there is willingness on the part of the leadership of many megachurches to empower members to create new ministries if none exist to address their issue. Thus, if a member who is a motorcyclist desires a group of bikers with whom he can share fellowship, discuss God's place in biker culture, and perhaps take trips, it is likely that his immediate pastor will encourage him to begin such a group. This ability to birth activities and ministries, based on the specific voluntaristic desires of its members and their needs, allows the church to minister to a wide variety of people.

The Challenges of Diversity

These efforts at creating and maintaining a diverse congregation are not without a cost. A pluralism of theological and social beliefs, worship styles, or subgroups can create a difficult situation for any church.

While a megachurch may more accurately represent diverse attitudes and styles in the larger culture, such variety can also diminish the doctrinal purity of the group or fracture the single body of Christ into clichés based on social characteristics. It is clear that the worship styles adopted by most megachurches mean that they are less likely to appeal to the oldest generations of Americans. While a majority of U.S. churches have members between the ages of sixty-five and eighty-five, it is unlikely that you will find more than 10 percent of the membership over the age of sixty-five in most megachurches.

This reality could be changing, however. In the past five years, the number of megachurches adding venues and services labeled "Traditions" or "Old Time Gospel" has grown. Some of this has been birthed by older adults that gravitated to the church following their children and grandchildren and asked for this specialized service. It might also be due to the tastes of baby boomers, maturing in their worship preferences. Other churches have begun to realize that not all young adults enjoy the high-decibel music and have created some more contemplative services. For whatever the reason, many churches are finding that the costs of adding the service are smaller than starting a new contemporary service. Usually these "traditions" services can be housed in smaller venues concurrently with other worship services and utilize common child-care spaces.

Additionally, if a church has a wide variety of social and political views represented within the membership, it is more likely that the pastor will be sensitive and attempt to walk a line between constituents with the hope of not offending any group when speaking on matters not crucial to the faith. The diversity across political parties and political positions, along with the separation of church and state and laws keeping clergy from endorsing candidates from the pulpit, ensures public political neutrality on the part of many megachurch pastors. In his study of three megachurches, Miller found that while the majority was politically conservative and affiliated with the Republican Party, roughly 30 to 40 percent of members diverged from the majority.[9] From our observations and conversations with megachurch members, it is clear that they see their faith and their pastor as influencing their political decisions, but there is a church/state separation even within the minds of many of these members. Contrary to the overt and highly publicized actions of a few megachurch pastors during the 2004 election cycle, the 2005 megachurch study found few churches engaged in public political actions with other churches. In our experience, there are relatively few megachurch pastors who take an active role in local, state, and national politics. They certainly hold personal political views, but rarely use their pulpits for dissemination of those views. They are more concerned about reaching and nurturing new believers than making overt political statements or encouraging attendees to vote for certain candidates.[10] Some strongly held beliefs with regard to marriage and family and important ethical concerns are addressed in due course from the teaching and preaching of the church, but they are framed as moral, not political, issues.

Another challenge whenever a diverse organization allows subgroups to organize into smaller self-selected units is how to promote cross-group interaction. This can clearly be seen within congregations composed of multiple races. A church can give each ethnic and racial group its own space, thus creating a multiracial reality, but not achieve true integration that might lead to real change in race perceptions or deep interracial friendships. The same dynamic could also become apparent if differing cultural and social groups have their own small fellowships, worship venues, or even off-site campuses. Segregating the diversity within the church can diminish the congregation's understanding of itself as the whole body of Christ, even though the effort is undertaken by the leadership to address each subgroup's distinct set of needs. This desire to minister to the diversity of members must always be balanced with an intentional intermingling of the population if the pluralism of a megachurch is to have a positive effect. On the basis of their size, structure, and vision, megachurches have a unique ability to hold together many different types of Christians so that "God may help us demonstrate his Kingdom through the diversity," as one megachurch pastor explained. If that is indeed a role they want to play, then the leadership of these churches will need to reflect on how to meet the needs of that diversity while also encouraging it to interact. True dialogue across diversity of any sort is never easy to maintain.

Contrary to how they appear from the outside or to a casual visitor, megachurches are not homogeneous collections of the same kind of person, neither by race, class, education, or political stance. Within most of these churches, significant pockets of diversity are apparent. It is true that megachurch attendees do have similar lifestyles, but this is due more to a common suburban milieu and unity around the vision of the church than anything intrinsic to the form of the megachurch itself. As regional churches, these congregations draw from a broad social spectrum. Although on average the memberships may appear uniform, a closer inspection of the congregation shows that these churches are reaching a wide array of individuals. This effort to reach a variety of persons has become a key task of many megachurches, and is likely to enhance the diversity within the congregation.

○

Applying What You Have Read

The focus of this chapter is on congregational diversity of race, class, and political views. This type of diversity is mostly seen in churches that are either very large (like megachurches) or very small. The medium-sized church (one hundred to four hundred) tends to have the hardest time building diversity.

In our experience, there are several factors to consider. One of our mentors told us the easiest way to build a racially diverse congregation was to divorce our present spouse and marry someone of another race. While we did not take their advice, we have noted that a number of racially diverse congregations do have a lead pastor that is married to someone of another race. Churches with a more Pentecostal and charismatic theology tend to be more diverse than other churches. Assuming that you are not going to change your spouse or your theology, what are the things you can do to broaden the diversity of your church?

For some congregations, including megachurches, one way to broaden the outreach of your church in a community is to invite a worshipping congregation of another racial group into your facility. Some might treat this group as a separate church planting, while others view the new congregation as an extension of the existing congregation. Some will start a congregation that worships in a language other than the existing congregation's primary language. Others choose to focus on a particular immigrant group who may speak the same language, but have divergent cultural styles or worship practices. Still another approach is to start a new congregation that focuses on the needs of younger adults within the community. This worship experience can have a different worship aesthetic and experience than the worship services of the currently existing congregation and may appeal to diverse groups in the community.

It is not enough to begin these groups or open your building and then assume the difficult task of making the church more diverse is over. The leadership will have to structure ways to interact and cause the lives of the members of the two congregations to intersect. Plan worship together. Begin biracial or bilingual small groups. Volunteer in a joint social ministry effort. Offer evenings where members of both congregations, racial groups, or other diversity groups come together for fun and fellowship, potlucks and singing. These and many other methods may be tried to have the groups get to know each other.

Diversity in the congregation can only happen if the existing "way we have always done it here" is relinquished, and a new way is forged together across subgroups. This is true whether the diversity is around age groups, racial groups, or other characteristics.

○ Closely examine the members of your congregation in terms of demographics (age, race, education, income, political party, gender, and so on). How diverse is the church?

○ Perhaps you can hand out a congregational survey with theological questions, collect it, and explore just how diverse the congregation is in terms of theology and social attitudes. (Our Web site will have suggestions about church inventories to use.)

○ How might diversity fit in the congregation's vision?

○ How does diversity fit into God's plan for the church?

○ What concrete steps might you take to make the church more diverse over the next five years?

"MEGACHURCHES GROW BECAUSE OF THE SHOW"

Megachurches attract their throngs the same way a business attracts customers: through marketing and friendly service, and by offering a compelling "product" that keeps people coming back for more. Sermons are typically delivered by a charismatic pastor through a top-notch sound system using video clips, live-music accompaniment, and even the occasional PowerPoint presentation.[1]

As with most megachurches, much of Calvary's growth is directly related to the senior pastor's energy and personal appeal. On that October morning, after twenty minutes of contemporary worship songs from singers accompanied by piano, sax, electric guitars and percussion, "pastor Bob," in a sport coat without necktie, makes his way inconspicuously to the pulpit from the wings. For the next hour and five minutes, seated for the most part on a stool to the pulpit's side, without notes and with just a few references to his open Bible, Coy conversationally mixes anecdotes with heartfelt messages. He is entertaining, animated, comedic, self-effacing, earnest—and he never stumbles.[2]

FOR MANY FIRST-TIME GUESTS to a megachurch, their experience begins in the parking lot, as smiling attendants point them to the closest parking spot. For those churches with extremely large parking areas, a shuttle takes people directly to the appropriate door at the church. If visitors have children with them, a greeter will point the way to the children's area. At many of these churches, children are registered and logged into the security system so that parents can feel their child is safe and they can be notified immediately if needed through a pager or electronic call board.

Once these first-time guests walk into the main worship space, the first thing that usually grabs their attention is the size of the sanctuary and the large projection screens. Before the worship service even begins, there is usually soothing recorded music playing in the background while images, announcements, photos, and items of interest are projected on the screens located in the front of the worship area. These same images play on the televisions and video screens throughout the atriums and gathering spaces outside the auditorium. The volume builds until it is time for the service to start. When the singing starts, the energy and volume crank up yet another notch. The song lyrics scroll across the projection screens along with accompanying images that reinforce the message. The music fades away as the song ends, and a smooth, articulate pastor in casual business clothes with a barely visible microphone comes forward to welcome the congregation. The pastor's smiling face is instantaneously projected onto the twenty-foot screen as he speaks. Welcome to worship at an American megachurch.

Let us begin with a few observations about worship in American Protestant churches. First, regardless of size, much of the worship in America is based on a preacher, pastor, minister, or other person standing in the front of a room and leading worshippers through various rituals in the worship of God. While there is a sense of worship as a community, it is usually led by someone who draws attendees into the worship of God. There may also be a choir, soloists, and a number of liturgists or Scripture readers, and deacons involved in the service. An organist or pianist and possibly several other instrumentalists will perform, and other members will collect the financial offerings during the worship service. Even with this activity, most of the attendees are fairly passive throughout the worship services. If their heads and hearts are not engaged, and they weren't required to stand to sing the hymns, they would sit the entire time with their eyes glazed over. For most congregants, the expectation is that the primary spiritual leader of the church will lead the corporate worship service. If this experience does not draw the congregant closer to God, the pastor gets the blame.

Most preachers and pastors seek meaningful ways to engage the attendees. A large number of publications, Web sites, sermon services, and books are written each year to help preachers (regardless of theological orientation or the size of the church) become more interesting. Even in smaller churches, pastors work with music leaders, Scripture readers, and others to create a better service that draws congregants into worship.

Countless books, articles, and services are available to help improve the worship service planning process.

For many megachurches, these two worship tasks—the sermon and service planning—are characteristics that are writ large. Worship in a megachurch can seem like a well-produced show instead of a body of believers worshipping together. The size of the auditorium alone with its ubiquitous projection screens, cameras, and sound mixing board, combined with the high quality of musical elements and pinpoint timing of smooth transitions from one activity to another, lead first-time visitors to marvel at the experience. Choirs at megachurches are often oversized and accompanied by a mini-symphony orchestra. For the majority of the churches that have a "praise band," the performers tend to be highly polished and professional. The megachurches with large auditoriums also frequently employ sophisticated sound, light, and visual projection systems that can overwhelm the senses of unsuspecting first-time guests. Indeed, some of these church leaders brag to the press about exactly how much was spent on these technological systems at the opening of their latest facility.

The megachurches that we labeled as following the Seeker model feel they should intentionally design the worship experience for the person who wants to remain anonymous and merely observe. Within this stream, the performance value of the worship presentation is very important. The entire worship experience includes a "down-to-the-second" production sheet with each element carefully scripted, rehearsed, polished, and delivered on the mark during the service. Afterward, the worship leaders gather to review the experience, tweak any elements for future worship services that weekend, and learn from any glitches before the next weekend. Some of these churches have even created the staff position of "weekend producer" to plan and execute all elements of the service.

These factors naturally lead many to feel that the Megachurch movement is driven by the "Sunday show"—its spiritual spectacle. Adding fuel to possible charges by critics are the waves of megachurches that have installed movie theater–style seating in the sanctuary, including some that have built-in cup holders. In the critics' view, this experience overwhelms congregants with comfort and functionality but does not lead to the true worship of God.

We have seen similar charges made against the other streams of megachurches in our typology, though seldom to the extreme of the Seeker model. To some degree, and with the exception of the theater seats, similar claims can be made with regard to the liturgical, "high church" worship services among certain mainline and Roman Catholic traditions. Each element of those traditions including processionals, the serving of the Sacrament, the reading of Scripture, and the collection of the offering is usually carried out with great planning, pomp, and precision. Likewise, even in older rural churches, a distinct order and formal system to the pattern of worship has developed over decades. Even in the most free-spirited, seemingly spontaneous Pentecostal service, there are well-ingrained patterns and paths for the spirit to follow freely in worship. Although none of these methods really measure up to the megachurch worship production in quantity, they are similar in quality.

With the megachurch, much of the criticism rests on the degree of the elaborateness of the "show." Throughout Christian history, believers have used various methods of spreading the Gospel: passion plays, religiously themed symphonies, oratorios, and concerts. These popular religious performances were in sync with their time and eventually made their way from the theater and auditorium into the churches and cathedrals. Similarly, the music and preaching styles used in camp meetings, open-air revivals, and stadium evangelistic events crept into the sanctuary as acceptable ways of doing church. Many of the innovations in music, sound and video projection, lighting and other factors have been adapted from popular culture and then baptized for use in the church. Each advance in worship throughout history has faced resistance, and so do the current innovations.

For some, the highly orchestrated nature of the Seeker model has led to a backlash against an overly structured worship experience. As such, many newer generation churches are returning to a simpler form of worship with fewer time constraints. But they still have the big projection screen and quality sound system.

How Worship Does and Doesn't Lead to Growth

While the critics may not understand or appreciate the worship experience at a megachurch, evidently many attendees do. A clear distinction between megachurches and other churches in terms of worship is the number of options available to participants, starting with the sheer number of worship services offered each week. Figure 9.1 illustrates the finding from the 2005 megachurch study that 97 percent of all megachurches hold multiple worship services. Over half of these churches have three or four worship services and over 11 percent have more than seven worship services per week. In addition to the number of worship services, over 50 percent of the churches say these services are "somewhat" or "very different" from each other.

Before we describe the different types of experiences offered, it's important to note that our survey found that almost 90 percent of

Figure 9.1. Number of Weekly Worship Services Offered by Megachurches.

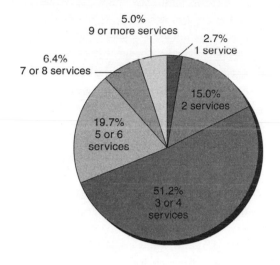

Table 9.1. Megachurch Worship Characteristics Compared with Those of Churches of All Sizes.

Congregations Saying This Term Describes Their Worship "Very Well"	2005 Megachurch Study (percentage)	2005 Faith Communities Today Study (percentage)
Reverent	16	20
Informal	20	11
Filled with a sense of God's presence	53	37
Joyful	50	30
Formal liturgy or ritual	2	15
Exciting	43	20
Inspiration	52	32
Thought-provoking	45	35

all respondents described the worship experience as "joyful," "inspirational," and "thought provoking." More than 80 percent of respondents agreed that the phrases "a sense of God" and "exciting" accurately characterized worship at their churches. These descriptions were used more frequently in megachurches than in smaller congregations from the Faith Communities Today 2005 study, as Table 9.1 shows.

For the past twenty-five years, growing numbers of churches, both large and small, have embraced "contemporary" worship. While there is not an exact meaning to the term, it generally implies the singing of simple praise songs rather than centuries-old hymns, the use of electric guitars and drums as musical accompaniment instead of organs, and the utilization of visual projection equipment to display song lyrics on a screen as a replacement for the hymnal. In some places, it also means the addition of visual projection to illustrate primary sermon themes or to move congregants through a message outline. Finally, it almost always means a more informal style of dress and cultural approach in the worship gathering.

For younger pastors and newer churches, what was called "contemporary" worship twenty years ago now seems tame given the high-decibel sound, elaborate video projection, and nightclub-like quality of worship in the group of churches we identify as New Wave megachurches. For them, the word "contemporary" takes on a whole new meaning. But in general, although the styles are slightly different, these New Wave megachurches would still fit into the broad contemporary worship style category.

It is clear that these worship styles continue to evolve at a rapid rate. A comparison of the 2000 megachurch study and the 2005 megachurch study in Table 9.2 illustrates some of the changes that have taken place in just five years. Likewise, the Faith Communities Today 2005 study showed an increase in contemporary worship generally across diverse sizes of churches, especially among churches within mainline denominational traditions.

Table 9.2. Characteristics of Megachurch Worship, 2000 and 2005.

How Often Is This Element Used in Worship?	Year	Percentage of Churches Responding				
		Never	Seldom	Sometimes	Often	Always
Piano (organ or piano in 2000)	2000	3	2	3	14	78
	2005	3	4	9	21	63
Electric or bass guitar	2000	1	6	14	17	61
	2005	2	1	4	13	80
Drums	2000	1	5	9	19	66
	2005	1	0	5	12	82
Visual projection equipment	2000	9	14	6	7	65
	2005	2	1	2	4	91

Table 9.2 shows that in 15 percent of the megachurches surveyed, always using the piano and organ in worship services has decreased. Instead, always playing the electric or bass guitar and drums in worship has risen in nearly 20 percent of these churches, and a whopping 91 percent of megachurches always make use of visual projection equipment. Whereas large church buildings fifty years ago were sometimes designed around the pipe organ, now the placement of various projection screens is carefully taken into consideration and given a place of prominence.

When these numbers are compared with the smaller Protestant churches in the 2000 study and the 2005 national Faith Communities Today (FACT) findings, the differences are indeed dramatic. In 2000, the megachurches were on average two to three times more likely to use these contemporary modes of music and worship, including strings and wind instruments and recorded music. By 2005, the FACT survey showed that smaller congregations were increasing their use of electronic guitars and drums; however, the megachurches still used these instruments at a significantly greater rate, as Table 9.3 shows.

Not all megachurches have abandoned a traditional worship format, however. A minority of churches in the "Program-Based" stream have worship services that could be considered "liturgical," "formal," and retaining some of the "high-church" characteristics of classic downtown, tall-steeple churches. In a few cases, megachurches in several of the streams offer venues characterized by more traditional forms of worship and music as one of the multiple service types. These "traditional" services employ time-honored hymns, recitation of creeds, and a quieter feel than the high-energy contemporary services in the main sanctuary. Often even those megachurches with loud, high-energy worship on Sunday have small prayer and reflection services at other times throughout the week to

---

**Table 9.3. Megachurch Worship Elements
Compared to Those of Churches of All Sizes.**

Congregations Using These Elements in Worship Services *Always* or *Often*	2005 Megachurch Study (percentage)	2005 Faith Communities Today Study (percentage)
Choir	53	56
Electric guitar or bass	93	33
Drums or other percussion	94	33
Visual projection	95	38

cater to members who prefer a quieter worship experience. Additionally, even the most contemporary worship services are beginning to build in periods of silent reflection and prayer.

We noted earlier that megachurch leaders see their services as joyful, exciting, inspirational, and thought-provoking. But is that how attendees see it as well? The answer is yes. When we ask long-term attendees of megachurches what drew them to the church, about half answer that it had something to do with the worship service style, as these quotes suggest:

> "The worship services just drew me in."
>
> "I felt the power of God when I was in the worship experience and when I left."
>
> "The quality in the worship service amazed me at first, but then I realized that this church had high quality in almost everything they do."

Judging more broadly from those who attended the largest Protestant churches in the U.S. Congregational Life Survey, 85 percent of these worshippers said they "always or usually" experience worship as inspirational, 84 percent as joyful, 86 percent as a sense of God's presence, and only 3 percent as boring or frustrating. Clearly the worship experience is essential to the growth of these organizations. Worship is perceived as high quality, inviting, and user-friendly. A megachurch may not have the best music compared to all other churches in an area. It may not have the hippest praise band, largest symphony orchestra, best sound system, or jazziest projection system. But it must have an adequate measure of all these elements to ensure quality and excellence in the service. Voices and instruments must be heard and the sound quality must be first-rate. Screens must be readable and the content well designed. The overall level of the worship experience must be perceived as excellent for the local context. The church is not only being judged in relation to other churches, but is also being compared to larger cultural criteria. In the minds of its attendees, the church's worship experience is measured against nightclubs, movies, television, and entertainment venues.

In addition to the worship experience, friendly faces and smiles are the order of the day. Ushers, greeters, informational booth attendants, parking lot attendants, and shop clerks are all trained to express the love of God in their assistance to those coming to the service. Congregants at large have also been exhorted and encouraged to reach out to other worshippers and to share with each other. Many of these churches place a high priority on physical touch with hugs, handshakes, and high-fives, actions that are modeled from the platform by musicians and worship leaders. This leads to a greater openness among the worshippers and a perceived sense of intimacy.

In our study, well over 50 percent of the churches describe their worship services as "informal." This is a description not only of the casual attire, but also of the attitudes of the worship leaders. At the same time, a large number of these churches also describe themselves as like a "close-knit family." In the 2005 study, 72 percent of megachurches agreed somewhat or strongly to this, while in all the FACT 2005 churches 90 percent agreed at these levels. While this attitude is significantly greater at the smaller churches in various studies, the presence of such an attitude at any gathering of thousands is surprising.

Megachurch worship styles are continually evolving. In the 2005 megachurch survey, a majority of the churches expressed a willingness to change their worship service. Only 15 percent of the churches say their format or style has not changed at all in the past five years. On the other hand, almost 60 percent said one or more of their weekend services has changed "some" or "a lot." These churches were also significantly more likely than smaller churches in both the 2000 and 2005 studies to say they were "willing to change to meet new challenges" and that they "welcomed innovation and change." Further exploration of the data showed that those megachurches growing most quickly were also the ones most likely to report they were embracing change.

The quality, informality, and friendliness of the worship services, however, do not fully explain how these churches grow to megasize or why most of them continue to expand. We feel that quality worship is crucial but not the only explanation. While worship may be the "front door" into a megachurch, there are equally significant side doors into the life of the church.

How Do Megachurches Grow?

Remember that megachurches don't start with a worship service of over two thousand people. Though some have grown quickly past that attendance level, we have yet to hear of one that started with two thousand on its first Sunday. (We probably will after the publication of this book, though.) The bottom line for megachurches is that they attract and retain more people over time than other churches. Worship and evangelism are factors directly related to this growth. The enthusiasm that attendees have about their church's worship is a key reason as well. At the same time, the complete answer to how these churches grow is multifaceted and complex. We can only begin to suggest some of the significant factors in this dynamic.

Outreach and evangelism are obviously key factors in a megachurch's growth, but this is a much less straightforward dynamic than one might think. Fifty-eight percent of megachurches claim that evangelism is a key activity for them (compared to 39 percent of all Faith Community Today 2005 congregations), and an additional 44 percent claim that it is a minor activity. In Table 9.4, it is evident that almost all megachurches (93 percent) encourage members to witness to others about their faith, but so do 90 percent of the congregations in the Faith Communities Today (FACT) 2005 study. Nearly every megachurch (94 percent) claims to encourage its members to invite others to worship, but again, so do almost all FACT 2005 churches (95 percent).

Megachurches take multiple approaches to outreach, but so do churches of all sizes. The megachurches offer more outreach programs in some areas than other size churches but these few differences are not statistically significant in explaining megachurch growth. Growth is not directly about the number or type of advertisements and outreach programs offered, although obviously any growing church will have them.

Table 9.4. Megachurch Outreach Elements
Compared with Those of Churches of All Sizes.

Congregations Reporting Using These Outreach Efforts in the Past Twelve Months	2005 Megachurch Study (percentage)	2005 Faith Communities Today Study (percentage)
Advertised on radio, on TV, or in newspapers	75	70
Mailed or distributed newsletter, letters, or flyers	77	67
Established or maintained a Web site	96	59
Developed a plan to recruit new members	60	52
Contacted people who recently moved into the area	41	48
Encouraged members to tell others about their faith	93	90
Encouraged members to invite others to worship	94	95
Sponsored a program or an event to attract visitors	84	67

Likewise, an important part of an evangelistic effort is how a church contacts its visitors after they attend a service. Not surprisingly, the megachurches follow up with first-timers quite a bit, but again so do other churches. In fact, smaller churches in both the 2000 and 2005 studies did a significantly better job of contacting visitors by personal visits. Table 9.5 shows that almost twice as many churches of all sizes in the FACT 2005 study did personal follow-up visits when compared with the megachurches. Interestingly, much larger percentages of megachurches contacted first-time visitors by passive means such as mail, phone, and e-mail than did all the congregations in the FACT 2005 study.

Megachurches embraced these less invasive ways to get in touch with visitors, rather than the face-to-face personal contact method often adopted by smaller churches. In part, this is in keeping with the perceived desire of visitors to remain somewhat anonymous and interact with the church on their own terms.

Another significant variable in the recruitment equation at mega-churches is the evangelistic activity of the congregational participants. When asked the question, "To what extent are your congregation's members recruiting other members?" 47 percent of megachurches said "a lot," and 38 percent reported "some" were active in this. Taken together, that means 85 percent of these churches report their members are engaged in significant outreach efforts. This pattern doesn't seem overly dramatic until these scores are compared with other congregations. Of the Faith Communities Today 2005 churches, only 14 percent said that their members are involved in recruiting "a lot." As noted in Table 9.4, these congregations said they encourage members to tell others about the faith and invite them to worship at a slightly greater rate than the megachurches did, but their attendees are seen by church leaders as doing less recruiting than megachurch attendees. The percentage of other churches with members engaged in "some" recruitment is

Table 9.5. Megachurch Follow-Up Elements
Compared with Those of Churches of All Sizes.

Congregations Indicating That They Use the Following Methods to Contact Visitors	2005 Megachurch Study (percentage)	2005 Faith Communities Today Study (percentage)
Mail	77	62
Phone	70	48
E-mail	38	19
Personal visit	29	45

about the same as for megachurches. However, when one looks at the percentage of churches that say their members are doing only "a little" recruitment, one sees another major difference: 14 percent of the megachurches said their members were slightly involved, but 42 percent of the FACT 2005 congregations reported their members at this marginal level. This difference between these groups of churches in how involved the participants are in recruiting is staggering.

When one compares the megachurches, not to smaller churches, but among themselves, an identical pattern unfolds. Those megachurches in the 2005 survey that reported the greatest levels of growth over the past five years also had the highest rates of members involved in recruitment.

Statistical analysis of the differing rates of growth among the megachurches yielded three significant findings: First, as we see in Table 9.6, the megachurches with the greatest percentage of five-year growth claimed the highest percentage of members who were involved "a lot" in recruitment. Second, the fastest-growing megachurches had the highest rates of worship described as "informal." Finally, the megachurches that grew the most rapidly also were most likely to describe their worship services as "exciting"—with this variable being the most powerful predictor of how rapidly an individual megachurch would grow over the five-year period.

Taken together, these three findings point to perhaps the most important and most often unacknowledged growth dynamic at these churches. The worship is perceived as exciting and informal, the attendees feel optimistic about the church's future because it is growing and successful, and their spiritual lives are fulfilling as they learn and act out their faith in ministry. These multiple dimensions of the committed attendee's intense satisfaction with the church create such excitement in them that they want to tell others; they are highly motivated to engage in active recruitment out of an intrinsic desire to express this excitement and satisfaction. They want to share the good news about the church and about what God is doing in their lives. While this sounds rather obvious, since church growth is nearly always derived from personal networks and word of mouth, it clearly is not happening in many churches. According to our data, it is happening in megachurches and to an even greater extent in the megachurches that are growing the fastest.

There is yet one other ingredient in this megachurch recipe for successful evangelistic outreach. It isn't enough to have your members bringing in new people if they just wander away in a few weeks because they haven't made any connections to the congregation. Megachurches excel at creating intentional efforts and planned procedures to help the interested newcomer become integrated into the church. There is a considerable

Table 9.6. Megachurch Member Recruiting and Growth Rates.

Megachurches, by Five-Year Growth Rate

Extent to Which Members Are Involved in Recruiting New Members	No Growth or Decline (percentage)	1 to 20 Percent Growth	21 to 50 Percent Growth	51 to 100 Percent Growth	More than 100 Percent Growth
Not at all	6.5	1.8	3.3	2.4	1.2
A little	32.3	21.8	9.9	14.3	7.1
Some	41.9	40.0	42.9	33.3	27.1
A lot	19.4	36.4	44.0	50.0	64.7

Table 9.7. Megachurch Follow-Up Practices Compared with Those of Churches of All Sizes.

Congregations Indicating That They Use the Following Methods to Integrate Interested Newcomers into the Congregation	2005 Megachurch Study (percentage)	2005 Faith Communities Today Study (percentage)
Designate people to extend hospitality to newcomers	58	22
Provide orientation class for new members	78	45
Invite newcomers to participate in a fellowship or other small group	88	64
Invite new people to volunteer to serve in the church or community	69	58

difference between the megachurches and other Faith Communities Today 2005 churches in this area. We address this characteristic in other chapters related to the numbers and types of small groups and specialized ministries, but the figures in Table 9.7 clearly show more megachurches are actively engaged in these efforts than other congregations.

The megachurches excel at creating the structures and programs that help new people become incorporated into the church rather than drift away, at least at higher rates than other churches. Additionally, these megachurches have more to offer in terms of programs and ministries, activities and fellowship groups. They make more effort to get a wide variety of people involved in the life of the church. This is much easier for these large churches since they also have a greater variety of groups and activities in which folks can get involved.

At the same time, nearly every megachurch will confess that they could retain people better. It is easy for new people to attend and then slip out the revolving back door. The leadership knows it happens too often. They are well aware exactly how many people visit, attend regularly, go through new members classes, and become involved only to drift away within six months to a year. And yet the data show these churches are growing because they invite, welcome, and attempt to incorporate their new people significantly better than most other congregations.

In addition to the megachurches' and their members' active involvement in evangelism and the integration of newcomers, there is yet another key ingredient to their evangelistic success. Like many things at the megachurch, evangelism really begins with the vision and passion of the pastor. In our experience, we find that those churches that have grown to megaproportions in a short period of time are led by senior pastors who have a personal passion, desire, and call to evangelism. Seeing more people meet and make an initial commitment to faith in Jesus Christ is the driving force in their lives. These pastors are concerned with discipleship, nurture, equipping, or other facets of the faith, but their zeal is to share the good news with others. The end goal for these pastors, almost every week, is to present a gospel message of redemption to as many people as possible. This passion isn't the pastor's alone; they communicate it actively to the attendees. The passion is also embedded in the ways the church as a whole responds to people who show a strong interest in participating. Then the congregation and leadership work hard to plan ways for the newcomer to be integrated into the life of the church.

Not long ago, Dave interviewed a senior pastor who planted a church in 1995 that grew to over ten thousand people in ten short years. The church currently has two Saturday evening services, two Sunday morning services, and multiple site locations in their area. He told Dave, "By five o'clock each Sunday evening, I get a call with a report of three critical numbers that help me gauge the day. They tell me the total number of people in worship services that day. They tell me the total number of people that said 'yes' to Jesus that day. And they tell me the total offering received during the services." In this church's tradition, a person is encouraged to go to a "yes table" in the worship venue to indicate that they want to know more about beginning a relationship with Jesus. This pastor feels that the number who say "yes" to following Christ is one of the biggest keys to keeping the church growing and healthy. This number is also reported in staff meetings each week. We have heard this story over and over with slight variations. The critical numbers vary, but fast-growth pastors generally want to know the number of those making serious inquiries about faith in Christ each week.

Even those megachurch pastors who do not have a personal gift for evangelism tend to have a sense of how many persons are making first-time commitments to Christ, though they may not track the number each week. In the conversation with these pastors, they can immediately recall how many commitments were made in the past month or the past year at their churches.

This emphasis on evangelism flows through the senior pastor to staff and to the attendees. But in our view, this passionate person-to-person evangelistic emphasis is one of the most important factors in megachurch growth. Some churches organize special weekend services designed to share Christ with those who are unbelievers. An excerpt from megachurch pastor Perry Noble's blog of September 26, 2006, exemplifies this passion. Perry is the pastor of New Spring Church in Anderson, South Carolina:

What we saw Sunday . . . it's NOT NORMAL!!! The e-mails we received yesterday blew us all away. There was a single mom who said she had contemplated suicide on Saturday night because she felt so hopeless . . . but didn't go through with it and so she got up on Sunday and came to church because a friend invited her . . . and she AND her daughter both accepted Christ.

There was a lady who told us that for the past eleven years her husband would not even say the name of Jesus . . . but on Sunday he walked forward and asked Jesus to come into his life.

There was the former atheist (notice I said former) who was here the week before and wanted to come back this week just to hear the message . . . yeah . . . he's not an atheist any longer! He received Jesus!

But folks—we can't sit back now and say "whew!" We saw this past Sunday what happens when we get passionate about our friends and family that do not know Christ. And there are STILL people out there that are one conversation, one invitation away from coming to church—hearing about Christ—and completely committing their life to Him.

Oh yeah . . . this Sunday—uh yeah, IT IS GOING TO BE JUST AS AMAZING! I promise you that this Sunday you will see something happen that 99.9 percent of you have NEVER seen take place . . . and that goes for those who grew up in church as well as those who are from an unchurched background. Pray hard . . . and if you have friends and family members that do not know Christ—GET THEM HERE![3]

This excerpt represents several things: first, the drive of those megachurch pastors with the gift of evangelism; second, the programming of special days specifically designed for evangelism; third, the evangelistic fervor and excitement that is being transmitted to the members, and the encouragement to get out and tell others about the wonderful things that are happening in the church; and finally, the church's continual contact with those who have received Christ and had their lives changed.

Calvary Church in Westlake Village, California, is housed in a former defense factory north of Los Angeles, just off Highway 101. Prior to this, worship services were held in a converted industrial warehouse. Though the space was small, the church made the most of it. In the years before they moved to their new space, the senior pastor encouraged attendees to make a list of those people in their family and friendship networks for whom they were regularly praying so that the attendee could share the good news of Jesus. He asked them to take a permanent marker and write the first names of those persons on a wall inside the entrance. Then over time, as those people either professed faith in Christ at the church or were found to have made a commitment in another faith setting, the member was encouraged to mark through the person's name.

The wall at this church had thousands of names on it, but more than half of them had a line through them. As the church began the process of moving to the new location, current members felt greater urgency to reach out to potential members. A video was made that shared the story of many of those people whose names were once "on the wall" and who had made a life-changing faith commitment. When the church did move to the larger new facility, they brought a small segment of the wall with them to the new building to remind them of those commitments. This type of physical reminder, be it a public wall or a personal pocket card completed with the name of a person being prayed for tucked into a Bible, is common in many megachurches.

Other Outreach Efforts

While we feel the person-to-person outreach efforts are a significant driving force behind the growth of these large churches, they do not ignore other outreach methods. A few megachurches are known for wide-scale media blitzes, complete with billboard, direct mail, and companion Web sites focused on a particular message. One of the more prominent campaigns in 2006 was conducted by Granger Community Church near South Bend, Indiana. This campaign was oriented around the image of four bare feet underneath a sheet with the title "My Lame Sex Life." The series of weekend services was intended to address the Bible's teaching about sex. These campaigns also utilize support materials such as large-format postcards, business card computer disks with audio and video invitations, and customizable e-mail "e-vites" that members can e-mail to friends. While these types of media campaign have increased in recent years, they are not widely utilized by the majority of megachurches.

Similarly, while many of the megachurches have small-scale radio programs and cable television broadcasts, not all do televangelism. Megachurches often do use basic advertising on these outlets as well as in newspapers (75 percent claim to do so). Some have confused the 30 to 40 percent of ministries that are driven by widespread radio and television ministries with the entire Megachurch movement. These ministries are certainly prominent and tend to have pastors who dominate the headlines, but they are in the minority.

The use of Web-based technologies to share the sermons and other teaching components with attendees and nonattendees has exploded in recent years. They are replacing the formerly ubiquitous tape- and CD-based sermon series. When asked about digitally recorded files being made available on their Web sites or on a download service such as Apple's iTunes, 83 percent of a small sample of megachurch Webmasters said they did so in 2005. A spot check of various megachurch Web sites shows it is hard to find one that does not have these electronic sermon files available. In addition, 31 percent of the churches in our megachurch Webmaster survey are now offering video files of primary messages on the Web in real time, as well as archival footage.

Ninety-six percent of the megachurches maintain a Web site about their church. While many of these sites seem simple in design, they are effective in giving basic information about the church's ministry and programs so that those seeking a church can learn more in a nonthreatening way. Web sites are now a requirement for a church, not a luxury. Recent analysis of the Faith Communities Today 2005 data showed that having a Web site was strongly correlated to the most rapidly growing churches of all sizes.[4] About 15 percent of the pastors, and almost all in the New Wave–type megachurches, post comments on a blog several times a week as an extra level of communication aimed at members and interested nonmembers.[5]

At some megachurches, low-key evangelistic programs are used to target special age or interest groups. These include sports programs for all ages that are designed to be less competitive than many public recreation programs and include elements of faith sharing. These programs have proven highly popular for many churches and offer yet another avenue in the life of the congregation.

After all of this chapter's information and argument, it is partly true that megachurches grow because of the show—at least somewhat. That is the interesting thing about these large churches; they are complex. No one formula could be created that would provide an easy answer about how megachurches grow, and certainly there is no easy "three-step process" by which a small church can quickly become a megachurch. The one dynamic that none of us have figured out is just how or why between two churches with similar programs, locations, fervent pastors, and committed members, one grows and becomes a megachurch and the other doesn't. Perhaps God and the Holy Spirit are involved in this more than we know.

We also are speaking from only one side of the conversation when we talk about how these churches grow. We are looking at the data and processes from the side of the church organization—and hopefully we have analyzed those dynamics to bring some clarity to what the church, its pastor, and members do to promote growth. However, we have little representative information about the other side of this growth dynamic—the individuals who come, those who stay, and those who don't stay. We are missing nuanced, in-depth interviews with many hundreds and thousands of potential, first-time, and new participants to find out why they came, what their needs were, what they were looking for in a church, and why they chose this church, not just over smaller ones but also over other large ones in the area. Also absent are conversations with long-time attendees to learn what they are getting out of worship, why they stay, and why they are committed at different levels and yet are still attending. And we need even longer conversations with those who come for a while, participate, and then drift away to understand why they leave, don't connect, or choose to go elsewhere. Until we have this rich set of information about a megachurch, the complete picture of what causes them to grow will remain a bit of a mystery.

The dynamics of church growth is a complex phenomenon—don't ever let a consultant or researcher tell you otherwise. None of us truly know what is going on ... well, except perhaps God. The rest of us only see through a glass darkly.

○

Applying What You Have Read

This chapter laid out some of the more pronounced differences between megachurches and churches of other sizes. We want you to focus on two key areas in the chapter as possibilities for your church.

The first area is the worship service. We know that changes in worship service practices are always hard on existing attendees. This is especially true when changing the music or altering the visual appearance of the worship space. The survey results between megachurches and other churches show that visual projection, drums, and the use of electric guitar or bass clearly illustrate the dramatic differences between the two. We are not suggesting that the use of these elements causes growth, but it is clear that megachurches do use these elements. Further, megachurch worship is characterized as significantly "inspirational," "joyful," and "filled with a sense of God's presence." As you are planning the worship experience, incorporate elements from your own tradition but consider ways to express these elements in a joyful and spontaneous manner.

It might be possible to start an entirely new worship service incorporating the practices mentioned above. If you choose to go in this direction, we would recommend that you find individuals both within your church and prospective attendees to work with you in planning for this service. It is possible to gradually move into this type of service by starting with a monthly, then biweekly gathering before moving to a weekly worship service.

The second area we call "simple tools and practices." These are low-cost ways in which megachurches are clearly distinct from other size churches, but that smaller churches should be able to apply to their daily functioning.

The first simple tool is a Web site. For any organization, a Web site has become like a phone listing. Even a simple Web site can inform others about your church, its worship times, and its ministries. A church does not need the fanciest or the most technologically advanced site. The site needs to have current information, but "current" does not mean that it has to be updated daily or weekly. Often this can be done by a volunteer in your church or within your church's extended family. Likewise, there are several online Web services designed for churches to help set up simple Web sites. The Web site that supports this book— www.megachurchmyths.com—provides several links that will help in creating a site for your church. Above all, make sure that whatever site you create reflects your congregation's identity and vision.

The second tool is the use of personal invitation by current attendees to prospective visitors. An emphasis on evangelism is more than just telling attendees to bring others to church, more than just learning the "Four Spiritual Laws" or the "Roman Road." Attendees have to want to bring others; they must be excited about their church and about being a Christian and want to share the experience with other people. If they do not exhibit such enthusiasm, why don't they?

A third tool or practice involves following up on people who visit your church and express an interest in continuing to come. In the surveys of megachurches and all churches, there is a clear difference in the frequency of follow-up practices in contacting interested people by mail, phone, and e-mail. All three of these approaches are low-cost activities for any church and less invasive for the potential new member.

The fourth practice involves intentionally integrating those people who visit and are interested in your church. When compared with other churches, megachurches are more than twice as likely to designate a team to extend hospitality to new attendees. Additionally, they are more likely to offer special orientation classes for new members, invite them to participate in a small group, and invite new people to serve in the church or on a community service project. Again, these are low-cost practices and tools that can be applied by any church no matter what your size.

○ How often each day do you use the Web to find times, information, and weather? If you don't have a Web presence for your church, you may not be found by those who are looking for a church home.

○ When was the last time you invited, or were challenged to invite, others to church?

○ If you enjoy your church and are spiritually satisfied there, what keeps you from wanting others to join you at this church?

○ Make a list of the ways your church responds to and follows up on visitors. Would you like to receive the attention or lack of it that your church gives to potential new members?

○ If someone expresses an interest in joining the church or makes a commitment for Christ, what mechanisms does your church have in place to help this person be integrated into the life of the congregation? How can they learn about what the church stands for and what the basic tenets of Christianity are?

10

"THE MEGACHURCH MOVEMENT IS DYING—YOUNG PEOPLE HATE THESE CHURCHES"

I'm becoming convinced that the brief reign of the megachurch as we know it (2,000-plus in worship) will begin to wane over the next twenty years. Not that megachurches will disappear, but two things will begin to happen. We will see fewer of them, and the largest ones will be "cyberchurches."[1]

Ironically, the very things that may attract baby boomers to megachurches are the very things that can turn off people in their late teens, 20s and early 30s. Megachurches that have good youth programs "hold on to their young people better,"
Gibbs [Eddie Gibbs, a professor at Fuller Theological Seminary in Pasadena, California] says. "But, for the unchurched youngsters, [megachurches] are a real turnoff. They don't like the megachurch. They don't like its entertainment or its professionalism. They don't like its programmatic emphasis. They don't like to be anonymous."[2]

UNLIKE SOME OF OUR OTHER MYTHS, pastors, church consultants, and Christian commentators often voice this one. They claim the megachurch era has ended—or will soon. Sure, megachurches still exist, they say, but they are dinosaurs and will slowly die off as the baby-boom generation ages. This is because the younger generations do not desire the same experiences in worship that the megachurch offers. Some of these leaders want to see this prophecy fulfilled. They serve in smaller churches and have a strongly held belief that megachurch attendance harms a person spiritually. Others may consult in larger churches, but have grown discontented with some of the practices they see in the megachurches. Many watch movements such as the "emerging church" and "house church" developments and suggest these characterize the desires of all later generations. Some critics believe that the megachurch is nothing more than a fad, a flash-in-the-pan phenomenon, which currently receives a lot of attention but eventually will lose the public's interest. This is the heart of this myth.

A careful look at our survey data and the megachurches themselves suggests a much different conclusion. We see the numbers of megachurches increasing in each of the last four decades. This is true for the number of churches, the overall size of the largest ones, and the speed at which the newest ones are growing. We have observed the continued adaptation of this movement, especially in the last decade or two, to reach new generations and devise new forms of ministry for the future. The social factors that produced the current generation of megachurches are still in place. They will continue to sustain the existing ones and facilitate the growth of new ones into the future. If megachurches did not just appear in relation to the boomer culture, but in relation to organizational and cultural changes in the institutions of American society themselves, then we expect these churches to be around at least until the societal characteristics that created them change. Finally, as a result of both the cultural continuity and the strategic adaptations taking place, we observe many young people worshipping at these churches, from children to young adults. While we wholeheartedly agree that the megachurch form is not for everyone, clearly there are large numbers of young adults in these churches—perhaps in greater percentages than in any other congregational size or form.

More Than Ever

The raw number of megachurches has grown tremendously over the past few decades. Some reports have the number growing from the low teens in the early 1960s to around 310 in 1990 to nearly 1,250 in 2007. By the latest tracking, we can see a fairly constant growth rate in both the number of these churches and the number of Americans who are choosing them.

In the 1960s and 1970s, there may have been a few more megachurches than were actually mentioned in press reports, historical accounts, and denominational rosters. Because these historic megachurches would have been isolated phenomena scattered throughout the country, some may have been missed. Additionally, there were almost no interactions between denominational and nondenominational churches, so information about certain independent and also nonwhite congregations might not have been widely available to scholars. The early forerunners of the phenomenon may have been undercounted, but it is not likely that the figure is off by more than a few churches.

In recent years, as these churches have become more common and more in the media's eye, it is much harder for megachurches to go unnoticed. In 2005, we worked diligently to find all the megachurches we could. After publishing the revised list to the Web site of the Hartford Institute for Religion Research, we received dozens of suggestions of additional megachurches, as well as many helpful corrections regarding those we had on the list. Over a year later, we still receive several e-mail nominations of churches to add to our list each month. On examination, a few of these have been megasized for some time and just escaped our attention, but many others recently crossed the two-thousand mark in attendance.

Not only are there a greater number of megachurches, but the largest ones have continued to grow larger. A few decades ago, only a handful would have been over ten thousand, and now sixty or more claim that size. The largest megachurch in the United States now reports an attendance of well above thirty thousand. Another interesting finding related to the growth of these massive churches in our 2005 study can be seen in Table 10.1. The newest churches are not only reaching megaproportions more quickly, they are also growing larger on average than those founded in other historical periods.

As denominational and mainstream press outlets have increasingly focused on the stories of megachurches, they are now seen as commonplace and almost "normal" to church observers. For many communities, megachurch pastors have assumed the role of public religious

---

Table 10.1. Megachurch Growth and Attendance by Founding Period.

Founding Date	Average Growth in Five Years (percentage)	Average 2005 Attendance	Median 2005 Attendance
Before 1946	47	3,158	2,600
1946–1970	56	3,734	2,700
1971–1990	89	3,544	3,000
1991–2005	228	4,290	3,440

spokesperson that was formerly filled by leaders of ministerial associations and local ecumenical groups or denominational executives. We are not arguing that megachurches are entirely commonplace throughout the country, but their notability and widespread dispersion across most of the United States doesn't make them seem so unusual and abnormal anymore.

With the growing acceptance of megachurches as a valid expression of American church life, more leaders and churches have begun to believe that they too can reach megaproportions. When smaller churches or interested pastors adopt the megachurch mental model, they often take practical steps that increase the likelihood that they will indeed grow larger. Some of these practical steps include land selection (buying larger rather than smaller plots), building design (constructing adaptable buildings with explicit plans for future expansion designed in stages of facility improvements), staffing (preparing staffing patterns for a target number of persons greater than current attendance), programming (planning worship times and schedules to accommodate future needs), and other items based on their vision of the future. It is now common for a brand-new church plant, not just the fast-growing one-thousand-person church, to factor these issues and others into their formal and informal planning systems. In doing so, this adjusted church planning enables a congregation to quickly move up to the two-thousand-attendee level.

Adaptation to New Generations

The fantastic growth of the early megachurches was paralleled by the coming of age of the baby-boom generation. As that generation pushed through the life cycle, they influenced every organizational form they encountered. It is no surprise that baby-boom generation pastors overwhelmingly lead the current crop of megachurches. These pastors intuitively understood their generation and knew what appealed to them. Because of this characteristic, some of those in later generations, born after 1964, have been most vocal in saying that their generation will not be a part of the Megachurch movement.

Perhaps some of the strongest and most visible critiques of megachurches come from younger leaders who are actively planting churches designed to reach today's young adults. Many of these leaders claim that today's young people are turned off by megachurches. Many have used the term *Emergent* to explain, among other things, their critique of the Megachurch movement. In their view, megachurches are too prepackaged, slick, and artificial. The music, worship, preaching, programming, and other components of these churches are criticized as being too consumer-oriented.

In this way, these Emergent leaders are similar to more conservative traditionalists who desire a return to formal, conventional, and even high-liturgical formats. Emergent pastors and churches are rediscovering some of the great truths and wonders of reflective worship that are common among some of these traditionalists. These leaders have their doubts about megachurches, which seemingly take the wonder and mystery out of the faith. The Emergent proponents dislike the showiness of megachurch worship. They are not crazy about the lighting, special effects, and so on. They equate megachurches with all the ills of suburbia and claim that future generations will not want to live in suburbia or attend a church of this type. We agree with some of these critiques, but at the same time this "future" is far from a current reality.

What is most interesting is that many of these Emergent leaders have roots in megachurches. Some were staff pastors at very large churches. A few older Emergent leaders are actually pastors of megachurches themselves. Some grew up in the suburban megachurch context and are now planting new churches to reach their generation.[3] They are changing the design of church to fit the new generation, and many of these congregations are growing rapidly, with several of them having reached megachurch proportions. We will say more about those later in this chapter.

Our perspective differs considerably from these critics' view of both the present and the future. First, many of the issues of identity, the connection to God, and an appropriate response to God's calling are the same issues that were faced by the baby-boom pastors as they attempted to start or lead existing churches populated by the rebellious boomers of the 1960s and 1970s. The language may be slightly different, but the issues have not changed that much. The next generation may come up with unique solutions and ways of articulating new perspectives, but the differences are in degree, not in kind.

An illustrative example from among the megachurches in Orange County, California, helps to make this case. Mariners Church, a boomer-oriented church in Newport Beach, actually helped to plant Rock Harbor Church nearby almost ten years ago. It was hoped that Rock Harbor could reach a new, younger group of people in a dynamic way. Both churches continue to grow and have large numbers of young adults. Rock Harbor has a majority of attendees under the age of thirty-five and talks about its faith journey vision in terms of "joining the revolution of Jesus." Mariners Church, on the other hand, describes its faith vision as "a step of commitment to live a Christ-centered life." The foundational theologies of both churches are the same. The articulation of those beliefs, however, attempts to appeal to different groups of people in the same geographical area.

While we agree that some megachurches have specific programs designed to target the baby-boom generation and thus will not be as attractive to younger adults, we also see that some megachurches have adapted tremendously to meet their needs, redesigning or reinventing themselves. We have watched some of these baby-boomer megachurches start worship services specifically targeting younger people and develop specialized ministries with a younger set of staff. These churches are flourishing.

One such example is McLean Bible Church, a thriving nondenominational megachurch located in the Virginia suburb of McLean near Washington, D.C. Senior pastor Lon Solomon has led the church for the past twenty-six years to its present ten thousand–plus size with the vision "to impact secular Washington, D.C., with the message of Jesus Christ!" The church has a total of fifty-one acres that include a former National Wildlife Federation property, a 280,000-square-foot multistory building, and a parking deck that holds twenty-five hundred cars. The main auditorium seats twenty-four hundred people, and the campus has a spacious lobby, gym, youth center, community room, adult classrooms, and creative arts space. It hosts four contemporary services on Saturday and Sunday and is often full of adults and families.

However, Sunday evenings at 5:30 and 7:30 P.M., McLean undergoes a metamorphosis and transforms itself into Frontline. Same church, worship space, and vision, but a radically different approach and a much younger congregation. These two evening services constitute a church-within-a-church whose focus is on young adults from age eighteen to thirty-five. Between one thousand and two thousand young adults attend each gathering. And these worship services are nothing like their parents' services.

The auditorium is nearly pitch black as one walks in, illuminated only by the timer playing on three huge projection screens counting down to the start of the service. In the background, recorded contemporary music is playing. The people gathered there are informally dressed, with equal numbers of males and females, individuals, couples, and small groups, and seemingly serious about their faith. The majority are white, but about 20 percent of the crowd are a mix of Asian, Hispanic, and African American persons. As the service starts, the spotlights focus on a young worship team with a stage band singing loud rock praise music accompanied by drums, electric guitar, and keyboard. The screens project the lyrics interspersed with cutaways of the singers and musicians. Throughout the praise portion of the service, fifteen hundred young people sway and sing along with the music.

After about forty minutes of singing, announcements, a low-key offering, and prayers, Todd Phillips, a thirty-something pastor of Frontline for the past few years, addresses the congregation in an informal, laid-back but sincere, conversational tone. He speaks from Exodus 17 relating it to the congregation, drawing practical applications for the group's situation. After about seventy-five minutes, with little fanfare, the service concludes with a prayer led by Pastor Todd. Many of the youth and young adults mill around the massive lobby after the service. Plans are being made for dinner, group meetings, and service projects for the week ahead. A first-time visitors' group of about fifty people meet and are introduced to the associate pastors, group leaders, and small group options. During this gathering, an evening trip is organized to have dinner at a local restaurant. Much of the conversation in the visitor orientation and later during dinner revolves around small group involvement and social and service ministries that folks can get involved in. It is clear from the leadership that Frontline is distinct from McLean, obviously in terms of age, but also both in worship style and options for social and service involvement. This is a megachurch within a megachurch, but one for a different generation.

In addition to this type of youth-oriented worship, there is an explosion of what we have called the New Wave or Re-Envisioned megachurches that are being established as independent churches and led by pastors of the post-1964 generation. Many of these churches have grown quickly to megasize. While the music may be louder and more diverse, the preaching and teaching more straightforward, and the programming somewhat simpler, the characteristics of these churches place them solidly in the broad river of the Megachurch movement. As one talks with these lead or senior pastors about the challenges they face personally and within their churches, they articulate problems similar to those that their baby boomer counterparts had twenty years ago. Some of these churches were planted and nurtured, received funding and administrative support, and were mentored in their development by existing megachurches. Overall, megachurches throughout the country have become adept at helping to plant and support other megachurches.

Pastors within the Emergent stream of American churches will cringe and disagree with what we are about to say. While we do see some qualitative differences in approach and emphasis from those who claim to be Emergent, nevertheless, as these leaders start families and begin to age, many of their views will begin to soften and change. The Emergent pastors will be forced to address child care, children's programs, and other issues relating to young families in a different way. Some of these idealists may move subtly away from their current strongly held views and create solutions and adaptations that parallel past generations' efforts.

Leadership Network has been privileged to work with both groups of pastors in its history. Over ten years ago, the Network helped to facilitate some early conversations among younger pastors. This group of clergy had a different view of the future of American church life, and Leadership Network actively encouraged them to pursue their vision. About half of those pastors have held fast to their vision and now lead midsized churches in cities around the country. These churches regularly receive coverage from secular and religious press. The other half of this group has grown larger, megasized churches. These churches are different from their mega predecessors, but not wildly dissimilar. The movement has adapted to the needs of the generation and to the necessities of a large organizational form.

A Continuity of Growth Factor Dynamics

Many of the factors in the culture that enabled the rapid growth of megachurches over the past decades and encouraged their acceptance by millions within the current generations are still in place. It is likely that these organizations will continue to appeal to new generations. The critics tend to ignore these cultural factors in their analysis of the future. The rapid increase of megachurches since the 1970s did not just take place in relation to the boomer culture or because there were more gifted preachers, but this was also in response to organizational changes in the institutions of American society. We expect these churches to be around at least until the societal characteristics that created them change dramatically. The continuity of these primary factors shaping the American culture and landscape ensure that young people will continue to flow into megachurches.

The suburbs and exurbs are still growing, and they are filling with people who are thirty-five and younger. While many city centers and urban areas are also growing and being revitalized, the strongest growth in numbers of younger families tends to be in the suburbs and exurbs of sprawl cities. These former farmlands continue to be fertile soil for megachurches. Many new and transplanted residents in these areas are looking for social and personal connections. In such contexts, existing megachurches grow larger and brand-new churches can quickly grow to megachurch size, filled with young couples. Critics would say that young adults don't want to live in the sterile suburbs, but the numbers tell a different story. According to demographer Joel Kotkin, 85 percent of the population growth in America since 2000 has occurred in the suburbs. In addition, 51 percent of all Americans state their preference is to live in the suburbs, while only 13 percent prefer an urban environment. He suggests, "The preference for suburban-style living continues to be particularly strong among younger families."[4]

Children, youth, and young adults are growing up in a world of large organizations. Just as the baby boomers were socialized in larger elementary, high schools, and universities than their parents were, so too are their children and grandchildren. Schools, grocery stores, big box retailers, malls, theaters, corporations, and a seemingly endless list of organizations are large and flourishing, and they are still accepted by a majority of Americans. While some Americans long for simpler times and smaller organizations, mass society does not. We have no evidence that there is a mass movement of young adults toward small-scale schools and businesses, or a downsizing of other spheres of life. When large organizations feel normal to vast numbers of Americans, there are few internal objections to attending a high-quality megachurch.

Today's young adults, like their parents, tend to want the best of everything for their children. Responding to this demand, megachurches are well positioned to provide superior programming for children, youth, and young adults. Most megachurches continue to increase the number of people reached and nurtured throughout the child-rearing years by providing special-purpose spaces with programs for children, youth, and their parents. These places are perceived as high-quality, relevant, and safe places for parents to leave their children. In the U.S. Congregational Life survey, a full 50 percent of attendees of the largest Protestant churches reported being "very satisfied" and another 26 percent were "satisfied" with what their churches offered for children and youth. This is a tremendous selling point for megachurches.

Our point is that many of these wider cultural factors that make megachurches appealing have not changed dramatically. These factors have conditioned the soil in which the megachurches are rooted. We don't see the generational appeal of megachurches changing until some of the contextual climate undergoes a transformation. Hedging our bets, though, in the next chapter we will address some potential discontinuities that could alter this optimistic assessment.

Just Look at the Numbers

The biggest challenge to those who insist the Megachurch movement is dying is the data. Our Megachurch 2005 study shows that these churches have many young attendees. In 2000 and 2005, our survey asked the church to estimate how many adults under the age of thirty-five attended their church. In 2005, 47 percent of the churches indicated that 40 percent or more of attendees were in this age group, another 46 percent of the churches said that 21 to 40 percent of their congregation was composed of these younger persons. In the 2000 survey, the megachurches reported a near identical pattern. When the megachurches in the 2000 study were compared with a sample of smaller Protestant churches from the Faith Communities Today 2000 study, the larger churches had significantly higher rates of persons thirty-five and under in the congregation. These megachurches were also located in areas that had greater percentages of persons from eighteen to thirty-four and an overall younger population based on the 2000 census data.

Looking at the concentration of households with children under eighteen in megachurches, one can see a similar pattern of youthfulness. In the 2005 survey, 62 percent of megachurches claimed that 40 percent or more of their congregations were composed of families with kids. The 2000 survey showed 53 percent of churches with this level of families with children. And these youths are not just spectators, either. The 2000 study showed that 94 percent of megachurches had programs for teens and youth. The churches were also asked to estimate what extent their members' teenage children were involved in the religious life of the congregation. Twenty-seven percent reported their teens were connected to a "very great extent," and another 42 percent claimed their youth were involved to a "large extent." Only 3 percent of megachurches said teens were involved to a "slight extent," and none of them reported their teenagers were "not at all" involved.

Another point from our 2005 survey is worth considering. Those churches founded before 1946, and which have not relocated in the past ten years, have fewer young people and families than other age groups. Part of this might be a church life-cycle issue. There are still young people and younger families attending, serving, and leading, but the numbers are comparatively smaller than those of the new churches formed since 1995. For the third of the churches in the 2005 study that were started between 1946 and 1995, the congregation is a mixed bag of young and old congregants. Some of this diversity is location dependent and some is possibly conditioned by the age of the lead pastor. Certain senior pastors of churches with this profile are genuinely concerned that their churches might not continue to reach younger generations, and they have begun targeted ministries, such as Frontline mentioned earlier in this chapter. Others have planted daughter churches nearby, as Mariners Church did, specifically intended to reach younger families—and thereby avoid making drastic changes in the mother church. These churches tend to place a high value on being a church for all ages. Older pastors in this range are also beginning to worry about succession and have begun making plans to transition the church to younger leadership.

Churches begun since 1995 that have reached megachurch status are full of young adults, parents, and kids. The average age of the senior or lead pastor of these churches is thirty-eight. And even at this age, they are older than many of the congregants. These churches are in constant capital campaign mode in order to build or find the space to put everyone.

Some observers feel that many young adults in postmodern America are not going to choose to attend church anywhere, no matter what size the church. The majority of these people can be identified as the "nevers" in American religious life. They have never attended any church with any regularity, and so the assumption is that they will never be connected to a church. It is these folks that many of the Emergent churches attempt to target. But it is also a target of the newer megachurches not in the Emergent stream.

Other observers point to data about another group of believers who grew up in a church and make the transition out of high school and out of church, no matter what the size. The assumption is that many never find their way back, and there is much truth to this perception. It is one of the reasons that many churches have designed their message to say, "find your way back to God" through our church. The assumption is that young people were connected once and need to reconnect. Many of these places of reconnection are megachurches or churches that will become megachurches. Community Christian Church, a multisite megachurch in the western suburbs of Chicago, states that "Our mission is to help people find their way back to God by multiplying congregations, campuses and churches that Celebrate, Connect and Contribute to the dream of God." Since they started in 1988, the church has grown to over four thousand regular attendees in eight locations. The bulk of these attendees are under forty-five.

Clearly, some young adults connect or get reconnected to a smaller-scale faith community. Indeed, there is an indication that the emerging House Church movement is partly composed of young adults who left megachurches some years ago and now find their faith community in these fellowships or in simple churches that meet in homes.[5] Some people connect to a smaller church in order to intentionally avoid the megachurch's style and trappings. Some of these churches express this difference through the aesthetics of their worship and by having longer periods of reflection and prayer. Other congregations lean toward simpler music and dialogical preaching. Many of the leaders of these efforts state they are attempting to create an intentional counterwave to megachurch worship.[6]

We are for people going to church in whatever expression fits them. We never argue that the megachurch is the be-all and the end-all for every person who worships in a community of faith. However, megachurch critics are mistaken to believe that young adults do not or will never attend a megachurch. It just isn't so according to the data and our experiences.

○

Applying What You Have Read

Two key issues arise when churches address the issue of reaching younger generations. The first issue is the retention of young people already within the church. The often-heard comment, "Our youth are the future of this church" relies on the assumption that those who are raised in the church will be its future leaders. This is often not the case, especially in megachurches. It is very much a catch-22 situation. Some smaller churches in small communities can retain younger adults who grow up in the church through the strength of family ties and the settledness of small town life. In suburban, megachurch contexts where new housing is targeted for younger generations, young adults may remain in the general metropolitan area. However, it is just as likely that those who are raised in the church will move away from the general area for college and employment and will find other churches to attend. This leads to the second key issue: attracting newer generations of young adults to the church.

In our consulting experience, many church leaders in smaller congregations stress the first issue. Emerging megachurches stress the latter issue. Megachurch leaders want their post-high-school adults to stay connected and will build programs to solidify that connection. But they are also realists and know that many people in this group will move to other places to establish their own residence and new associations. Instead of grieving about this reality, they address it proactively and encourage their young adults to find places of worship and service wherever they go. Many times church leaders will suggest potential church homes in the selected regions. Numerous megachurches actively help launch new churches more in tune with younger generations to help retain and reach other young adults in the growth areas of their region.

So what is a church leader to do? First, face the reality that many young people who grew up in your church will not live in the area anymore.

There is a good chance you can connect to many of the younger people who do live in your area through family and friendship ties, but reaching large numbers has to come through more intentional processes. Do you know how many younger people live in your area? A quick check of census reports will give you some current estimates. Most pastors are surprised to discover that there are more young adults in their community than they thought!

The most likely younger persons to connect with quickly are those who have recently moved to the area. They have few community ties, are looking for connections, and need supportive people to help orient them to the neighborhood. Marketing service companies sell lists of names and addresses of new residents, and other companies can help design direct mail and other strategies aimed at raising awareness of your church. Remember that younger generations use the Internet to find new connections and services, so an informative Web site is also a priority. Most churches are not visible enough in their community for young adult newcomers to know that your church exists without advertising.

The next step is to intentionally design ministries and programs to reach younger generations. For some churches, this means starting an additional worship service targeting these prospective attendees. For others, the efforts might include ministries that help parents of young children or a community orientation. Our advice is to gather a group of newcomers in these age groups and ask them to help shape your church plan for reaching out to people like them.

For church leaders who seriously want to reach younger generations, we encourage you to connect with the leaders of the churches in your area who are successfully reaching younger adults and in humility ask to be mentored by them. This "reverse mentoring" approach pays dividends in many ways with both sets of church leaders, but when an older leader approaches a younger leader and asks for this mentoring it can be a very powerful moment.

Don't assume that you can reshape your church's leadership into something that resembles the younger church's leadership; that is not the point to being mentored. The point is to engage in a mutual learning experience in which the established church leader can learn to see the younger generations through the younger leader's eyes and understand the needs, concerns, and aspirations of these generations from their point of view. This will help the entire leadership of the existing church in making decisions for the future.

Finally, we encourage you to take the leadership team of your existing church to a church that is reaching many younger adults and observe with a friendly, uncritical eye. Encourage your team to ask the attendees why they have chosen that church. Ask them what two or three things your church could do to reach these generations. You won't be able to do them all. There are no magic bullets here.

WHAT MIGHT THE FUTURE HOLD?

WHAT DOES THE FUTURE HOLD for American megachurches? Predicting what is yet to come is always an imperfect and messy business. Some predictions turn out to be correct, and others turn out to be way off base. The first part of this chapter reflects on the future of events and issues already evident, also known as predictions based on continuity. Later, we delve more into predictions based on some discontinuous factors that don't currently present themselves.

This country is in the midst of a shift in religious practice, beliefs, and organizational forms, both inside institutional religious bodies and externally in the larger spiritual world. Many of these religious changes are in reaction to cultural and social changes that have taken place over the past fifty years. Some changes come from within the church community, and many of them come directly from megachurches.

There are clear reasons that these large churches are so appealing. They offer a form of organized religious life that responds to the needs of modern Americans. There is considerable resonance between what ordinary people in society value and what the megachurches have to offer. While this form of church isn't for everyone, for millions of Christians each week it is the way they worship God and experience the communion of the saints.

Megachurches will continue to be around for many more decades. The more than twelve hundred megachurches that currently exist show few signs of imminent collapse. Likewise, the pattern of increase in the numbers of megachurches over the past two decades suggests that many more very large congregations may come into existence in the first half of the twenty-first century. In nearly every sector of society, the trend continues toward large-scale societal forms. As members of society continue to be raised in and nurtured by these megainstitutional realities, it seems unlikely that the entire U.S. population will reject this church form, which has so much in common with the rest of our large-scale world.

Adaptation

Megachurches have proven to be excellent at developing new forms and methods to adapt to current realities that will continue to serve them well into the future. The model, however, does need to be continually challenged and encouraged to guard against the potential difficulties of borrowing too much from secular culture, giving members just what makes them feel good, being only about money, and being the big bully in the neighborhood, as well as many more potential traps.

The primary lessons to be gleaned from a study of megachurches are not necessarily theological or programmatic; rather, they are the common strategies that underlie the megachurches' ministry efforts. We are convinced that part of their success has been their ability to read and adapt to the changing patterns and cultural needs of contemporary society. This is the genius of megachurches. If congregations of all sizes and theologies are to remain relevant, they must learn this ability. All churches have to reach out to both current and potential members in ways that fit a changing social reality. Underlying the forms and structures of megachurches are assumptions about the context of modern America that ensure a fit between their programs and the needs of a contemporary world.

Already we see signs of such change. The Faith Communities Today 2005 survey showed that three-quarters of the national sample of congregations had changed the format or style of at least one of their worship services in the past five years. Megachurches seem to have the willingness and aptitude to try, fail, and abandon ideas that are not working and then try something else. Observing what is working in megachurches can aid other churches in their ministry development.

Simplified Structure

While we have described a complex array of ministries and involvements in megachurches, others are speculating that the next wave of innovation will come through simple churches and house churches. Although we see clear growth in house church movements, we don't expect them to gain the prominence that megachurches currently have.[1] However, we do see some trends that suggest that megachurches are moving in much simpler directions.

This shift among megachurches works in two ways. First, new church plants that are growing to megaproportions in short periods of time tend to have a much simpler structure than the previous generation of megachurches. This is expressed in fewer core programs with ministries flowing through worship celebrations and small groups. For example, many New Wave churches are not adding weekday children's, women's, or men's programs. They are delivering basic Bible teaching in the weekend services and through their small groups. They are also less likely to offer multiple programs during the day. Our survey even showed that the newest megachurches have the least number of staff and the lowest ratio of pastors and staff to attendees. While this simpler staffing pattern could just be a life-cycle phenomenon, where the churches become more complex as they age and get larger, many leaders of these churches are focused, at least for now, on simpler models.

The second way the trend toward simplicity shows up is when older megachurches mature and have become overgrown with organization and programs. The 2005 megachurch survey hinted at this phenomenon as well, showing that megachurches that were older and had gone through a senior pastor change were growing slowly or not at all and also had the most staff and the highest ratio of staff to attendees. We are seeing some churches begin the pruning process by ending many longtime programs and ministries. This process is painful at times for leaders and congregants, but it represents another way that megachurches are adapting to changing contexts and realities.

Melting Pot

The multiracial nature of many megachurches has been a surprise to many church observers. It reflects a change not just in congregational dynamics but also in housing patterns and the increasing pluralism of our society. Whereas residential areas were once quite segregated, they are now more integrated. Many of the megachurches are intentionally designing their approaches to reach the broadest range of residents in their community. While this seems to be most common in Anglo churches in suburbs that hire persons of other races in staff roles, urban church plants are also hiring multiracial staffs from the beginning and reaching a broad swath of city dwellers. Even in exurban and more rural areas, we find churches with significant minority participation. For example, many megachurches have begun Spanish-speaking ministries and services or launched Spanish-speaking churches as new plants. While this was formerly the case for select areas of the country, it is now widespread as Latino and Hispanic immigration has grown. A case in point is Marcus

Witt's Spanish service held on Sunday afternoon in the sanctuary of Joel Osteen's Lakewood Church. This service presently has over five thousand attendees and is among the largest Spanish-speaking worship services in the country. We fully expect that in the next decade many new Latino megachurches will arise not only in Florida, Texas, New York, and California but in other parts of the country as well.

Parallel with the rise of other ethnic groups in the United States, a number of megachurches representing ethnic communities have also emerged. Numerous churches led and populated by Korean Americans and Chinese Americans have reached megastatus in the past decade or two. Some Asian-born pastors have immigrated to the United States to build churches. A growing number of second-generation immigrant children are also starting churches designed to reach the crossover cultures represented by the assimilation into American ways and values.

Likewise, if we were writing this book a generation ago, even the African American megachurches would have looked radically different. At that time, most of the African American megachurches would have been classified as "urban." They would have been smaller, and their pastors would have had little name recognition outside their local community. Today, an African American megachurch is just as likely to be suburban as urban. Many of the largest megachurches in the country now fit this description, and pastors like T. D. Jakes and Creflo Dollar are national figures. Most of the power preachers in today's African American megachurches are suburban.

Continuing this ethnic expansion of megachurches, in the near future there will be an increase in the number of African-led churches addressing the spiritual needs of first-generation immigrants from Africa. Many church leaders in various African nations view the United States as a great untapped mission field for their missionaries. They have begun to send lay Christian believers and pastors both to this country and to Europe to start churches. The largest church in Europe is said to be a Pentecostal congregation of thirty thousand in Kiev, Ukraine, named the Embassy of the Blessed Kingdom of God for All Nations. That church is led by an African immigrant, Sunday Adelaja, who states on his Web site that his plan is to plant 250 churches in the United States and 300 in Europe.[2] It must be remembered that megachurches are a worldwide phenomenon, not limited to the United States. Indeed, many international megachurches have considered creating locations in the United States, not only to connect with transplanted congregants, but also to plant churches with their model of ministry here.

Relocations and Franchises

In the future, megachurches will be even more scattered throughout the country. They are already plentiful in metropolitan areas, but we expect them to spread into second- and third-tier cities across the nation. As suburban sprawl and technology continue to advance, distance from a center city matters less. The newer suburbs have a preponderance of these churches. We now see them popping up in the outermost rings of large cities and in some formerly rural areas. Newcomers to these areas often left a suburb where they attended a megachurch and desire one in their new place of residence. When a new church starts with a vision similar to the megachurch they left, they are attracted and join. New megachurches may also spring up in resort and retirement areas and draw an upscale retirement population. These churches may never reach the super-megasizes, but they could grow to the two thousand–attendee level.

We also expect the multisite approach among megachurches to continue as a way both to reach shifting populations and also to maintain the advantages of a large-scale organization. In recent years, we have seen an increase in the number of churches of all sizes willing to create satellite congregations. We have also observed existing churches seeking to become satellite campuses of large, successful megachurches. Rather than joining a megachurch's network, independent congregations may seek to merge with the megachurch to become a franchised subsidiary of the larger church itself.

Internet Campuses

Megachurches have pioneered the use of new technologies, such as the Internet, to connect members, transmit daily inspirational messages, link satellite congregations, and provide outreach. This use of new technology will continue to grow. We know of at least one megachurch that now has a legitimate, functional "Internet campus." Life Church in Oklahoma (www.lifechurch.tv) has recently started an online "campus" designed both for members who cannot get to a regular worship service and for people around the world who want to connect with Life Church. Three live Internet-delivered worship services are held each week in addition to the archives of past services offered via podcast. A "lobby chat" area opens before and after worship to connect with other Internet campus attendees, and a blog allows interested people to interact with others throughout the week. The church has appointed an Internet campus pastor whose role is to serve and minister to these members. This "church" also has its own support staff. Our guess is that cyberspace will become a viable venue for a number of other megachurches. It is just one small step beyond the live Internet broadcasts, blogs, and online leadership training classes now offered by many megachurches on their Web sites.

Challenges That Are Coming

While we are optimistic about the future of megachurches in the United States, we also see a number of challenges on the horizon. The first concerns land for the expansion of these churches. This challenge also raises the question of the future of the tax-exempt status for congregations with large acreage and programs, such as shops, cafés, and health clubs, that stretch the definition of religious activity. Additionally, the question of who will lead these megachurches as their current founding senior pastors age remains one of their greatest challenges.

Land Use

Nearly every week, there is a newspaper story about a municipality trying to deny a megachurch a building permit for a current or future site. These cases can get ugly at the local level. The church usually appeals to religious freedom laws to argue its case. While these laws do offer some protection regarding a church's land use, often the debates and challenges drag on and cost both government and church massive amounts of money in legal fees. In some land use cases against megachurches, environmental concerns, increased traffic, and other potential problems are raised. Most of the megachurches work hard with planners and architects to mitigate those concerns, but their plans do not always satisfy all the citizens or legislators of an area. In recent years, most cases have been settled eventually in favor of the churches. As megachurches' land needs continue to expand and as they add more bookstores, gyms, and coffee shops to their campuses, the challenges will continue to grow. But megachurches have proven adaptable to these challenges. Some of the most prominent multisite churches have developed other campuses as an alternative to the expense of litigation. As more and more megachurches adopt the multisite approach, this could be one of the solutions to the land use challenge. However, the movement for megachurches to have multiple sites may raise similar neighborhood and municipality issues, as many of these sites may also grow quite large.

Taxation

In the United States, tax-exempt organizations (including churches and other nonprofit groups) receive preferential tax treatment. The biggest issue for megachurches is exemption from property taxes for church properties. As megachurch sites have grown and as these churches have purchased desirable properties in growing areas, many municipalities have complained about removing these properties from the tax rolls. With megachurches including restaurants, cafés, bookstores, and other revenue-generating programs in their ministries, some claim that these churches have an unfair advantage over other businesses that must pay taxes. Additionally, the argument is made that these activities are not of a religious nature and therefore should be taxed. The complaint arises that church facilities still need police, fire, and other services provided by the municipalities that they don't pay to support. In a few locales, megachurches have compromised with the communities by declaring specific sections of their property exempt and other areas taxable. Certain municipalities have used various fees, such as "stormwater fees" and "impact fees," to offset some of the servicing costs. In addition, we know of some megachurches that have made large contributions to cities and communities on a voluntary basis, such as the gift of a new fire engine, ambulances, land for a park, and lighting for a public ball field, to demonstrate that although they do not pay property taxes, they are contributing to the community. However, this battle will continue, and megachurches could lose at least a part of their tax-exempt status someday.

Pastoral Succession and Replacement

As mentioned previously, there are considerable concerns that individual megachurches will decline in size and vitality when their pastors retire. Commentators fuel worries by using stories of past churches that did decline after a long-serving pastor left. They point to empty buildings where handfuls of worshippers struggle to maintain a large out-of-date structure. Others identify pastors, long past retirement age, who refuse to step down, appearing to want to hang on to the pulpit and its power rather than relinquish leadership to a younger generation.

There is truth in these observations, but there are also circumstances that help explain the situations. Many of those nearly empty older churches were built on small sites with limited off-street parking, in more inaccessible locations than today's megachurches. They are often in urban areas where the "remnant" constituency no longer lives.

Pastoral transitions are tricky in these large churches. For every story we hear of a pastor who has stayed too long, we hear another story of a successful transition. No matter what the outcome, these leadership shifts are difficult and are seldom without a cost to the church. Nevertheless, the healthier the staff, lay teams, and other systems in the church are, the more likely the transition will lead to stability and growth. But it does not happen without planning or willful responsible action on the part of the clergy, staff, and congregation.

Discontinuous Changes

It is rarely the continuous changes that radically transform a society. When there is a discontinuous change, an unexpected disruption of daily life, everything adjusts around that change following the initial shock. It is possible to imagine feasible significant shocks to our society that could dramatically change the functioning of entire systems and would greatly affect the growth of megachurches. We offer a few of these scenarios not to predict that they will happen but to describe the vulnerability of these large organizations and also to suggest how they might adjust.

Economic Depression

Though we are grateful that we did not live through the economic depression in the last century, our parents and grandparents did. Unlike many smaller churches, many megachurches carry megadebt on their facilities. If there were widespread economic collapse, a number of megachurches would be vulnerable. We feel that these churches would adjust to the new reality, but it would certainly change their functioning. Staff would be reduced, and debt would be renegotiated unfavorably. The era of continual construction and elaborate programming could well draw to a close. While it is our belief that the total attendance at all churches might increase if a major economic depression occurred, we also believe that the growth in the total number of megachurches would slow dramatically.

Prolonged Oil Embargo

Megachurches are regional churches that draw from a large area that require attendees to drive fairly long distances. Over the past few years, Americans have shown that even significant rises in gas prices do little to change consumption. Nevertheless, if gas prices suddenly doubled or tripled due to tensions in other parts of the world, this might cause adjustments in the driving habits of megachurch attendees. Megachurches would most likely adjust to this reality by organizing car pools, increasing bus ministries, moving to alternative schedules, and creating multiple sites, especially with the help of technology. But this scenario would likely reduce the growth in the number of large regional churches in their current form.

Widespread Airborne Disease

There has been much talk of "bird flu" and other communicable diseases that could spread rapidly across the globe. In some cases, the symptoms do not appear until after the individual has spread the disease to others. If a pandemic of this type were to occur, all large gathering places would likely be avoided. Megachurches would not be an exception. Unlike some of the scenarios above, this one could prove very troublesome for megachurches. Knowing how adaptable most megachurches are, we think they would find a way to survive and continue their ministry. We know of several megachurches that recently strategized about how to respond to just such a scenario. They came up with ways to serve people affected by the disease and explored how to carry on the church's mission if they could not meet corporately for some period of time. Certainly, these and many other megachurches would draw on the strength of their small groups and advanced technological skills to adapt to the situation.

Into the Future

We don't want to end this book with worst-case scenarios or dire problems. The megachurches we know are very positive places with a track record of overcoming obstacles. Therefore, we wish to offer a few positive observations. We suspect that by the planned megachurch 2010 study, we will be reporting perhaps fifteen hundred churches over the two thousand–attendee level. Our hunch is that megachurches will still clearly be at the center of American Christianity for another decade or two. We have observed a growing number of scholars thinking and writing on the subject. New research is yielding some excellent papers and dissertations. There is much still to learn about this religious phenomenon. But ten years from now, we may have a much better picture of how megachurches function and the role they play in society.

In addition to increased focus on megachurches with over two thousand attendees, Leadership Network regularly tracks churches that have an average attendance of at least one thousand. This group of large churches also seems to be expanding at a rapid rate. In the near future, we hope to research these churches to explore what significant differences there might be with congregations of one thousand to two thousand.

We also see secular groups wanting to track, connect, and market to megachurches, their pastors, and constituents. Two of these, interestingly enough, are the major political parties. It is not surprising that the Republican and Democratic parties would want to build connections to large gatherings of people. Both have held conferences and hired consultants in the faith-based arena. Strategists and consultants interested in finding ways to reach this audience have approached both of us. Additionally, major think tanks and policy analysts who desire to add megachurch expertise to their staff and "fellow rosters" have inquired about training and informational sessions. These communications indicate that these organizations see the power and influence of megachurches and want to keep their secular constituents informed about those developments.

Media companies, especially filmmakers and distributors, also want to connect with megachurches. The success of the 2004 film *The Passion of the Christ* was just the tip of the iceberg of this phenomenon. Major movie studios and television networks are fighting for audience attention and dollars. They see megachurches as a way to influence consumers and more easily target the religious market. This increased attention by groups formerly antagonistic to religious faith leads us to believe that megachurches will continue to attract the interest of a secular audience.

If the secular public pays such close attention to megachurches, how much more should they have the attention of pastors and denominational leaders? Megachurches have had the interest of some religious leaders, but as we have suggested, that attention has been focused on the wrong things. We argue that the greatest contribution of megachurches is not about growth or being large so much as it is about learning how to address the contemporary needs of people in the community. In many cases, megachurches have figured out how to do this in ways that resonate with their neighbors—an insight that has great value to congregations of all sizes.

In the past decade, megachurches have become a mainstream phenomenon. Given all the attention these churches have gotten, Americans, whether religious or not, have formed all kinds of opinions and stereotypes about them. Which of these ideas are myth and which are reality? With so many megachurches setting the pace for how to address the contemporary needs of Americans, they cannot be ignored. Nor can our opinions be based only on the myths. This book has attempted to lay a factual foundation for a significant religious reality that will continue to be widely discussed—and studied—for years to come.

APPENDIX: SURVEY DATA
DETAILS

THROUGHOUT THIS BOOK, we use questionnaire data from several surveys of megachurches completed by their leaders and from a few surveys of the attendees of these churches. Rather than footnoting every time we cited this material, we have noted in the text from which study the information came. The majority of the material we quote comes from statistical analyses of the data sets of these individual studies.

This Appendix describes the scope, sample size, and methods of each of the studies from which we drew our information. We also point to Internet locations where it is possible to find further information about these studies. We trust that in drawing on these different sources of information we are able to provide a richer picture of the dynamics and characteristics of megachurches in the United States.

Megachurches Today 2005

In early 2005, Scott Thumma, the primary investigator of the Megachurches Today 2000 study, joined with Warren Bird and Dave Travis of Leadership Network to redo the earlier study in a more comprehensive manner. We combined our separate databases of known megachurches, and then augmented these databases with lists of possible churches with over two thousand people in attendance from seven additional sources. The resulting list of potential candidates totaled 1,838. At the time we did not know the actual attendance of many of these churches. A paper and online questionnaire duplicated parts of the 2000 survey as well as matched the national Faith Communities Today 2005 survey.

The Megachurches Today 2005 survey was mailed to 1,236 churches and e-mailed to 600 for which we had accurate e-mail addresses for a total of 1,836 potential megachurches. E-mail reminders, along with other efforts, including press releases in newsletters, other Christian and secular publications, and notices to networks of megachurch pastors, were used as reminders to complete the questionnaires. The result was a total of 667 full and partial responses or a 36 percent response rate. The total number of fully completed surveys was 529, with 146 of these having an attendance of less than two thousand. The total number of confirmed, complete surveys of megachurches with an attendance of eighteen hundred or more persons is 406, and of those, 383 with an attendance of two thousand or more. The analysis reported in this book is based on the questionnaires of these 406 churches. We have included churches with eighteen hundred or more attendees because attendance fluctuates, and these congregations may reach the two thousand mark at times throughout the year. Additionally, these churches exhibit many of the same characteristics as churches with two thousand or more in attendance.

Along with this survey effort, we attempted to contact and confirm several facts about all the churches in the total list of 1,838 in order to determine, as accurately as possible, the entire population of megachurches in the country. This effort entailed sending e-mails, checking Web sites, communicating with many denominational research offices, and calling well over 500 churches. This procedure resulted in the confirmation of 1,210 congregations who reported having an average worship of two thousand or more attendees. Based on these 1,210 churches, the 383 completed questionnaires represent 32 percent of the U.S. megachurches.

Because we undertook the considerable effort to confirm the total population of megachurches in the United States, we were able to weight the survey respondent questionnaires to approximate the total U.S. megachurch population. We believe that these findings generally represent the total group of megachurches in the United States

The profile of the total population of these 1,210 megachurches can be found at http://hirr.hartsem.edu/megachurch/megastoday2005_profile .html. A listing of all the megachurches in the country is also available at http://hirr.hartsem.edu/megachurch/database.html.

The questionnaire used for this study has many questions in common with the Faith Communities Today 2005 study, a larger national random survey of congregations. This allows us to make comparisons between the megachurches and smaller congregations. Likewise, many of the questions replicate the Megachurches Today 2000 survey; therefore, it is also possible to explore how megachurches changed over those five years. Caution should be used in drawing firm conclusions from these data because it is not known exactly how representative the earlier study was, and several questions had slightly different wording. Nevertheless, putting these two surveys side by side is very interesting with respect to their similarities and differences as well as in the potential implications regarding the possible changing nature of the megachurch phenomenon. A direct comparison of the two studies can be seen at http://hirr.hartsem.edu/megachurch/megastoday2005_comparison.html.

Faith Communities Today 2005 (FACT 2005)

The interfaith coalition of denominations and faith groups that conducted the Faith Communities Today 2000 national study of congregations determined to continue a regular survey initiative under the name of the Cooperative Congregational Studies Partnership (CCSP) under the auspices of Hartford Institute for Religion Research, Hartford Seminary, Hartford, Connecticut. The first survey in this series, FACT 2005, went into the field on April 2005.

The survey was administered by the Institute for Social Research at Calvin College, Grand Rapids, Michigan. The questionnaire was mailed to a random sample of three thousand congregations and included the option of completing the questionnaire online. The sample was originally generated by American Church Lists and was then reviewed and cleaned up by CCSP denominations and faith groups. Random replacements for nonresponding congregations were drawn from an American Church Lists shadow sample and from denominational yearbook samples.

The administrators received 884 usable questionnaires.

"To enhance national representation, responses were weighted to the population parameters for region and faith family provided by Hadaway and Marler and for size of congregation and rural/city/suburban location found in the FACT 2000 national survey of 14,301 congregations. Sampling error for such a survey can only be estimated. We estimate it to be plus or minus 4 percent at the 95 percent confidence level."[1] The principal investigator was David A. Roozen, chair of the CCSP Advisory Committee and director of the Hartford Institute for Religion Research, Hartford Seminary.

Related Publications and Resources

Research findings and summary reports are available at http://fact.hartsem.edu/research/fact2005/index.html.

Megachurches Today 2000

The pastors of a total of six hundred megachurches were mailed a questionnaire in 1999 that contained the core Faith Communities Today 2000 questions plus several additional items. These six hundred churches were from an existing database of known megachurches. After e-mail reminders, a total of 153 usable forms were collected, for a response rate of 25.5 percent. Scott Thumma was the principal investigator for this study.

Related Publications and Resources

Research findings and summary reports are available at http://hirr.hartsem
.edu/megachurch/megachurches_research.html.

Faith Communities Today 2000 (FACT 2000)

The Faith Communities Today 2000 research project was the largest
survey of congregations ever conducted in the United States. The Faith
Communities Today data brought together twenty-six individual surveys
of congregations representing forty-one denominations and faith groups.
The forty-one participating denominations and faith groups include
about 90 percent of worshippers in the United States. Project participants
developed a common core questionnaire. Faith groups then conducted
their own surveys of a sample of congregations. More than 14,300
congregations participated in the survey. Usually, the congregation's
leader completed the questionnaire.

The Hartford Institute for Religion Research at Hartford Seminary,
Hartford, Connecticut, initiated the Faith Communities Today project.
Codirectors of the project are Carl S. Dudley, professor emeritus of
Church and Community at Hartford Seminary, and David A. Roozen,
director of the Hartford Institute for Religion Research and professor of
Religion and Society at Hartford Seminary.

In a few instances, we used a subset of the full 14,300 congregation
survey limited to a 400-church random sampling of Protestant churches
drawn by Warren Bird; these instances are noted in the text.

Related Publications and Resources

Research findings and many topical reports are available at http://fact
.hartsem.edu/research/fact2000/index.html.

The data from this study are available at http://www.thearda.com/
Archive/FCT.asp.

U.S. Congregational Life Survey

More than three hundred thousand worshippers in over two thousand
congregations across America participated in the U.S. Congregational
Life Survey, making it the largest survey of worshippers in America ever
conducted. Three types of surveys were completed in each participating
congregation: (1) an Attendee Survey completed by all worshippers aged
fifteen and older who attended worship services during the weekend of

April 29, 2001; (2) a Congregational Profile describing the congregation's facilities, staff, programs, and worship services completed by one person in the congregation; and (3) a Leader Survey completed by the pastor, priest, minister, rabbi, or other leader. Together this information provides a unique three-dimensional look at religious life in America. "The National Opinion Research Center (NORC) at the University of Chicago identified a random sample of U.S. congregations attended by individuals who participated in the General Social Survey (GSS) in the year 2000. All GSS participants who reported that they attended worship at least once in the prior year were asked to name the place where they worshipped. Since the GSS involves a national random sample of individuals, congregations identified by GSS participants comprise a national random sample of congregations. NORC researchers verified that each nominated congregation was an actual congregation and then invited each congregation to participate in the project"[2]

Sixty-one percent agreed to participate. Of those, 53.76 percent returned completed forms. Of invited congregations, 33 percent returned completed forms. The principal investigators for this study were Cynthia Woolever, professor of Sociology of Religious Organizations, Hartford Institute for Religion Research, Hartford Seminary, and Keith Wulff, coordinator of research services, Presbyterian Church (USA), with Deborah Bruce, associate research manager, Presbyterian Church (USA), project manager, and Ida Smith-Williams, associate for information, Presbyterian Church (USA), data management specialist.

For this book, we received permission to use a subset of the data for attendees from the largest Protestant churches in the survey. These 6,349 persons were from ten churches with an average attendance of 1,000 to 2,837.

Related Publications and Resources

Woolever, Cynthia, and Bruce, Deborah. *A Field Guide to U.S. Congregations: Who's Going Where and Why.* Louisville, Ky.: Westminster/John Knox, 2002.

Woolever, Cynthia, and Bruce, Deborah. *Beyond the Ordinary: 10 Strengths of U.S. Congregations.* Louisville, Ky.: Westminster/John Knox, 2004.

Other reports are listed at http://www.USCongregations.org.

The data from this study are available at http://www.thearda.com/Archive/USCLS.asp.

New Evangelical Movement Congregations Study

This survey included attendees at four congregations: Anaheim Vineyard Fellowship (1,402), Calvary Chapel Downey (1,060), Hope Chapel Kaneohe (441), and Hope Chapel Hermosa Beach (678). Surveys were distributed at four consecutive Sunday services in 1992 and 1993 at each of the four churches. Although the churches did not have membership lists, the estimate is that between 50 and 60 percent of those regularly attending the churches completed the surveys.[3] Donald E. Miller was the principal investigator for this study.

Information used in this book comes entirely from Appendix 2 of Donald Miller's *Reinventing American Protestantism: Christianity in the New Millennium.*[4]

Related Publications and Resources

Miller, Donald E. *Reinventing American Protestantism: Christianity in the New Millennium.* Berkeley, Calif.: University of California Press, 1997.

Perrin, Robin D., Kennedy, Paul, and Miller, Donald E. "Examining the Sources of Conservative Church Growth: Where Are the New Evangelical Movements Getting Their Numbers?" *Journal for the Scientific Study of Religion,* 1997, 36(1), 71–80.

The data from this study are available at http://www.thearda.com/Archive/GrpOther.asp.

Nondenominational Megachurch Study

As a part of the five-year study (1988–1992), Scott Thumma randomly surveyed the worship participants of the Atlanta nondenominational charismatic megachurch that he was researching for his dissertation at Emory University. Approximately two thousand questionnaires were distributed in the fall of 1991 during worship services for three consecutive weeks. Respondents returned a total of 694 usable questionnaires. This response of 35 percent was not considered representative of the entire church at the time, as it overrepresented the most committed. Nevertheless, it offers another look at the attitudes of megachurch members.

Related Publications and Resources

Thumma, Scott. *The Kingdom, the Power, and the Glory: Megachurches in Modern American Society.* Doctoral dissertation, Emory University, 1996.

NOTES

Introduction

1. Schaller, Lyle E. *The Very Large Church*. Nashville, Tenn.: Abingdon Press, 2000, p. 16.

Chapter 1: The Scale and Scope of Megachurches in America

1. Drucker, Peter F. "Management's New Paradigms." *Forbes*, Oct. 5, 1998, p. 169.

2. Barna, George. *The State of the Church, 2006*. Ventura, Calif.: Barna Group, 2006, p. 8.

3. Ibid., p. 35.

4. Hadaway, C. Kirk, and Marler, Penny Long. "How Many Americans Attend Worship Each Week? An Alternate Approach to Measurement." *Journal for the Scientific Study of Religion*, 2005, 44, 307–322.

5. Barna, *State of the Church, 2006*, p. 35; Gallup Poll, "Religion," Jan. 15–18, 2007. Accessed Mar. 21, 2007, at http://www .galluppoll.com/content/Default.aspx?ci=1690&pg=1& VERSION=p.

6. Gallup Brain, Sept. 15–17, 2006. Accessed Feb. 20, 2007, at http://brain.gallup.com/content/default.aspx?ci=1690&pg=1.

7. Hadaway and Marler, "How Many Americans . . . ?" We follow Hadaway and Marler's well-argued estimate of 331,000 total congregations in the country, but we add 4,000 to the count to augment the independent and nondenominational Christian count and then remove the non-Christian congregations to come up with this total of 320,000 Christian churches.

8. Chaves, Mark. *Congregations in America*. Cambridge, Mass.: Harvard University Press, 2004, p. 18.

9. Carroll, Jackson W. *God's Potters: Pastoral Leadership and the Shaping of Congregations*. Grand Rapids, Mich.: Eerdmans, 2006,

p. 8. We suggest that the number is greater than six hundred thousand because Carroll's numbers did not include counts of pastors in independent and nondenominational traditions.

10. Chaves, *Congregations in America*, p. 18.

11. Chaves, Mark. "All Creatures Great and Small: Megachurches in Context." *Review of Religious Research*, 2006, 47, 329–346.

12. Vaughn, John. *Megachurches and America's Cities: How Churches Grow*. Grand Rapids, Mich.: Baker Books, 1993, p. 117.

13. Ibid., pp. 77–80.

14. See Roozen, David A., and Hadaway, C. Kirk. "The Growth and Decline of Congregations." In C. Kirk Hadaway and David A. Roozen, *Church and Denominational Growth*. Nashville, Tenn.: Abingdon, 1993; Marler, Penny Long, and Hadaway, C. Kirk, "New Church Development and Denominational Growth (1950–1998): Symptom or Cause?" In Hadaway and Roozen, *Church and Denominational Growth*; and Olson, Daniel V. A. "Church Friendships: Boon or Barrier to Church Growth?" *Journal for the Scientific Study of Religion*, 1989, 28, 432–447.

15. Miller, Donald E. *Reinventing American Protestantism: Christianity in the New Millennium*. Berkeley: University of California Press, 1997, p. 168.

Chapter 2: "All Megachurches Are Alike"

1. Petty, Kelly. "Megachurches: The New Corporate Face of Religion in America." *Georgia State Signal*, Oct. 25, 2005. Accessed Dec. 11, 2006, at http://www.gsusignal.com/media/storage/paper924/news/2005/10/25/Perspectives/Megachurches-1761663.shtml?norewrite200607210832&sourcedomain=www.gsusignal.com.

2. Veith, Gene Edward. "Packed, but Still Empty: 'Contemporary' Churches Aren't Attracting Many Contemporaries." *World Magazine*, Aug. 20, 2005. Accessed Jan. 5, 2007, at http://www.worldmag.com/articles/10943.

3. For excellent accounts of these and other early large churches, see Loveland, Anne C., and Wheeler, Otis B. *From Meetinghouse to Megachurch: A Material and Cultural History*. St. Louis: University of Missouri Press, 2003; Kilde, Jeanne Halgren. *When Church Becomes Theatre*. Oxford: Oxford University Press, 2002; and Vaughn, John L. *Megachurches and America's Cities: How*

Churches Grow. Grand Rapids, Mich.: Baker Books, 1993, pp. 17–28.

4. Vaughan's *Megachurches and America's Cities* clearly makes this argument throughout.

5. There is often confusion regarding the nondenominational/independent label. Some independent Christian churches fiercely claim no denomination, but in concert with other churches act very much like a denomination. In addition, some Baptist churches are independent of a denomination but carry the Baptist name and strongly cling to a Baptist heritage. Also, movements such as the Vineyard, Calvary Chapel, and even the Assemblies of God eschew being called a denomination. Several of the categories in Table 2.2 require estimations on our part. It is unknown exactly how many nondenominational churches there are. Estimates based on recent national studies place the figure at roughly 12 percent of congregations in the United States. Likewise, the categories of "Other Baptists," "Christian," and "Churches of Christ" are approximations. See Thumma's work on nondenominational churches at http://hirr.hartsem.edu/cong/nondenom.html.

6. We believe the recent influx of Latino immigrants over the last few decades will lead to an increase in the number of Latino-oriented megachurches in the next twenty years.

Chapter 3: "That Church Is Just Too Big!"

1. Schwartz, Christian. *Implementation Guide to Natural Church Development*. St. Charles, Ill.: ChurchSmart Resources, 1998, p. 200.

2. Spinelli, Tony, and Brophy, Andresy. "Growing Protest over Church's Relocation," *Connecticut Post*, Dec. 3, 2006, p. A11.

3. Chaves, Mark. *Congregations in America*. Cambridge, Mass.: Harvard University Press, 2004, p. 19.

4. Woolever, Cynthia, and Bruce, Deborah. *A Field Guide to U.S. Congregations*. Louisville, Ky.: Westminster/John Knox, 2002, pp. 18–19.

5. Chaves, *Congregations in America*, p. 20.

6. More information about the Religious Land Use and Institutionalized Persons Act can be accessed at http://www.RLUIPA.com. The Beckett Fund, a legal organization that specializes in defending religious freedom, has created an extensive

resource of litigation with the implications of this act, including this Web site. Many news reports have been written about church land use battles, including the following: Alter, Alexandra. "Megachurches: Battle over Bigness." *Miami Herald*, Apr. 27, 2006, p. 1A. Accessed Jan. 6, 2007, at http://www.miami.com/mld/ miamiherald/living/religion/14438116.htm; Jennings, Rob. "High-Powered Help May Take Role in Christ Church Fight: Rockaway Twp. Talks to Attorney Who Won Religious Land Use Case." *Daily Record*, May 2, 2004, p. A1. Accessed Jan. 6, 2007, at http://www.dailyrecord.com/news/articles/news2-marci.htm; Jennings, Rob. "DEP Wants More Info on Christ Church's Plans." *Daily Record*, Jan. 4, 2007, p. A12. Accessed on Jan. 6, 2007, at http://www.dailyrecord.com/apps/pbcs.dll/articleAID=/20070104/ COMMUNITIES43/701040319/1203/NEWS01; O'Connor, Lona. "Churches Contend Palm Beach County Proposal to Limit Sizes Bullies Pulpits." *Palm Beach Post*, Apr. 24, 2006, p. 1A. Accessed Jan. 6, 2007, at http://www.palmbeachpost.com/localnews/content/ local_news/epaper/2006/04/24/c1amegachurch_0424.html; and Gorski, Eric. "Church Projects Don't Get Neighbors' Blessing: Conflicts over Traffic, Noise Prompt Lawsuits." *Denver Post*, Aug. 3, 2003, p. A1.

7. Surratt, Geoff, Ligon, Greg, and Bird, Warren. *The Multisite Church Revolution*. Grand Rapids, Mich.: Zondervan, 2006, pp. 55–56.

Chapter 4: "Megachurches Are Cults of Personality"

1. Zoll, Rachel. "Superstar Pastors Pose Challenge," SFGate.com, Nov. 10, 2006. Accessed Dec. 28, 2006, at http://www .religionnewsblog.com/16519/superstar-pastors-pose-challenge.

2. Hartman, Greg. "You Wanna Supersize That Church?" Plain Truth Online, Sept.-Oct. 2003. Accessed Feb. 20, 2007, at http://www .ptm.org/03PT/SepOct/supersizeChurch.htm.

3. Based on the 2000 megachurch study, over a third (38 percent) of megachurches produce their own television programs, and 44 percent can be heard through their radio programs. Increasingly, megachurches are also using streaming media, podcasts, and RSS feeds to get their message out by means of the Internet.

4. A good treatment of this branding phenomenon within megachurches, although less so of the pastors of these churches, can be found in Twitchell, James B. *Branded Nation: The Marketing of*

Megachurch, College Inc., and Museumworld. New York: Simon & Schuster, 2004, pp. 47–108.

5. Carroll, Jackson W. *God's Potters: Pastoral Leadership and the Shaping of Congregations*. Grand Rapids, Mich.: Eerdmans, 2006, pp. 73–74.

6. In the recent 2006 Leadership Network Annual Salary survey, adjusting for churches with two thousand in attendance. There are other surveys, such as the National Association of Church Business Administrators, with similar figures. However, personal experience leads us to believe the average is closer to $145,000 after interviewing numerous pastors in the past year. Pastors can receive part of their compensation in the form of a housing allowance, so this amount is included in the higher figure.

7. For example, one church we know of compares the pastor's salary to the salaries of long-tenured high school principals, a local college president, the head of the local hospital, and the executive director of the largest United Way agency in that city. The salaries are surprisingly similar overall.

8. Carroll, *God's Potters*, p. 90.

9. All statements on Blackhawk Church's mission and values are from Blackhawk Church. "Vision and Values." 2007. Accessed Mar. 22, 2007, at http://www.blackhawkchurch.org/about/vision.php.

Chapter 5: "These Churches Are Only Concerned About Themselves and the Needs of Their Attendees"

1. Brown, Patricia Lee. "Megachurch as Mini-Towns." *New York Times,* May 9, 2002, sec. F, p. 1.

2. Ibid.

3. *Support* is defined as a material or financial contribution, member volunteer time, or space in a building.

4. A conference paper report titled "A Mighty Fortress: The Social and Economic Foundations of the American Megachurch Movement," by Irwin Morris, Wayne McIntosh, Kim Karnes, and Shanna Pearson-Merkowitz, makes this argument. Paper presented at the annual meeting of the American Political Science Association, Washington, D.C., Sept. 1, 2005. Accessed Feb. 20, 2007, at http://www.allacademic.com/meta/p41353_index.html.

5. Swanson, Eric. *Churches Moving into the Community*. Dallas, Tex.: Leadership Network, 2004.

6. Thumma, Scott, and Petersen, Jim. "Goliaths in Our Midst:
Megachurches in the ELCA." In *Lutherans Today: American
Lutheran Identity in the Twenty-First Century*, ed. Richard Cimino.
Grand Rapids, Mich.: Eerdmans, 2003, pp. 102–124.

Chapter 6: "Megachurches Water Down the Faith"

1. Baird, Julia. "The Good and Bad of Religion-Lite." *Sydney*
(Australia) *Morning Herald*, Feb. 23, 2006. Accessed Jan. 6,
2007, at http://www.smh.com.au/news/opinion/the-good-and-
bad-of-religionlite/2006/02/22/1140563858123.html.

2. Sheler, Jeff. "Interview: Alan Wolfe." *Religion and Ethics
Newsweekly*, Apr. 30, 2004. Accessed Jan. 6, 2007, at
http://www.pbs.org/wnet/religionandethics/week735/interview
.html.

3. "25 Most Influential Evangelicals Photo Essay: Bill Hybels." *Time*,
Nov. 1, 2005. Accessed Jan. 6, 2007, at http://www.time.com/time/
covers/1101050207/photoessay/12.html.

4. Goldberger, Paul. "The Gospel of Church Architecture, Revised."
New York Times, Apr. 20, 1995, pp. B1, B4. The architecture of
megachurches is thoroughly and beautifully explored in Loveland,
Anne C., and Wheeler, Otis B. *From Meetinghouse to Megachurch:
A Material and Cultural History*. St. Louis: University of Missouri
Press, 2003.

5. Quest Community Church. "Frequently Asked Questions." 2007.
Accessed Mar. 23, 2007, at http://www.questcommunity.com/
subindex.php?id=faq.

6. Bird, Warren. "Megachurches as Spectator Religion: Using Social
Network Theory and Free-Rider Theory to Understand the Spiritual
Vitality of America's Largest-Attender Churches." Doctoral
dissertation, Fordham University, 2006. Bird explored a similar
theme in his dissertation using the Faith Communities Today 2000
and Megachurches Today 2000 data and also found that the larger
the church, the more likely it was to assert that it held strong
beliefs. A slightly different finding resulted from Nancy Martin's
analysis of the National Congregations Study, in which she found
that megachurches were similar to smaller churches on most moral
behavioral rules, less strict in prohibiting alcohol and smoking, but
more strict in encouraging giving and restricting women from
positions of authority over men. See Martin, Nancy J. "On Rules
and Ruling: Strictness and the Politics of Gender in American

Megachurches." Paper presented at the annual meeting of the Association for the Sociology of Religion, Philadelphia, Aug. 13–15, 2005.

7. Banerjee, Neela. "Intimate Confessions Pour Out on Church's Web Site." *New York Times,* Sept. 1, 2006. Accessed Nov. 6, 2006, at http://select.nytimes.com/gst/abstract.html?res=F20D14F9355A0 C728CDDA00894DE404482&showabstract=1.

Chapter 7: "These Churches Are Bad for Other Churches"

1. This story is recounted in the superb article about one pastor's interaction with a local megachurch and the positive outcome for his congregation living in the shadow of the megachurch. See Asimakoupoulos, Greg. "In the Shadow of a Giant." *Enrichment Journal*, Fall 2001, p. 4. Accessed Jan. 6, 2007, at http://enrichmentjournal .ag.org/200104/056_in_the_shadow.cfm. Other such stories include Delgado, Berta. "In the Shadow of Prestonwood: Smaller Congregations Say There's Room for Everybody near Megachurch." *Dallas Morning News*, May 1, 1999; and Tornquist, Chris W., and Aker, John B. "The Shadow of a Megachurch: Neighboring Churches, Big and Small, Can Enjoy a Healthy Coexistence." *Leadership Magazine*, Oct. 1, 1990. Accessed Jan. 6, 2007, at http://ctlibrary.com/13712.

2. This competitive context is described in Roger Finke and Rodney Stark's excellent book *The Churching of America, 1776–2005: Winners and Losers in Our Religious Economy*. New Brunswick, N.J.: Rutgers University Press, 2005. The authors describe an economic, free-market approach to the religious history of the United States in which the largest market share of participants goes to those churches or traditions that adapt and best serve the spiritual needs of Americans.

3. An interesting, similar story is told by Nancy Eiesland, an Emory University professor, in a chapter titled "Contending with a Giant: The Impact of a MegaChurch on Exurban Religious Institutions." In *Contemporary American Religion: An Ethnographic Reader*, ed. Penny Edgell Becker and Nancy L. Eiesland. Walnut Creek, Calif.: AltaMira Press, 1997, pp. 191–220. Eiesland has a fuller treatment of the religious ecology of the same exurban Georgia area in her book *A Particular Place*. New Brunswick, N.J.: Rutgers University Press, 2000.

4. Nancy Eiesland and Stephen Warner describe this religious ecology idea in their chapter titled "Ecology: Seeing the Congregation in Context." In *Studying Congregations: A New Handbook*, ed. Nancy T. Ammerman, Jackson W. Carroll, Carl S. Dudley, and William McKinney. Nashville, Tenn.: Abingdon Press, 1998, pp. 78–104.

5. Eiesland, *A Particular Place*, p. 201.

6. Bibby, Reginald, and Brinkerhoff, M. B. "Circulation of the Saints, 1966–1990." *Journal for the Scientific Study of Religion*, 1994, *33*, 273–280.

7. Baylor Institute for Studies of Religion. "American Piety in the 21st Century." Sept. 2006, p. 8. Accessed on Jan. 6, 2007, at http://www.baylor.edu/isreligion/index.php?id=40634.

8. Eiesland, *A Particular Place*, p. 215.

9. Thumma, Scott, and Petersen, Jim. "Goliaths in the Midst: Lutheran Megachurches." In *Contemporary American Lutheranism*, ed. Richard Cimino. Grand Rapids, Mich.: Eerdmans, 2003, p. 111.

10. Thumma, Scott. "The Kingdom, the Power, and the Glory: Megachurches in Modern American Society." Doctoral dissertation, Emory University, 1996.

11. Eiesland, *A Particular Place*, p. 213.

12. Thumma and Petersen, "Goliaths in the Midst," p. 111.

13. Parrott, Les, and Perrin, Robin D. "The New Denominations." *Christianity Today*, Mar. 11, 1991, pp. 29–33.

Chapter 8: "These Churches Are Full of People of the Same Race, Class, and Political Preferences"

1. Wells, David. *Above All Earthly Pow'rs: Christ in a Postmodern World*. Grand Rapids, Mich.: Eerdmans, 2005, p. 289.

2. Democratic Leadership Council. "Understanding Megachurches." *New Democratic Dispatch,* Mar. 22, 2006. Accessed Jan. 6, 2007, at http://www.ndol.org/ndol_?kaid=127&subid=177&contentid=253793.

3. Christian Smith and Robert Faris tested this assumption and found that socioeconomic variables continue to separate denominations in the United States. See their "Socioeconomic Inequality in the American Religious System: An Update and Assessment." *Journal for the Scientific Study of Religion*, 2005, *44*, 95–104.

4. Miller, Donald E.. *Reinventing American Protestantism: Christianity in the New Millennium.* Berkeley: University of California Press, 1997.

5. Emerson's research has spawned a number of books on the subject, including Emerson, Michael O., and Smith, Christian. *Divided by Faith: Evangelicals and the Problem of Race in America.* New York: Oxford University Press, 2000; Deyoung, Curtiss Paul, Emerson, Michael O., Yancey, George, and Kim, Karen Chai. *United by Faith: The Multiracial Congregation as an Answer to the Problem of Race.* New York: Oxford University Press, 2003; Christerson, Brad, Emerson, Michael O., and Edwards, Korie L. *Against All Odds: The Struggle for Racial Integration in Religious Organizations.* New York: NYU Press, 2005; and Emerson, Michael O. *People of the Dream: Multiracial Congregations in the United States.* Princeton, N.J.: Princeton University Press, 2006.

6. Thumma, Scott. "The Kingdom, the Power, and the Glory: Megachurches in Modern American Society." Doctoral dissertation, Emory University, 1996.

7. Miller, *Reinventing American Protestantism.*

8. For a more detailed description of this multisite trend, see Surratt, Geoff, Ligon, Greg, and Bird, Warren. *The Multisite Church Revolution.* Grand Rapids, Mich.: Zondervan, 2006.

9. Miller, *Reinventing American Protestantism.*

10. Meyer, Andrew R. "With Firmness in the Right: Ohio Megachurch Sermons During the 2004 Presidential Election." Master's thesis, University of Ohio, 2004, p. 31.

Chapter 9: "Megachurches Grow Because of the Show"

1. "Understanding Megachurches." *North Denver News*, Mar. 23, 2006. Accessed Feb. 26, 2007, at http://northdenvernews.com/content/view/266/39.

2. Vogel, Mike. "Big Box Worship." *Florida Trend Magazine*, Dec. 2005. Accessed Jan. 6, 2007, at http://www.floridatrend.com/issue/default.asp?a=5681&s=1&d=12/1/2005.

3. Nobel, Perry. "A Fresh Perspective." Sept. 26, 2006. Accessed Feb. 20, 2007, at http://www.perrynoble.com/2006/09/26/a-fresh-perspective.

4. Hadaway, C. Kirk. "FACTs on Growth." Hartford, Conn.: Faith Communities Today of the Hartford Institute for Religion Research

and Hartford Seminary, Nov. 2006. Accessed Dec. 27, 2006, at
http://fact.hartsem.edu/CongGrowth.pdf.

5. For additional information on blogging and churches, see Bailey,
   Brian, and Storch, Terry. *The Blogging Church*. San Francisco:
   Jossey-Bass, 2007.

Chapter 10: "The Megachurch Movement Is Dying—Young People Hate These Churches"

1. Easum, William. "The End of the Megachurch?" *Net Results*,
   Nov.-Dec. 2000, pp. 20–21. Bill Easum, our friend and Dave's
   coauthor on an earlier book, has now recanted this position,
   but it is still widely held by other commentators. Bill's recent book
   Go Big: How to Lead Your Church to Explosive Growth
   (Nashville, Tenn.: Abingdon, 2006) was written with a megachurch
   pastor.

2. Przybys, John. "Baby Boomers Behind Change in Ministerial
   Approach." *Las Vegas Review-Journal*, Apr. 25, 2002.

3. For example, three of the chief spokespersons in the Emergent
   churches are Doug Pagitt, Tony Jones, and Brian McLaren. Doug
   and Tony were staff members of megachurches. Brian helped plant
   a church that grew to megasize.

4. Kotkin, Joel. "In Praise of Suburbs." *San Francisco Chronicle*, Jan.
   29, 2006. Accessed Dec. 26, 2006, at http://www.newamerica.net/
   publications/articles/2006/in_praise_of_suburbs.

5. Barna, George. *Revolution: Finding Vibrant Faith Beyond the Walls
   of the Sanctuary*. Carol Stream, Ill.: Tyndale House, 2005, pp.
   64–65. See also Ed Stetzer's research in "New Research on the Rise
   of House Churches and Alternative Faith Communities." *Center for
   Missional Research Insights Newsletter*, Dec. 18, 2006.

6. Scott Thumma has argued that both the small house church model
   and the megachurch approach ideally fit the contemporary cultural
   situation of American society. The existence of both these forms of
   religious organization is not contradictory, nor do they demand the
   survival of one form and the demise of the other. See Thumma,
   Scott. "The Shape of Things to Come: Megachurches, Emerging
   Churches, and Other New Religious Structures." In *Faith in
   America: Changes, Challenges, New Directions*. Vol. 1: *Organized
   Religion Today*, ed. Charles Lippy. Westport, Conn.: Praeger,
   2006, pp. 185–206.

Chapter 11: What Might the Future Hold?

1. Thumma, Scott. "The Shape of Things to Come: Megachurches, Emerging Churches, and Other New Religious Structures." In *Faith in America: Changes, Challenges, New Directions*. Vol. 1: *Organized Religion Today*, ed. Charles H. Lippy. Westport, Conn.: Praeger, 2006.

2. Pastor Sunday Adelaja has been featured in several magazines and news outlets in recent years. See Fawkes, Helen. "Nigerian Pastor Finds New Flock in Ukraine." BBC News, Oct. 20, 2006. Accessed Feb. 20, 2007, at http://news.bbc.co.uk/2/hi/uk_news/6098658.stm; and Jewel, Dawn Herzog. "From Africa to Ukraine." *Today's Christian*, Nov.-Dec. 2005. Accessed Feb. 20, 2007, at http://www.christianitytoday.com/tc/2005/006/4.42.html. Also see the pastor's own Web site and updates regarding his ministry at www.pastorsunday.com.

Appendix: Survey Data Details

1. Hadaway, C. Kirk. "FACTs on Growth." Faith Communities Today of the Hartford Institute for Religion Research and Hartford Seminary, Nov. 2006. Accessed Dec. 27, 2006, at http://fact.hartsem.edu/Cong.Growth.pdf. The reference is to Hadaway, C. Kirk, and Marler, Penny Long. "How Many Americans Attend Worship Each Week? An Alternate Approach to Measurement." *Journal for the Scientific Study of Religion*, 2005, 44, 307–322.

2. Woolever, Cynthia, and Bruce, Deborah. *A Field Guide to U.S. Congregations: Who's Going Where and Why*. Louisville, Ky.: Westminster/John Knox, 2002.

3. See Perrin, Robin D., Kennedy, Paul, and Miller, Donald E. "Examining the Sources of Conservative Church Growth: Where Are the New Evangelical Movements Getting Their Numbers?" *Journal for the Scientific Study of Religion*, 1997, 36, 71–80.

4. Miller, Donald E. *Reinventing American Protestantism: Christianity in the New Millennium*. Berkeley: University of California Press, 1997, pp. 195–212.

BIBLIOGRAPHY

Alter, Alexandra. "Megachurches: Battle over Bigness." *Miami Herald*, Apr. 27, 2006, p. 1A. Accessed Jan. 6, 2007, at http://www.miami.com/mld/miamiherald/living/religion/14438116.htm.

Asimakoupoulos, Greg. "In the Shadow of a Giant." *Enrichment Journal*, Fall 2001, p. 4. Accessed Jan. 6, 2007, at http://enrichmentjournal.ag.org/200104/056_in_the_shadow.cfm.

Bailey, Brian, and Storch, Terry. *The Blogging Church*. San Francisco: Jossey-Bass, 2007.

Baird, Julia. "The Good and Bad of Religion-Lite." *Sydney* (Australia) *Morning Herald*, Feb. 23, 2006. Accessed Jan. 6, 2007, at http://www.smh.com.au/news/opinion/the-good-and-bad-of-religionlite/2006/02/22/1140563858123.html.

Banerjee, Neela. "Intimate Confessions Pour Out on Church's Web Site." New York Times, Sept. 1, 2006. Accessed Nov. 6, 2006, at http://select.nytimes.com/gst/abstract.html?res=F20D14F9355A0 C728CDDA00894DE404482&showabstract=1.

Baylor Institute for Studies of Religion. "American Piety in the 21st Century." Sept. 2006. Accessed Jan. 6, 2007, at http://www.baylor.edu/isreligion/index.php?id=40634.

Bibby, Reginald, and Brinkerhoff, M. B. "Circulation of the Saints, 1966–1990." *Journal for the Scientific Study of Religion*, 1994, 33, 273–280.

Bird, Warren. "Megachurches as Spectator Religion: Using Social Network Theory and Free-Rider Theory to Understand the Spiritual Vitality of America's Largest-Attender Churches." Doctoral dissertation, Fordham University, 2006.

Brown, Patricia Lee. "Megachurch as Mini-Towns." *New York Times*, May 9, 2002, sec. F, p. 1.

Carroll, Jackson W. *God's Potters: Pastoral Leadership and the Shaping of Congregations*. Grand Rapids, Mich.: Eerdmans, 2006.

Chaves, Mark. *Congregations in America*. Cambridge, Mass.: Harvard University Press, 2004.

Chaves, Mark. "All Creatures Great and Small: Megachurches in Context." *Review of Religious Research*, 2006, 47, 329–346.

Chaves, Mark, Konieczny, Mary Ellen, Beyerlein, Kraig, and Barman, Emily. "The National Congregations Study: Background, Methods, and Selected Results." *Journal for the Scientific Study of Religion*, 1999, *38*, 458–477.

Christerson, Brad, Emerson, Michael O., and Edwards, Korie L. *Against All Odds: The Struggle for Racial Integration in Religious Organizations*. New York: New York University Press, 2005.

Dalton, Ray Philip. "Sources of Attraction to the Megachurch: Factors Influencing the Individual's Decision to Participate." Doctoral dissertation, University of Tennessee, Knoxville, 2002.

Delgado, Berta. "In the Shadow of Prestonwood: Smaller Congregations Say There's Room for Everybody near Megachurch." *Dallas Morning News*, May 1, 1999.

Democratic Leadership Council. "Understanding Megachurches." *New Democratic Dispatch*, Mar. 22, 2006. Accessed Jan. 6, 2007, at http://www.ndol.org/ndol_ci.cfm?kaid=127&subid=177&contentid=253793.

Deyoung, Curtiss Paul, Emerson, Michael O., Yancey, George, and Kim, Karen Chai. *United by Faith: The Multiracial Congregation as an Answer to the Problem of Race*. New York: Oxford University Press, 2003.

Drucker, Peter F. "Management's New Paradigms." *Forbes*, Oct. 5, 1998, pp. 152–177.

Easum, William. "The End of the Megachurch?" *Net Results*, Nov.-Dec. 2000, pp. 20–21.

Easum, William. *Go Big: How to Lead Your Church to Explosive Growth*. Nashville, Tenn.: Abingdon Press, 2006.

Eiesland, Nancy L. "Contending with a Giant: The Impact of a Megachurch on Exurban Religious Institutions." In *Contemporary American Religion: An Ethnographic Reader*, ed. Penny Edgell Becker and Nancy L. Eiesland. Walnut Creek, Calif.: AltaMira Press, 1997, pp. 191–220.

Eiesland, Nancy L. *A Particular Place*. New Brunswick, N.J.: Rutgers University Press, 2000.

Eiesland, Nancy L., and Warner, R. Stephen. "Ecology: Seeing the Congregation in Context." In *Studying Congregations: A New Handbook*, ed. Nancy T. Ammerman, Jackson W. Carroll, Carl S. Dudley, and William McKinney. Nashville, Tenn.: Abingdon Press, 1998, pp. 78–104.

Ellingson, Stephen. *The Megachurch and the Mainline: Remaking Religious Tradition in the Twenty-First Century*. Chicago: University of Chicago Press, 2007.

Emerson, Michael O. *People of the Dream: Multiracial Congregations in the United States*. Princeton, N.J.: Princeton University Press, 2006.

Emerson, Michael O., and Smith, Christian. *Divided by Faith: Evangelicals and the Problem of Race in America*. New York: Oxford University Press, 2000.

Fawkes, Helen. "Nigerian Pastor Finds New Flock in Ukraine." BBC News, Oct. 20, 2006. Accessed Nov. 13, 2006, at http://news.bbc.co.uk/2/hi/uk_news/6098658.stm.

Finke, Roger, and Stark, Rodney. *The Churching of America, 1776–2005: Winners and Losers in Our Religious Economy.* New Brunswick, N.J.: Rutgers University Press, 2005.

Goldberger, Paul. "The Gospel of Church Architecture, Revised." *New York Times,* Apr. 20, 1995, pp. B1, B4.

Gorski, Eric. "Church Projects Don't Get Neighbors' Blessing: Conflicts over Traffic, Noise Prompt Lawsuits." *Denver Post,* Aug. 3, 2003, p. A1. Accessed Nov. 15, 2004, at http://www.denverpost.com/cda/article/print/0,1674,36%7E53%7E1548896,00.html.

Gregory, Joel C. *Too Great a Temptation: The Seductive Power of America's Super Church.* Fort Worth, Tex.: Summit Group, 1994.

Hadaway, C. Kirk. "FACTs on Growth." Faith Communities Today of the Hartford Institute for Religion Research and Hartford Seminary, Nov. 2006. Accessed Dec. 27, 2006, at http://fact.hartsem.edu/Cong.Growth.pdf.

Hadaway, C. Kirk, and Marler, Penny Long. "How Many Americans Attend Worship Each Week? An Alternate Approach to Measurement." *Journal for the Scientific Study of Religion,* 2005, 44, 307–322.

Jennings, Rob. "High-Powered Help May Take Role in Christ Church Fight: Rockaway Twp. Talks to Attorney Who Won Religious Land Use Case." *Daily Record,* May 2, 2004. Accessed Jan. 6, 2007, at http://www.dailyrecord.com/news/articles/news2-marci.htm.

Jennings, Rob. "DEP Wants More Info on Christ Church's Plans." *Daily Record,* Jan. 4, 2007. Accessed Jan. 6, 2007, at http://www.dailyrecord.com/apps/pbcs.dll/article?AID=/20070104/COMMUNITIES43/701040319/1203/NEWS01.

Jewel, Dawn Herzog. "From Africa to Ukraine." *Today's Christian,* Nov.-Dec. 2005. Accessed Jan. 18, 2007, at http://www.christianitytoday.com/tc/2005/006/4.42.html.

Kilde, Jeanne Halgren. *When Church Becomes Theatre.* Oxford: Oxford University Press, 2002.

Kotkin, Joel. "In Praise of Suburbs." *San Francisco Chronicle,* Jan. 29, 2006. Accessed Dec. 26, 2006, at http://www.newamerica.net/publications/articles/2006/in_praise_of_suburbs.

Loveland, Anne C., and Wheeler, Otis B. *From Meetinghouse to Megachurch: A Material and Cultural History.* St. Louis: University of Missouri Press, 2003.

Martin, Nancy J. "On Rules and Ruling: Strictness and the Politics of Gender in American Megachurches." Paper presented at the annual meeting of the Association for the Sociology of Religion, Philadelphia, Aug. 13–15, 2005.

Meyer, Andrew R. "With Firmness in the Right: Ohio Megachurch Sermons During the 2004 Presidential Election." Master's thesis, University of Ohio, 2004.

Miller, Donald E. *Reinventing American Protestantism: Christianity in the New Millennium.* Berkeley: University of California Press, 1997, pp. 195–212.

Morris, Irwin, McIntosh, Wayne, Karnes, Kim, and Pearson-Merkowitz, Shanna. "A Mighty Fortress: The Social and Economic Foundations of the American Megachurch Movement." Paper presented at the annual meeting of the American Political Science Association, Washington, D.C., Sept. 1, 2005. Accessed Jan. 5, 2007, at http://www.allacademic.com/meta/p41353 _index.html.

O'Connor, Lona. "Churches Contend Palm Beach County Proposal to Limit Sizes Bullies Pulpits." Palm Beach Post, Apr. 24, 2006, p. 1A. Accessed Jan. 6, 2007, at http://www.palmbeachpost.com/localnews/content/local_news/ epaper/2006/04/24/c1a_megachurch_0424.html.

Olson, Daniel V. A. "Church Friendships: Boon or Barrier to Church Growth?" *Journal for the Scientific Study of Religion*, 1989, 28, 432–447.

Olson, Richard. *The Largest Congregations in the United States: An Empirical Study of Church Growth and Decline.* Doctoral dissertation, Northwestern University, 1988.

Parrott, Les, and Perrin, Robin D. "The New Denominations." *Christianity Today*, Mar. 11, 1991, pp. 29–33.

Perrin, Robin D., Kennedy, Paul, and Miller, Donald E. "Examining the Sources of Conservative Church Growth: Where Are the New Evangelical Movements Getting Their Numbers?" *Journal for the Scientific Study of Religion*, 1997, 36, 71–80.

Pritchard, G. A. *Willow Creek Seeker Services: Evaluating a New Way of Doing Church.* Grand Rapids, Mich.: Baker Books, 1996.

Przybys, John. "Baby Boomers Behind Change in Ministerial Approach." *Las Vegas Review-Journal*, Apr. 25, 2002.

Roozen, David A., and Hadaway, C. Kirk. *Church and Denominational Growth.* Nashville, Tenn.: Abingdon Press, 1993.

Sargent, Kimon H. *Seeker Churches: Promoting Traditional Religion in a Non-traditional Way.* New Brunswick, N.J.: Rutgers University Press, 2000.

Schaller, Lyle E. *The Seven-Day-a-Week Church.* Nashville, Tenn.: Abingdon Press, 1992.

Schaller, Lyle E. *The Very Large Church.* Nashville, Tenn.: Abingdon Press, 2000.

Schwartz, Christian. *Implementation Guide to Natural Church Development.* St. Charles, Ill.: Church Smart Resources, 1998.

Sheler, Jeff. "Interview: Allen Wolfe." *Religion and Ethics Newsweekly*, Apr. 30, 2004. Accessed Mar. 22, 2007, at http://www.pbs.org/wnet/religionand ethics/week735/interview.html.

Spinelli, Tony, and Brophy, Andresy. "Growing Protest over Church's Relocation," *Connecticut Post*, Dec. 3, 2006, p. A11.

Smith, Christian, and Faris, Robert. "Socioeconomic Inequality in the American Religious System: An Update and Assessment." *Journal for the Scientific Study of Religion*, 2005, 44, 95–104.

Surratt, Geoff, Ligon, Greg, and Bird, Warren. *The Multisite Church Revolution.* Grand Rapids, Mich.: Zondervan, 2006.

Swanson, Eric. *Churches Moving into the Community.* Dallas, Tex.: Leadership Network, 2004.

Thumma, Scott. "Sketching a Megatrend: The Phenomenal Proliferation of Very Large Churches in the United States." Paper presented at the annual meeting of the Association for the Sociology of Religion, Miami, Florida, 1993.

Thumma, Scott. "The Megachurch: A Sacred Power in a Secular Society." Keynote lecture given at the Catholic University of America's School of Architecture, June 1995.

Thumma, Scott. "Exploring the Megachurch Phenomena: Their Characteristics and Cultural Context." Revised excerpt from "The Kingdom, the Power, and the Glory: Megachurches in Modern American Society." Doctoral dissertation, Emory University, 1996. Accessed Jan. 6, 2007, at http://hirr .hartsem.edu/bookshelf/thumma_article2.html.

Thumma, Scott. "The Kingdom, the Power, and the Glory: Megachurches in Modern American Society." Doctoral dissertation, Emory University, 1996.

Thumma, Scott. "Megachurches of Atlanta." In *Religions of Atlanta*, ed. Gary-Laderman. Atlanta: Scholars Press, 1996.

Thumma, Scott. "Megachurches Today 2000: Summary of Data from the Faith Communities Today Project." Apr. 2001. Accessed Jan. 6, 2007, at http://hirr.hartsem.edu/org/faith_megachurches_FACTsummary.html.

Thumma, Scott. "The Shape of Things to Come: Megachurches, Emerging Churches, and Other New Religious Structures." *In Faith in America: Changes, Challenges, New Directions.* Vol. 1: *Organized Religion Today*, ed. Charles H. Lippy. Westport, Conn.: Praeger, 2006, pp. 185–206.

Thumma, Scott, and Petersen, Jim. "Goliaths in Our Midst: Megachurches in the ELCA." *In Lutherans Today: American Lutheran Identity in the Twenty-First Century*, ed. Richard Cimino. Grand Rapids, Mich.: Eerdmans, 2003, pp. 102–124.

Thumma, Scott, Travis, Dave, and Bird, Warren. "Megachurches Today 2005: Summary of Data from the Faith Communities Today Project." Feb. 2006

Accessed Jan. 6, 2007, at http://hirr.hartsem.edu/megachurch/megastoday 2005_summaryreport.html.

Tornquist, Chris W., and Aker, John B. "The Shadow of a Megachurch: Neighboring Churches, Big and Small, Can Enjoy a Healthy Coexistence." *Leadership Magazine*, Oct. 1, 1990. Accessed Jan. 6, 2007, at http://ctlibrary.com/13712.

Towns, Elmer L. *The Ten Largest Sunday Schools and What Makes Them Grow.* Grand Rapids, Mich.: Baker Books, 1969.

Tucker-Worgs, Tamelyn. "Bringing the Church "Back In": Black Megachurch and Community Development." Doctoral dissertation, University of Maryland, 2002.

Tucker-Worgs, Tamelyn. "Get on Board, Little Children, There's Room for Many More: The Black Megachurch Phenomenon." *Journal of the Interdenominational Theological Center*, 2001–2002, 29, 177–204.

"25 Most Influential Evangelicals Photo Essay: Bill Hybels." *Time*, Nov. 11, 2005. Accessed Jan. 6, 2007, at http://www.time.com/time/covers/ 1101050207/photoessay/12.html.

Twitchell, James B. *Branded Nation: The Marketing of Megachurch, College Inc., and Museumworld.* New York: Simon & Schuster, 2004.

Vaughn, John L. *The World's Twenty Largest Churches.* Grand Rapids, Mich.: Baker Books, 1984.

Vaughn, John L. *Megachurches and America's Cities: How Churches Grow.* Grand Rapids, Mich.: Baker Books, 1993.

Veith, Gene Edward. "Packed, but Still Empty: Contemporary Churches Aren't Attracting Many Contemporaries." *World Magazine*, Aug. 20, 2005. Accessed Jan. 5, 2007, at http://www.worldmag.com/articles/10943.

Vogel, Mike. "Big Box Worship." *Florida Trend Magazine*, Dec. 2005. Accessed Jan. 6, 2007, at http://www.floridatrend.com/issue/default.asp?a=5681& s=1&d=12/1/2005.

Warren, Rick. *The Purpose Driven Church.* Grand Rapids, Mich.: Zondervan, 1995.

Wells, David. *Above All Earthly Pow'rs: Christ in a Postmodern World.* Grand Rapids, Mich.: Eerdmans, 2005.

Woolever, Cynthia, and Bruce, Deborah. *A Field Guide to U.S. Congregations.* Louisville, Ky.: Westminster/John Knox, 2002.

ABOUT THE AUTHORS

SCOTT THUMMA is a professor of sociology of religion at Hartford Seminary and conducts research for the seminary's Hartford Institute for Religion Research. In addition to being a faculty member for the past eight years, he is also the seminary's information technology director and the administrator of the school's Web sites and its distance education program.

Scott has a doctorate in religion from Emory University, a master of divinity degree from the Candler School of Theology, and a bachelor of arts degree from Southwestern University.

Scott has studied megachurches since 1988. For his Ph.D. dissertation, he did a five-year study of one megachurch in Atlanta. He has since published articles and chapters on megachurches and conducted two national academic studies of U.S. megachurches, in 2000 and 2005. His research on megachurches has been quoted in hundreds of U.S. and international newspapers, including the *New York Times, Wall Street Journal, Christian Science Monitor, Atlanta Journal and Constitution, Los Angeles Times, USA Today,* and *Dallas Morning News.* His work has also been featured in national and international magazines and on television programs including the BBC, CNN, *Good Morning America,* the CBS *Early Show,* and numerous local television stations.

He has also written about and taught on such topics as congregational studies, Pentecostalism, the intersection of homosexuality and evangelicalism, and the role of the Internet in congregational life.

Prior to his appointment at Hartford Seminary, Scott taught at several institutions in and around Atlanta, as an adjunct faculty member. Since 1992, his consulting company, Congregational Consultants, has helped numerous church, denominational, and secular organizations come to a better understanding of their organizations. Scott has consulted with such denominations as the United Methodist Church, the Church of the Nazarene, and the Evangelical Lutheran Church in America, as well as with over fifty individual congregations.

Scott grew up as an independent Baptist and has been involved over the years with Methodist, Presbyterian, Disciples, and Southern Baptist congregations, with nondenominational megachurches, and with small independent charismatic fellowships. He has been married to his wife, Jennifer, for twenty-five years. They have three children: Katherine, Benjamin, and Madeline.

○

DAVE TRAVIS is the executive vice president of church innovations at Leadership Network, heading a large field team that works with innovative churches and ministries across the United States and Canada. Leadership Network is a nonprofit organization whose mission is to identify, connect, and help high-capacity Christian leaders multiply their impact. The organization helped nurture the Megachurch movement and other movements in American Christianity through its forums and events over the past twenty years. Dave has been with the organization since 1995 and served it in several roles before assuming his current position in 2002. Throughout his tenure at Leadership Network, Dave has had the privilege of working with hundreds of pastors and leaders of large churches in the United States and Canada and is known as a trusted adviser to many of them.

Prior to joining Leadership Network, he was a denominational leader, pastor, church staff member, and engineer and served as a consultant to numerous congregations on issues of growth and development.

Like his coauthor, he is frequently sought out and quoted by major news outlets on the topic of megachurches and church innovation. His previous book, *Beyond the Box: Innovative Churches That Work* was cowritten with Bill Easum and published by Group Publishing.

Dave is a graduate of Georgia Tech and of the Southern Baptist Theological Seminary. He and his wife, Lynne, have two daughters, Stephanie and Claire. They reside near Atlanta.

INDEX

A

Adaptation, need for, 183
Adelaja, S., 185
Advertising. *See* Outreach
Age, of senior pastor, 59–60
Airborne disease, 190
America: and influence of
megachurches, 18–19; and
megachurch growth, 14–17; as
religious nation, 3–6, 120
Anderson, L., 21
Anonymity, 136–137
Architecture, 34, 93–94
Assemblies of God, 37
Attendance: distribution of, 5–17; and
founding date, 25; growth trends
in, 8, 169–171; and size, 23–24,
44–54
Attendees: classification of, 102–111;
integration of, 46–50, 158–160,
166; and making commitments,
111–115; and potential new
members, 132–133; socioeconomic
class of, 139; and transfer
membership, 119–128
Audience, of ministry, 28–30, 42
Azusa Street Revivals, 37

B

Baby-boom generation, 171–175
Bay Life Church (Brandon, FL), 41
Beliefs, 91–117
Ben Hill United Methodist Church
(Atlanta, GA), 37
Bible colleges, 131–132
Bigness, benefits of, 126–132
"Bird flu", 190
Blackhawk Church (Madison, WI), 63
Brown, C., 71

Budgets, 13–14
Burke, D., 74–75
Butler, D., 38
Butler, K., 38

C

Calvary Chapel (Costa Mesa, CA),
26–27, 128, 138–139, 147
Calvary Chapel Fellowship of
Churches, 26–27, 47
Calvary Church (Westlake Village,
CA), 118, 162–163
"Change Conferences", 131
The Chapel (Akron, OH), 37
Chapel Hill Harvester Church
(Atlanta, GA), 83
"Charismatic movement", 37
Charismatic/Pastor-Focused stream,
31–35, 37–38
Chaves, M., 6
Choirs, 100–111. *See also* Worship
styles
Christ Community Church (Omaha,
NE), 85
Christ the King Church (Skagit Valley,
WA), 26
Christian education, 33, 100–111,
131–132
The Church of God (Cleveland, TN),
37
The Church of God in Christ
(COGIC), 37
Church/state separation, 143
Church Without Walls (Tampa, FL),
38
Clergy, number of, 5
Cleveland, TN, 37
Commitments, 100–115, 161
Communion. *See* Worship styles

OTHER BOOKS OF INTEREST

The Present Future
Six Tough Questions for the Church
Reggie McNeal

Cloth
ISBN: 0-7879-6568-5
ISBN13: 978-0-7879-6568-6

"This is the most courageous book I have ever read on church life. McNeal nails the problem on the head. Be prepared to be turned upside down and shaken loose of all your old notions of what church is and should be in today's world."
—George Cladis, senior pastor, Westminster Presbyterian Church, Oklahoma City, Oklahoma and author, *Leading the Team-Based Church*

"With humor and rare honesty Reggie McNeal challenges church leaders to take authentic Christianity back into the real world. He's asking the right questions to help us get back on track."
—Tommy Coomes, contemporary Christian music pioneer and record producer, artist with Franklin Graham Ministries

"Reggie McNeal throws a lifeline to church leaders who are struggling with consumer-oriented congregations wanting church for themselves. *The Present Future* will recharge your passion."
—Rev. Robert R. Cushman, senior pastor, Princeton Alliance Church, Plainsboro, New Jersey

In *The Present Future*, Reggie McNeal identifies the six most important realities that church leaders must address including: recapturing the spirit of Christianity and replacing "church growth" with a wider vision of kingdom growth; developing disciples instead of church members; fostering the rise of a new apostolic leadership; focusing on spiritual formation rather than church programs; and shift, from prediction and planning to preparation for the challenges in an uncertain world. McNeal contends that by changing the questions church leaders ask themselves about their congregations and their plans, they can frame the core issues and approach the future with new eyes, new purpose, and new ideas.

REGGIE MCNEAL is the director of leadership development for South Carolina Baptist Convention. Drawing on twenty years of leadership roles in local congregations, and his work over the last decade with thousands of church leaders, McNeal counsels local churches, denominational groups, seminaries and colleges, and para-church organizations in their leadership-development needs. He lives in Columbia, South Carolina, with his wife and two daughters.

OTHER BOOKS OF INTEREST

The Present Future DVD Set
Reggie McNeal

DVD
ISBN13: 978-0-7879-8673-5

In this 4-DVD set, Reggie McNeal personally presents the ground-breaking ideas and insights in his best-selling book, *The Present Future*.

Filmed live before a studio audience, these DVDs show Reggie at his most appealing and compelling best. His blend of humor, personal story, and challenging approach has captivated thousands of people. Package includes leader's guide and participant's guide to facilitate use of the DVD with church groups and leaders.

As in the book, in the *Present Future* DVDs McNeal takes up the challenges of leadership for the church--what must leaders do in order to move beyond "churchianity" to Christianity, to move from church growth the kingdom growth, to develop followers of Jesus rather than just church members, to shift from planning and programs to new ways of moving into a missional future.

By changing the questions church leaders are asking themselves about their congregation and their plans for the future, McNeal seeks to frame the issues so that the future can be approached with new eyes, new purpose, and new ideas.

OTHER BOOKS OF INTEREST

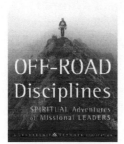

Off-Road Disciplines
Spiritual Adventures of Missional
Leaders
Earl Creps
Foreword by Dan Kimball

Cloth
ISBN: 0-7879-8520-1
ISBN13: 978-0-7879-8520-2

"As a well-traveled explorer of the Church over many years, Earl offers more than a description of the latest cool topics in leadership. . . . You hold something that is rich, cured, and aged to sink into your mind and heart in a way that couldn't happen without breadth of experience behind it. This isn't a book about a quick fix to break an attendance barrier, or bringing new music or a new design for a worship gathering. It isn't about how to give better sermons. Earl writes about the most important thing he has discovered in all his exploring of the Church: the life of the missional leader and its effect on a missional organization."

—from the Foreword by Dan Kimball

In *Off-Road Disciplines*, Earl Creps reveals that the on-road practices of prayer and Bible reading should be bolstered by the other kinds of encounters with God that occur unexpectedly—complete with the bumps and bruises that happen when you go "off-road." Becoming an off-road leader requires the cultivation of certain spiritual disciplines that allow the presence of the Holy Spirit to arrange your interior life. Earl Creps explores twelve central spiritual disciplines—six personal and six organizational—that Christian leaders of all ages and denominations need if they are to change themselves and their churches to reach out to the culture around them.

Earl Creps explores each of these off-road disciplines and shows how to make them part of normal daily life so that they can have a transformative effect. Creps provides a map of the cultural terrain leaders must navigate and offers insight on the ways in which the process of personal spiritual formation can lead to changes in organizations.

Visit the Leadership Network Website, www.leadnet.org, for more information.

Earl Creps—a popular speaker and leader—is director of the Doctor of Ministry program and associate professor at the Assemblies of God Theological Seminary (AGTS) in Springfield, Missouri. He has been a pastor, ministries consultant, and university professor. Along the way, Creps earned a Ph.D. in communication at Northwestern University and a doctor of ministry degree in leadership at AGTS.

OTHER BOOKS OF INTEREST

The Blogging Church
Sharing the Story of Your Church
Through Blogs
Brian Bailey, Terry Storch

Paper
ISBN-10: 0-7879-8487-6
ISBN-13: 978-0-7879-8487-8

"I had a lot of questions about blogs and their value for my church. I'm thankful that Brian and Terry are sharing their experiences to answer those questions. Their insights are for everyone in ministry. Whether you are reading blogs, writing blogs, or just trying to figure out how to use the word in a sentence, this book is for you."
—Mark Beeson, Senior Pastor, Granger Community Church

"My talking head is limited to the pulpit proper. I thank God that there's a tool to reach outside the church, to those that are sadly, outside the church. Thank you Terry and Brian for *The Blogging Church*.
—Pastor Bob Coy, Senior Pastor, Calvary Chapel, Ft. Lauderdale

The Blogging Church offers church leaders a field manual for uitilizing the social phenomenon of blogs to connect people and build communities in a whole new way. Inside you will find the why, what, and how of blogging in the local church. Filled with illustrative examples and practical advice, the authors answer key questions learned on the front lines of ministry: Is blogging a tool or a toy? What problems will blogging solve? How does it benefit ministry? And what motivates the user? You will be inspired to implement blogs in your church and equipped with the tools to make it happen.

Includes contributions from five of the most popular bloggers in the world–Robert Scoble, Dave Winer, Kathy Sierra, Guy Kawasaki, and Merlin Mann, as well as interview with blogging pastors such as Mark Driscoll, Craig Groeschel, Tony Morgan, Perry Noble, Greg Surratt, Mark Batterson, and many more.

BRIAN BAILEY (Dallas/Ft. Worth, TX) is the Web Director at Fellowship Church, one of the five largest churches in America with more than 20,000 members. Brian leads the design and development of the church's four websites. A staff member for five years, he has spent the last three championing weblogs in the church, leading to the launch of official Fellowship Church blogs, as well as numerous staff and internal blogs.

TERRY STORCH (Dallas/Ft. Worth, TX) is the Chief Operations and Technology Pastor for Fellowship Church. As a member of the Executive Team, he is responsible for the technology and business operations for the church. Terry has spoken at many different conferences across the country and is widely considered by the experts to be a true church technology visionary.